Forgiving the Gift

Medieval & Renaissance Literary Studies

Originally titled the *Duquesne Studies: Philological Series* (and later renamed the *Language & Literature Series*), the **Medieval & Renaissance Literary Studies Series** has been published by Duquesne University Press since 1960. This publishing endeavor seeks to promote the study of late medieval, Renaissance, and seventeenth century English literature by presenting scholarly and critical monographs, collections of essays, editions, and compilations. The series encourages a broad range of interpretation, including the relationship of literature and its cultural contexts, close textual analysis, and the use of contemporary critical methodologies.

Foster Provost	Albert C. Labriola	Richard J. DuRocher
EDITOR, 1960–1984	EDITOR, 1985–2009	EDITOR, 2010

Forgiving the Gift

The Philosophy of Generosity in Shakespeare and Marlowe

SEAN LAWRENCE

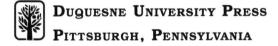 **DUQUESNE UNIVERSITY PRESS**
PITTSBURGH, PENNSYLVANIA

Published in the United States of America by
DUQUESNE UNIVERSITY PRESS
600 Forbes Avenue
Pittsburgh, Pennsylvania 15282

Library of Congress Cataloging-in-Publication Data

Lawrence, Sean.
    Forgiving the gift : the philosophy of generosity in Shakespeare and
Marlowe / Sean Lawrence.
        p. cm.
    Includes bibliographical references and index.
    Summary: "Original readings of Dr. Faustus, The Merchant of Venice,
Edward II, King Lear, Titus Andronicus, and The Tempest, in which
Sean Lawrence challenges the tendency to reflexively understand gifts as
exchanges or negotiations. Lawrence uses the philosophies of Levinas and
Derrida to argue that these plays depict a radical generosity that breaks the
cycle of self-interest" — Provided by publisher.
    ISBN 978-0-271-09296-6 (paper : acid-free paper)
    1. Shakespeare, William, 1564–1616 — Criticism and interpretation.
    2. Marlowe, Christopher, 1564–1593 — Criticism and interpretation.
    3. Generosity in literature. I. Title.

    PR3001.L39 2012
    822.3'3 — dc22

                                                                2011050540

∞ Printed on acid-free paper.

P. B. O.

CONTENTS

ACKNOWLEDGMENTS

"Beggar that I am, I am even poor in thanks."
— *Hamlet*

Acknowledgments constitute a distinct genre, as Daniel Pennac shows to hilarious effect in his monologue, *Merci*. If I frustrate generic expectations, it is not because I fear acknowledging my debts. On the contrary, I have argued in what follows that we should be less anxious in the face of gifts and less driven to repay them in order to free ourselves from the debts they impose.

I wish to remain in debt to those who have helped me instead of repaying my debts, however symbolically. Levinas claims that the true gift should be met with ingratitude. He exaggerates, and I am not ungrateful, but I should not wish a public expression of gratitude to become confused with some sort of payment or suspected of an effort at network building like the dedication at the beginning of a Renaissance poem. I must appear ungrateful here if I am to maintain my gratitude against accusations of covert exchange, name-dropping, or schmoozing.

Even if I wanted to, however, repaying my debts would be impossible in practice. Acknowledgments at the beginnings of monographs remain absurdly inadequate, even when they swell into epic lists. Certainly, the notes and bibliography come nowhere near to inventorying what I owe. To contemplate the extent of one's debts is to recognize the ubiquity of generosity and how poorly theories of exchange describe our lived experience. Repaying what we owe in gratitude is impossible in practice but also in theory. What I owe others defies repayment, for it is as infinite as their difference from me.

What one owes to the dead illustrates how a debt can exceed our ability to repay. I am grateful to Izaak Walton Killam and Dorothy Brooks Killam, whose estate funded a good deal of my research, especially on *The Merchant of Venice*, during a post-doctoral appointment at Dalhousie University. The Killams were generous, and I am grateful, but we do not enter into an exchange. In something of the same spirit, I would like to publicly thank the second reader chosen by Duquesne University Press, who offered many useful suggestions. The gift of his or her advice has no donor, at least none I can know, and therefore my gratitude does not constitute one side of an exchange. The reader's generosity, like that of the Killams, furnishes a concrete repudiation to claims regarding the ubiquity of self-interested, reciprocal gift exchange.

In fact, every reader's attention is more than I have earned. This includes a number of colleagues, friends, and mentors who have read portions of this book and provided valuable advice, but it also includes the reader holding this book in her or his hands. Thank you, whoever you are.

The Satanic Pact

The central and initiating event of Christopher Marlowe's *Doctor Faustus* is an exchange. The episodic plot achieves narrative unity in following "the form of Faustus' fortunes, good or bad," as the prologue to the play promises us, through the 24 years of his contract with Lucifer.[1] The play opens with his determination to enter into the pact and ends with its consummation as devils drag him down to Hell. Practically everybody who has heard of the play, let alone those who have viewed or read it, knows that it depicts the story of a man who enters into a pact with the devil.

According to David Hawkes, the Faust myth, as presented by Marlowe and others, dramatizes our own postmodern fascination with signification. "Faustus's basic sin is semiotic," Hawkes declares. The protagonist's confusion of representations with reality closely parallels our own era's "philosophy, psychology, linguistics and, above all, its economics." Hawkes therefore finds it "impossible to avoid the conclusion that the Western world has sold its soul to Satan." Rather than arguing, like Hawkes, that the play shows a general fear of representation including theater as a form of witchcraft,[2] I read the play as a dramatization of the sixteenth century's—and our own—fascination with exchange. The pact represents a particular type of signification, which is marked as diabolical in that it signifies an exchange that is the logical and moral opposite of the gift of grace. The definition of damnation established by the play indeed applies to our postmodern world, because the notion of exchange bewitches us as well as Faustus.

The play and the story it dramatizes arose in a particular moment in religious history, when Saint Augustine of Hippo's doctrine of salvation by grace attracted renewed interest throughout western Christendom.[3] Several of its most eloquent exponents remained staunch Roman Catholics; however, the doctrine attained explosive force in the powerful and sin-tormented mind of the Augustinian monk, Martin Luther. His insistence that justification cannot be earned exceeded even Augustine's own, because in Luther's theology, justification remains external to the sinner even after its receipt.[4] The sale of indulgences implied, on the contrary, that grace could be retailed. Luther therefore responded to an aggressive marketing campaign by making increasingly angry denunciations, which catalyzed the European Reformation, to the surprise of Luther and everyone else.[5] As both Michael Keefer and Hawkes show at some length, the Faust myth originated in Lutheran Germany. Luther even mentioned Faustus in his table talk. In one early version of the story, Faustus debates Philipp Melanchthon, Luther's colleague.[6] Luther's insistence that grace can only be received from without led him and, more famously, John Calvin to a doctrine of predestination. Keefer follows Jonathan Dollimore in declaring that the play interrogates this doctrine.[7] My point is neither that the play expounds a consistent doctrine of predestination nor that it illustrates a consistently Lutheran suspicion of the sign, as Hawkes argues, but that it dramatizes in Faustus's career an extreme alternative to the gift of salvation by faith alone. For a period heavily invested in this doctrine, the pact appears exemplary of the demonic. Faustus does not merely reject gratuitous grace but substitutes its opposite:

reciprocal exchange. If our world has sold its soul, it is because we too reject the possibility of a gift, for which grace furnishes the exemplary theological expression.

Dollimore reads the play as "an exploration of subversion through transgression" in which the doctrine of predestination is called into doubt by its own dramatization. More generally, it exposes the Calvinist God as, in words Dollimore quotes from Michael Walzer, "an arbitrary and wilful, omnipotent and universal tyrant," who holds man responsible for his damnation, while withdrawing from the reprobate the power of working their own redemption."[8] As Keefer argues, "A Calvinist orthodoxy may appear to win out at the end of this play, but it does so at the cost of being exposed, in the moment of its triumph, as intolerable."[9] Such a collapse of a theological paradox into a straightforward contradiction, Dollimore concludes, anticipates the demystification of tyrannous power in Jacobean tragedy.[10] However, Lucifer rather than God appears in terms closely approximating a secular ruler. Dollimore asks, as many others have done before, "how is evil possible in a world created by an omnipotent God?"[11] Faustus, however, does not ask this question and expresses little curiosity toward the metaphysical origins of evil. A commitment to and belief in exchange serves as a sort of mental handicap, rendering Faustus incapable of accepting forgiveness.

A doctrine of predestination, in either its Lutheran or Calvinist expressions, follows from the logically prior doctrine of salvation by grace. The young Luther broke with his training as a lawyer and with the quasi-economic theology of the late Middle Ages by ascribing salvation to God and not to any action on the part of man.[12] The theologians in whose works Luther was steeped followed William of Ockham in treating works as a token currency, ascribed value by a pact between God and man. Luther, however, found no comfort in the claim that man can be saved by performing what works he is able.[13] Trenchantly defending predestination against Desiderius Erasmus's humanist insistence on free will, Luther describes the doctrine as a liberation: "But now that God has taken my salvation out of the control of my own will, and put it under the control of His, and promised to save me, not according to my working or running, but according to His own grace and mercy, I have the comfortable certainty that He is faithful and will not lie to me, and that He is also great and powerful, so that no devils or opposition can break Him or pluck me from Him." Doctrines of predestination are unsettling, but they follow from an effort to break with economic models of salvation that seemed, at least to Luther, to lead everyone inevitably to damnation. "By the power of 'free-will,'" he declares, "none at all could be saved, but every one of us would perish."[14] This is precisely the case for Faustus, who can and does choose his own damnation. What Keefer and Dollimore take to be examples of a disquieting ideology are perhaps better understood as indications of grace's status as gift.

The play presents Faustus's pact as the opposite of grace and therefore in the language of contract. As its initiator, Faustus instructs Mephistopheles to tell the devil that "he surrenders up to him his soul" (1.4.90). Faustus uses a legal and now largely obsolete use of the word "surrender" meaning to "to give up (a copyhold estate) to the lord of the manor."[15] Marlowe foregrounds the legal deed, having Faustus read the whole aloud and deploying the physical document as a theatrical property. "Then hear me read," says Faustus (2.1.95), somewhat heavy-handedly. The pact's exposition and then its text emphasize reciprocal obligations. "Here Mephastophilis," Faustus concludes,

> receive this scroll,
> A deed of gift, of body and of soul:
> But yet conditionally, that thou performs
> All articles prescrib'd between us both. (2.1.89–92)

The first five articles of the pact consist entirely of "conditions" that the devil must fulfill, before Faustus reciprocates with his soul. The pact, like all contracts, makes an exchange, in which each party's obligations are conditional upon the discharge of reciprocal obligations. It gives Faustus to Lucifer but at the expi-ration of "four and twenty years,...the articles being inviolate" (2.1.108–09). The devil may "fetch or carry the said John Faustus, body and soul, flesh, blood, or goods" (2.1.109–10) but only upon the performance of the devil's side of the bargain.

Faustus's pact may be the most famous example of a deal with the devil, but it exemplifies a belief central to the contemporary construction of witchcraft. King James declared that the devil "is glad to mooue...to a plaine and square dealing" with a necro-mancer by the mechanism of a pact.[16] Jean Bodin declared that "every kind of idolatry and superstitious observance" constitutes a "tacit, or implicit" pact. This implies that evil, if not good, can be freely chosen but also positions contractual agreement as the diabolical inverse of salvation. The pact made by magicians such as Faustus distinguishes itself only by being overt: "[I]t is some-times made verbally, and without writing. Or sometimes Satan, to be sure of his people, makes them write down their obligation and sign it if they can write, before they can obtain what they ask. Sometimes he makes them sign with their blood, in the man-ner of the ancients who used this practice to confirm oaths and friendships."[17] Bodin could be describing a scene in Marlowe's play, though there is no evidence that either writer drew direct influence from the other. Instead, both express a belief common in the late sixteenth century, that necromancers enter into an explicit pact with Satan. So central was the pact to the early mod-ern construct of witchcraft that Reginald Scot took it as the weak point in the entire construct of demon-mania: "If the league be untrue, as are the residue of their confessions, the witchmon-gers arguments fall to the ground: for all the writers herein hold this bargaine for certeine, good, and granted, and as their onelie maxime. But surely the indentures, conteining those covenants, are sealed with butter; and the labels are but bables."[18]

Historians recognize that the possibility and validity of a pact with the devil is central to early modern debates about witchcraft. Keith Thomas declares that "the notion that the witch owed her

powers to having made a deliberate pact with the Devil" constituted a new belief, original to the late Middle Ages and serving to distinguish European beliefs "from the witch-beliefs of
other primitive peoples."[19] While noting much earlier examples,
Jeffrey Burton Russell marks the early modern period as the high
point of belief in a demonic pact: "The idea that witches were
worshipers of Satan and had signed a literal, explicit pact with
him was the heart of the witch craze."[20] Marlowe's play gives
dramaturgical expression to a belief held widely in the period of
its composition.

The mere existence of a widely shared belief that the devil
makes formal pacts with his followers does not, however, explain
why the belief attained such power, either in Marlowe's play or
the culture whose beliefs it expresses. The devil may be, as the
Geneva Bible says, "a liar, and the father thereof,"[21] but both he
and Faustus show admirable trustworthiness in fulfilling their
respective sides of the pact. The critical problem of the play is
not why Faustus sells his soul but why he keeps his word. "Is
not thy soul thy own?" Faustus asks himself with characteristic
solipsism, as he watches his blood congealing in revulsion at his
signature (2.1.68). Scot offers a response to Faustus's query, in the
context of a story about a woman suffering anguish in the deluded
belief that she has sold her soul. "[T]his thy bargain is void and
of none effect," her husband reassures her, "for thou hast sold
that which is none of thine to sell; sith it belongeth to Christ,
who hath bought it, and deerelie paid for it, even with his bloud,
which he shed upon the crosse; so as the divell hath no interest
in thee."[22] Lucifer makes an equally legalistic but of course dia-
bolically inverted claim: "Christ cannot save thy soul, for he is
just; / There's none but I have interest in the same" (2.3.85–86).
Lucifer's argument relies on a narrowly legalistic understanding
of "justice" following Roman Law. Luther only overcame this
idea when he discovered that the Hebrew *sdqh* had very different implications from the Latin *iusticia* and would allow a just
God to save sinners rather than merely punish them.[23] Not only

is Lucifer's case defective in law—Faustus could not give away a soul he does not own, so Lucifer can have no interest in it—but the possibility of forgiveness violates the reciprocal obligations of contract and law in general. Lucifer bases his claim on an untenable reading of law, which itself is irrelevant to salvation. He therefore reveals his claim on Faustus's soul as doubly invalid.

The play's insistence upon the possibility of forgiveness emphasizes the weakness of Lucifer's claim. His despair notwithstanding, Faustus recognizes this possibility, at least intellectually, in his final torturous vision of "Christ's blood...in the firmament" (5.2.71). Earlier, the Old Man nearly inspires him to repentance with a description of "an angel /...with a vial full of precious grace," who "Offers to pour the same into thy soul" (5.1.53–55). In both cases, grace would come from without, in keeping with Protestant doctrine. In dialogue with the angels at the beginning of act 2, Faustus asks about "contrition, prayer, repentance: what of them?" (2.1.16). Two scenes later, he announces his intention to "renounce this magic and repent" (2.3.11). The good angel assures him later in the same scene that it is "Never too late, if Faustus can repent" (2.3.80). Even returning to Wittenberg to meet the devil and consummate his pact, he assures himself that "Christ did call the thief upon the cross" (4.2.37), borrowing the same example as in the Elizabethan homily "Against the Fear of Death."[24] At least once, Faustus exaggerates the possibility of redemption. "Be I a devil," he declares, "yet God may pity me" (2.3.15). In this statement, he exceeds the confidence offered by Augustinian theology, drawing instead on the beliefs of Origen, who suggested that even devils could be saved. Faustus does not draw upon doctrines of predestination to despair in reprobation, at least not in this instance; on the contrary, he draws upon the opposite doctrine, favored by Erasmus, Luther's polemical opponent on the subject.[25] The play returns repeatedly and even hyperbolically to the power of forgiveness. In all instances, however, forgiveness would have to come from without. The Old Man precedes his image of grace being poured into Faustus by ascribing, with perfect orthodoxy, the possibility of salvation to the "mercy, Faustus, of thy Saviour sweet, / Whose blood alone must wash away thy guilt" (5.1.45–46). Salvation always remains a possibility in the play but a possibility that Faustus cannot actively choose.

Where the receipt of grace would place Faustus in a position of passivity, at least initially and concerning his salvation, the pact ratifies his identity and power. Faustus signs with his full name, place of residence, and academic title: "John Faustus of Wittenberg, Doctor" (2.1.105). He roots his extravagant desires for the services of spirits in regional and professional loyalties:

> I'll have them wall all Germany with brass
> And make swift Rhine circle fair Wittenberg;
> I'll have them fill the public schools with silk
> Wherewith the students shall be bravely clad.   (1.1.89–92)

Despite the desire that he adds almost immediately to "reign sole king of all our provinces" (1.1.95), he remains a loyal, modest, and even entertaining servant of the emperor, promising "to do whatsoever your Majesty shall command me" (4.1.15–16). The demonic pact does not seriously undermine his position as a subject and even reinforces it by making him subject to another lord, Lucifer. Humiliated by Faustus, a knight at the imperial court demands, "How darst thou thus abuse a gentleman?" (4.1.78), but Faustus excuses himself to the emperor: "My gracious lord, not so much for the injury he offered me here in your presence, as to delight you with some mirth, hath Faustus worthily requited this injurious knight" (4.1.85–87). He proceeds to warn his victim to "hereafter speak well of scholars" (4.1.89). The entire episode shows Faustus bound by national, class, and professional identities. At its end, the emperor promises him "a bounteous reward" (4.1.93). Faustus's sycophantic entertainment of Charles V might contrast with Luther's dignified defiance of him at the Diet of Worms.[26] In any case, exchanges of favors and entertainments ratify the relationship with the emperor, as with the devil. Faustus certainly transgresses—the epilogue accuses him of practicing "more than heavenly power permits" (Epilogue.8)—but the pact does not undermine social order.

In fact, it mirrors the social order, binding Faustus to Lucifer as to a feudal lord. Lucifer is referred to more than once in terms recalling a political ruler. Faustus conjures Belzebub as "Orientis princeps" (1.3.17–18) and extends the same title to Lucifer, "Prince of the East" (2.1.106), albeit in translation. Lucifer explains this joint sovereignty by referring to Belzebub as his "companion prince in hell" (2.3.88). Mephistopheles adopts the language of feudalism when he describes himself as "a servant to great Lucifer" (1.3.40) and again when he claims that Lucifer desires Faustus's soul to "Enlarge his kingdom" (2.1.40). Later, Mephistopheles threatens to "arrest thy soul / For disobedience to my sovereign lord" (5.1.66–67). In fact, the devil's self-presentation as a monarch was a convention of Elizabethan interludes[27] and in Saint Luke's gospel the devil claims power over "all the kingdomes of the worlde," though a marginal note in the Geneva text helpfully adds that "he is but prince of the worlde by permission."[28] In any case, it is hardly surprising that throughout *Faustus*, the devil's power is described in terms that might describe a secular ruler's.

Lucifer's power over Faustus appears political in that it relies, like feudal power, on the force of an oath to command loyalty. Such is the legitimacy of the pact, at least in Faustus's mind, that he resists the call to salvation as he would a temptation. At the beginning of act 2, Faustus calls upon himself to "be resolute" when "something soundeth in mine ears" (2.1.6–7). Following one of the interventions by the good angel and the evil angel, Faustus distorts two biblical statements and a hymn, applying them to the devil rather than to God (2.1.29–30 and note). After a further flirtation with repentance, Faustus asks Lucifer to "pardon me in this" (2.3.94). After another, he begs Mephistopheles to "entreat thy lord / To pardon my unjust presumption" (5.1.69–70). In all these blasphemous inversions, Faustus treats the thought of forgiveness as itself a sin to be forgiven.

Only the terms of the pact render Faustus's interest in salvation disloyal. The pact directs Faustus's loyalty to Lucifer, whom he promises to worship with "an altar and a church, / And offer lukewarm blood of new-born babes" (2.1.13–14). Even contemplating the sight of "Christ's blood," Faustus recognizes the right, or at least power, of Lucifer to "rend…my heart for naming of my Christ" in keeping with the terms of the bond (5.2.71–73). At the beginning of his dramaturgically abbreviated final hour, he ascribes to his damnation the inevitability of time itself: "time runs, the clock will strike, / The devil will come, and Faustus must be damn'd" (5.2.68–69). In asking that the stars "draw up Faustus like a foggy mist" in order that "My limbs may issue from your smoky mouths, / So that my soul may but ascend to heaven" (5.2.85, 88–89) he offers his body in exchange for his soul, proposing another trade. This desperate offer reverses the pact, which exchanges Faustus's soul for "all voluptuousness" (1.3.92), but it is still an exchange. His last full sentence, being carried away, offers to "burn my books," as if trying to reverse the contract by returning the benefits he has received (5.2.115). Salvation remains available to Faustus but requires a violation of the pact, the legitimacy of which Faustus never seriously questions. According to Bodin, a physical copy of a pact with the devil would constitute damning evidence of witchcraft, though only "if the witch's signature is acknowledged by him."[29] Bodin's condition threatens even the strongest prosecutorial case, but it is hard to imagine Faustus ever denying his signature. Faustus believes in the power of the pact more than he believes in the power of grace.

Like any tyrant, Lucifer enforces his power with the threat of violence. The evil angel tells Faustus that if he repents, "devils shall tear thee in pieces" (2.3.81). Speaking to the scholars near the end of the play, Faustus explains his entire career of nonrepentance by claiming that "the devil threatened to tear me in pieces if I named God, to fetch both body and soul if I once gave ear to divinity" (5.2.42–43). The scholars only discover "Faustus' limbs / All torn asunder by the hand of death" (Appendix A 5.3.6–7) in the later and inferior text of the play, but in the early as well as the later text, Lucifer possesses and incarnates the power of a Renaissance state to destroy its subjects in spectacular violence. Nevertheless, Lucifer's power reveals itself as more or less imaginary. When the evil angel threatens Faustus with being torn "in pieces," the good angel assures him that "they shall never raze thy skin" (2.3.82). Were Faustus to repent, the devil's ability to harm him would be no greater than Mephistopheles's ability to harm the Old Man (5.1.78–80). The devil's power and authority to harm Faustus, including the power to drag him down to hell, derives from the pact itself and its claim to legitimacy. His threats of violence depend for their realization, as well as their legitimacy, on the very pact they enforce.

The pact not only affirms Faustus's social identity as an accomplished academic and subject of the empire but also ratifies his agency. Wolfgang Musculus's *Commonplaces of Christian Religion*, which David Riggs describes as the most popular theological handbook in Marlowe's Cambridge,[30] argues that unregenerate man is free but only to do evil: "there is in man free will, notwithstanding that he is subjecte unto the bondage of sinne and Satan. For he is of so corrupte and perverse a disposition, that the evill which he committeth in his bondage, he doeth it not as compelled and restrayned, but with moste free wil and desire."[31] Musculus proceeds to argue that man "newe borne by the grace of Christ" receives a greater liberty, but obviously this is not Faustus's case. Instead, he exercises the only free will of which he is capable and does evil. In surrendering his soul, he claims ownership over it. The pact ratifies not only his position as a subject, to the emperor, for instance, or Lucifer, but also his subjectivity.

In addition to social and existential reassurance, the pact also offers epistemological reassurance. Faustus demands, among other things, political, philosophical, and even metaphysical knowledge. He anticipates that the spirits will "read me strange philosophy, / And tell the secrets of all foreign kings" (1.1.87–88). As soon as he has the pact in hand, Mephistopheles invites Faustus to "ask me what thou wilt," and Faustus demands to know "about hell" (2.1.115–16). Later, he pushes aside thoughts of repentance by turning to metaphysical speculation: "Come Mephastophilis, let us dispute again, / And reason of divine astrology" (2.3.33–34). As the name of the topic anticipates, this leads him from science to theology, about which anything Mephistopheles could say would be "against our kingdom," as he helpfully explains (2.3.73). The wisdom Faustus buys with his soul consists, he complains, in nothing but "freshmen's suppositions" (2.3.56). Like Scot's witch, he might accuse Lucifer of breach of contract.

On the other hand, a number of his questions are answered in short order. His inquiries about both hell and heaven are answered experientially, in fact. Lucifer answers Faustus's desire to "see hell, and return again," with a guided tour: "I will send for thee at midnight" (2.3.163–64). Later, his travels include a voyage "to scale Olympus' top" in order to "To know the secrets of astronomy / Graven in the book of Jove's high firmament" (3.0.2–5). Mephistopheles, however, refuses to answer Faustus regarding "who made the world" (2.3.68). Creation, like salvation, comes from outside the world itself. Choosing necromancy over all other studies, Faustus declares that "his dominion that exceeds in this / Stretcheth as far as doth the mind of man!" (1.1.61–62). It stretches, therefore, to "Jove's high firmament," which Faustus can know and at least metaphorically visit, but not to the act of creation by which the cosmos came to be. Dollimore argues that the power of God serves as "the limiting structure of Faustus's universe"[32] but it seems rather that the power of God exceeds Faustus's mental universe, constricted instead to "the mind of man." Faustus indeed achieves all knowledge of which he is capable but only by severely restricting his horizons. This restriction at least partly results from his own self-censorship, obedient to Lucifer's command to "Talk not of Paradise, nor creation" (2.3.105). In Marlowe's principal source, *The English Faust-Book*, the doctor complains that "the gift that is given me from above" has not provided him "any such learning or wisdom that can bring me to my desires."[33] He enters the pact in rejection of God's gift, which it displaces. By avoiding the disquieting possibility of a gift, exchange maintains the commonsensical supposition that, as King Lear tells the fool, "nothing can be made out of nothing."[34] Faustus masters wisdom but only of a limited kind.

The struggle over Faustus's salvation is between the legitimacy of a reciprocal agreement, freely entered into, and the power of a gift, coming from without. Both Faustus's fate and, more fundamentally, his mind seem delimited by the principle of exchange rendered overt in his pact with Lucifer. Rather than accepting the gift of grace, Faustus prefers to trade. Marlowe's depiction of Faustus's stunted character associates credulousness toward the power of the demonic pact with a general belief in the legitimacy of exchange, whereas incredulousness toward grace appears as a rejection of the possibility of a pure gift that is not chosen, earned, or reciprocated. Such hyperbolic fidelity to exchange offers Faustus certain advantages: it leaves his agency intact and ratifies the structures of society, from which he derives social identity. Moreover, it offers him a position of knowing, albeit by excluding everything not immediately comprehensible. He can learn everything except what matters.

A belief in exchange also offers some consolation for the critic or reader. The party to an exchange may be understood as a self-seeking agent and therefore becomes amenable to a psychology, anthropology, or criticism that would remain quite simple, at least in its premises. An assumption derived from anthropology, that reciprocal exchanges are ubiquitous always and everywhere, has come to dominate the study of Renaissance drama. Such a model limits not only how one can read the plays but also how one can understand the world in general. Reading early modern drama as an endless series of exchanges provides us with knowledge, certainly, but only because we, like Faustus, severely restrict our horizons, indulging in the fascination with exchange that seals his damnation. If we have entered a demonic pact, it is in our skepticism toward gift and corresponding credulity toward exchange.

Forgiving the Gift

Introduction

Marlowe's *Faustus* makes a reciprocal exchange the basis of its plot but also presents exchange as the diabolical opposite of saving grace. In our own time, by contrast, few things attract suspicion as reliably as generosity, which we dismiss almost reflexively as some sort of ruse. Adriaan Peperzak observes that "some postmodern authors, very much impressed by critical analyses of abnormal and normal behavior, social structures, economic mechanisms, linguistic and ideological patterns, have dogmatically affirmed that all human actions, even those that seem most generous, are selfish, egotistic, narcissistic."[1] Those authors, in other words, seem to filter the world through the mind of Faustus, incredulous toward generosity, credulous toward exchange, and damned.

Such a dogmatic belief in the ubiquity of exchange blinds us to the belief in the gift that was central to early modern drama and to the culture in which it arose. The belief in ubiquitous exchange nevertheless commands importance in criticism of Shakespeare and his contemporaries, though as Peperzak observes, it arises from the social sciences. Specifically, the notion that every gift anticipates recompense achieves theoretical expression in the ethnology of Marcel Mauss. Within criticism of early modern drama, this assumption finds its strongest expression in the work of Stephen Greenblatt and the school he founds, New Historicism.

Rather than tracing how Greenblatt comes to be influenced by Mauss, by way of Clifford Geertz and Greenblatt's interest in cultural anthropology,[2] I am content to show that Mauss and Greenblatt share similar ideas. Where Greenblatt finds "a network of trades and trade-offs"[3] in the early modern world and its drama, Mauss finds networks of exchange in every society he considers. The 1924 publication of Mauss's *The Gift* as an extended essay in *l'Année Sociologique* marks a watershed in theoretical consideration of gift-giving practices. Mary Douglas credits this text with providing ethnology "a new criterion of sound analysis"[4] and it certainly influenced many disciplines in the humanities as well as in the social sciences. Mauss's essay, moreover, gives overt form to the assumptions that inform much criticism of early modern drama and therefore opens these assumptions to criticism.

When we assume that self-interest motivates characters in works of drama, we employ a set of ideas enunciated by ethnography to describe societies. Our critical understanding of fictive worlds therefore betrays the influence of ideas about the world itself. Conversely, however, the readings we make of fictive worlds and characters influence our understanding of our own being-in-the-world. If we come to view Faustus as a self-interested agent or the product of a society that gives itself to be exhaustively described as a series of exchanges, we endorse a particular worldview. While the social sciences clearly contribute to the study of literature, literary criticism also influences our understanding of the world. In this sense, literary criticism is always philosophical.

Emmanuel Levinas suggests in *Time and the Other* that "the whole of philosophy is only a meditation of Shakespeare."[5] Richard A. Cohen suggests that the phrasing calls to mind the title of René Descartes's *Meditations on First Philosophy* and, as a result, "carries enormous philosophical weight, even more than might be imagined at first glance." In the original French, "de Shakespeare" has the force of a possessive, causing Cohen to comment: "What this means is not that all of philosophy is a meditation about Shakespeare, which by itself would already be a remarkable and thoughtworthy possibility, but rather that the whole of philosophy is a meditation by Shakespeare, Shakespeare's meditation."[6] Levinas refers to Shakespeare frequently throughout *Time and the Other*; moreover, he places references to Shakespeare in parallel with references to philosophers. After listing "Pascalian, Kierkegaardian, Nietzschean, and Heideggerian anxieties," he argues that the "the fool of the Shakespearean tragedy" offers an alternate response to the terror of solitude. Earlier in the same book, sandwiched between Albert Camus's and Martin Heidegger's definitions of absurdity, he discusses the attitudes of Hamlet, Macbeth, and Juliet toward suicide. Particularly in this early work but also throughout his career, Levinas does not treat Shakespeare's plays as mere illustrations but as philosophical meditations, on par with those of Heidegger. This is not to say that Levinas defers to Shakespeare's authority any more than he defers to Heidegger's or Descartes's. In fact, Levinas occasionally introduces Shakespeare's works in order to disagree with them, as if with an interlocutor. In *Time and the Other*, he quotes Hamlet's "To be or not to be" in the original English, finding in Shakespeare's most famous soliloquy a consideration of "the impossibility of annihilating oneself."[7] Hamlet's words echo through Levinas's career. In an essay first published in 1981 he anticipates this question with his own answer: "To be or not to be: the question *par excellence* probably does not lie therein."[8] He concludes a 1984 essay by asking rhetorically, "To be or not to be—is that the question? Is it the first and final question?"[9] At Levinas's funeral, Jacques Derrida quoted Maurice Blanchot as crediting Levinas with questioning "our facile reverence for ontology."[10] Cohen argues that Levinas praises Shakespeare because literature, for which "Shakespeare" stands as a metonym, "is closer to the humanity of the human, to the transcendence constitutive of the ethical category of the human, than are the abstract reflections of philosophy."[11] In any case, Levinas respects Shakespeare's plays as addressing the same issues to which Levinas directs phenomenology.

Levinas does not extend his use of Shakespeare to a discussion of gifts on the Elizabethan and Jacobean stage, but it seems legitimate to draw Levinas's philosophy back into dialogue with the texts he so much respects, albeit on a different topic. In particular, Levinas's emphasis upon the radically nonreciprocal opposes Mauss's axiom that there is no free gift and therefore allows new readings of early drama. If one were to nominate any particular donation as a pure gift, a doctrinaire follower of Mauss could simply declare the motives of the participants to be misunderstood, unconscious, socially conditioned, or otherwise marking these participants as the dupes of exchange. Mauss presents an *a priori* assertion that is impossible to disprove; moreover, he is inconsistent in simultaneously praising generosity and dismissing its very possibility. His praise of generosity presupposes a possible gift and therefore actually requires a Levinasian understanding of generosity.

Ironically, as Derrida points out, Mauss's book seems to be about "everything but the gift," because he dismisses the possibility of a true gift, one given without thought of recompense.[12] Exchanges of services, Mauss argues, "Almost always...have taken the form of the gift, the present generously given even when, in the gesture accompanying the transaction, there is only a polite fiction, formalism, and social deceit, and when really there is obligation and economic self-interest."[13] Mauss's essay ranges across cultures, from the coast of British Columbia to ancient and contemporary Europe, by way of Polynesia and India, discovering in every culture it examines evidence for a relentless thesis, that gifts are not really generous but obligatory and even aggressive. Ilana F. Silber comments on the "essentializing and homogenising thrust of his argument."[14] Mauss argues, for instance, that while potlatches held by members of First Nations in British Columbia stage exchanges of service, such "'service' on the part of the chief takes on an extremely marked agonistic character. It is essentially usurious and sumptuary." Mauss even marks the word "service" as ironic with single quotation marks. Later, he italicizes an entire sentence: *"The obligation to give is the essence of the potlatch."*[15] In reference to the practice of *kula* in the Trobriand Islands, he declares, "The aim of all this is to display generosity, freedom, and autonomous action, as well as greatness. Yet, all in all, it is mechanisms of obligation, and even of obligation through things, that are called into play." Mauss uses the term *gift* narrowly, to designate an exchange that imposes an obligation. Where Bronislaw Malinowski finds non-reciprocal donation in a customary payment of a husband to his wife, Mauss finds nothing but what Douglas calls "a kind of salary for sexual services rendered" transforming a conjugal ceremony into a prostitute's wage, as Jonathan Parry also notes.[16] In this instance, Mauss exposes an apparent exception as one might expose an imposter. His suspicion of gift exchange extends from the cultures he studies to that in which he lives: "Yet are we sure that it is any different in our own society, and that even with us riches are not above all a means of lording it over our fellow men?"[17] His denunciation of the possibility of a truly generous gift becomes explicit at discrete points but remains implicit throughout.

Though insistent, Mauss's dismissal of generosity is also inconsistent. He is touched that "Our much regretted friend [Robert] Hertz" made a note to pass on some research to him, for instance, rather than rejecting Hertz's intellectual generosity as a threat. More generally, his essay crescendos into a call for social solidarity, through a rediscovery in the archaic past of "the joy of public giving; the pleasure in generous expenditure on the arts, in hospitality, and in the private and public festival." Shortly before this, however, he claims that contemporary practices of charity as well as of potlatch reveal what he follows William James in calling the "fundamental motives for human activity: emulation between individuals of the same sex, that 'basic imperialism' of human beings."[18] Mauss seems intent on denouncing the gift as both impossible and insidious, a contradiction to which Simon

Jarvis draws attention;[19] moreover, he praises the gift as a source of social solidarity that anticipates the welfare state, while also denouncing it as a means of aggression that renders itself more dangerous by adopting a pretense of disinterestedness. So great is the apparent incoherence of Mauss's position that Parry observes, "it is claimed as the *fons et origo* of quite divergent theoretical positions." Parry derives a very sophisticated reading and claims that the belief that "the notion of a 'pure gift' is mere ideological obfuscation which masks the supposedly *non*-ideological verity that nobody does anything for nothing…has distorted our reading of Mauss's essay." Even he, however, complains that Mauss's writing is excessively "elliptical."[20] The association of Mauss's name with the notion Parry describes is Mauss's own fault; moreover, it undermines his own goals.

Mauss attempts to overcome the contradiction between his praise and denial of generosity by avoiding the binary of generosity and interest altogether. "These concepts of law and economics that it pleases us to contrast" he writes, "liberty and obligation; liberality, generosity, and luxury, as against savings, interest, and utility—it would be good to put them into the melting pot once more." Mauss certainly questions the distinction between gift and commerce. In his only allusion to Shakespeare, he claims, "The life of a monk and the life of a Shylock are both equally to be shunned" in favor of a "new morality" described as a "good but moderate blend of reality and the ideal." The new moralist, he continues, "must have a keen sense of awareness of himself, but also of others, and of social reality," asking rhetorically in parentheses, "in moral matters is there even any other kind of reality?"[21] A countercultural moral act seems not to occur to Mauss, even as a possibility. Instead, he treats generosity as part of a socially mandated moral system.

Having questioned the independence of gift from exchange, Mauss conversely questions the independence of economics as a discipline and view of the world, insisting that it incorporates the practices of what we might otherwise be tempted to call pre-economic cultures. "In these societies," he declares, "we shall see the market as it existed before the institution of traders and before their main invention—money proper." In a long note, he argues in favor of retaining the term "primitive money" to describe the "other things, stones, shells and precious metals in particular, that have been used and have served as a means of exchange and payment." They still, he argues, "discharge debts." He later describes how "[t]hrough gifts made and reciprocated" Melanesians "have robustly replaced a system of buying and selling." Though potlatch may demand the destruction rather than accumulation of wealth, it nevertheless qualifies as "a system of law and economics."[22] The gift, in Mauss's understanding, does not stand over and against economics or law, with the reciprocity of exchanges they imply, but explains both economics and law as a cause explains an effect. He insists that trade does not account for all exchanges, even in our own society: "We possess more than a tradesman morality. There still remain people and classes that keep to the morality of former times, and we all observe it, at least at certain times of the year or on certain occasions." He opposes "the so-called natural economy, that of utilitarianism" by arguing that "this whole economy of the exchange-through-gift lay outside the bounds" of it.[23] Mauss attacks utilitarianism, but not by questioning its premises and by arguing that individuals are fundamentally generous or denouncing human happiness as irrelevant. Instead, he claims to reveal a deeper structure. Douglas places Mauss's work within a polemical context where "the real enemy, the open enemy of French political philosophy was Anglo-Saxon utilitarianism," but even she concedes, "The gift cycle echoes Adam Smith's invisible hand: gift complements market in so far as it operates where the latter is absent."[24] Each serves as a means for the distribution of goods. Mauss can therefore compare his exemplary participants in gift exchange to investors: "One might really say that the Trobriand or Tsimshian, although far removed from him, proceeds like the capitalist who knows how to dispose of his ready cash at the right time, in order to reconstitute at a later date this mobile form of capital."[25] While he posits a broader, gift-based economics underlining a narrowly utilitarian economics, Mauss nevertheless describes an economic system.

Mauss enables comparison between widely divergent cultures not by universalizing a "primitive economy" based on utilitarian assumptions, but by universalizing gift exchange. "This moral-ity," of gift exchange, he declares, "is eternal; it is common to the most advanced societies, to those of the immediate future, and to the lowest imaginable forms of society. We touch upon funda-mentals. No longer are we talking in legal terms: we are speaking of men and groups of men, because it is they, it is society, it is the feelings of men, in their minds and in flesh and blood that at all times spring into action and that have acted everywhere." For Mauss, gift exchange is doubly universal, explaining not only every society but also everything about every society. "In these 'total' social phenomena," he argues, "all kinds of institutions are given expression at one and the same time — religious, juridical, and moral, which relate to both politics and the family; likewise economic ones, which suppose special forms of production and consumption, or rather, of performing total services and of distri-bution."[26] Though Mauss denies the universality of trade, he falls into universalizing his own construct of gift as exchange. There is something almost painfully ironic in how his efforts to avoid the excessive claims of an economic theory lead him to propose what he italicizes as the *"system of total services,"* and later as *"total social facts."*[27] While his universalizing assumption allows Mauss to describe society as a whole and, as Douglas credits him, to vastly advance ethnology from an earlier, empirically descriptive form,[28] it also effectively abolishes other possibilities for being in the world.

Mauss ends his book with a call to action: "Thus, from one extreme of evolution to the other, there are no two kinds of wisdom. Therefore let us adopt as the principle of our life what has always been a principle of action and will always be so: to emerge from self, to give, freely and obligatorily. We run no

risk of disappointment."[29] One might accuse Mauss of confusing an ethnographic observation with an ethical imperative.
Indeed, Christian Arnsperger argues that "any serious reader of
Mauss" must ask whether Mauss promotes an ideal of generosity
or provides "a phenomenology of unveiling which describes the
way our society *in fact operates* without our being aware of it."
Arnsperger observes that Mauss slips from descriptive observation to normative prescription when he calls nostalgically for a
return to a more authentic human community. "[W]ith alarming
lightheadedness," Arnsperger continues, Mauss "amalgamates
the idea of 'generosity' with practices which, personally, I would
certainly never want to see generalized in society."[30] It is hard to
understand why what Mauss describes as "a polite fiction, formalism, and social deceit"[31] should function as any kind of moral
imperative at all.

Mauss's universalizing of gift giving into a total system has
other disturbing consequences. For one thing, this totality conflates the human and inhuman: "Everything holds together,
everything is mixed up together.... The circulation of goods follows that of men, women, and children, of feasts, rituals, ceremonies, and dances, and even that of jokes and insults." For Mauss,
exchange unites the human and the inhuman and thereby implicitly denies the strong ethical claim of human beings against treatment as things. He insists that gift exchange predates our modern
and "strict distinction...between real rights and personal rights,
things and persons."[32] In fact, his argument explaining the return
of gifts requires such a conflation, so that, as Parry writes, "The
gift contains some part of the spiritual essense of the donor."[33]
In praising systems of gift exchange that include exchanges of
people, Mauss seems to justify or at least naturalize the slavery
practiced by the societies he studies. His intentions obviously
lie elsewhere, but Mauss's exaggeration of the importance of
exchange nevertheless generates disturbing corollaries.

Mauss denies not only the extraordinary status of the human
but also the independence of the individual, and he insists that
"it is not individuals but collectivities that impose obligations

of exchange and contract upon each other." Though he later concedes that some exchanges might involve barter between individuals, wider social obligations always already imbricate these individuals: "barter is hardly carried on except between relatives, allies or partners in the *kula* and the *wasi*."[34] Mauss demotes the individual in favor of "*persons* who enter into the exchanges...as incumbents of status positions and [who] do not act on their own behalf."[35] Marin Terpstra argues that Mauss makes it a central thesis that "human relations cannot hold if people are only motivated by self-interest."[36] Like interest and profit, Mauss argues, the individual represents a relatively new idea: "The victory of rationalism and mercantilism was needed before the notions of profit and the individual, raised to the level of principles, were introduced." He therefore continues to universalize exchange, while denouncing what he terms "The brutish pursuit of individual ends...harmful to the ends and the peace of all, to the rhythm of their work and joys."[37] Mauss's ethnology becomes all-embracing by raising the social to a position both prior to and superior to the individual; the study of society thereby becomes the study of everything by excluding the individual who would stand over and against society.

While Mauss seeks to combat "the brutish pursuit of individual ends," his blanket dismissal of the individual would also disqualify a possible recipient of charity. In fact, Mauss cites Ralph Waldo Emerson on the injuriousness of charity,[38] a point amplified by Douglas's introduction, which opens by trenchantly declaring, "Though we laud charity as a Christian virtue we know that it wounds."[39] Mauss describes a world in which other people appear either as the apparent agents of exchanges truly commanded by social convention or as the objects exchanged, like slaves.

Mauss excludes other people with their ethical claims upon us but also and more radically refuses to allow the gods to stand over and against the all-embracing logic of exchange. He refuses to understand sacrifices, for instance, as violations of self-interest and therefore pure giving, instead labeling them as the most reciprocal of exchanges: "The purpose of destruction by sacrifice is precisely that it is an act of giving that is necessarily reciprocated." Such reciprocation provides the gods with their very reason to be; they "are there to give a considerable thing in the place of a small one."[40] Parry argues that Mauss completely misunderstands gift giving to temples and Brahmins in the Hindu tradition, where a "pure asymmetry must obtain," and that "much the same theme recurs in Theravada Buddhism, where indeed we find the gift without a recipient at all."[41] More relevant to early modern drama, the contrast with the theology of grace that forms the background to *Faustus* is considerable, and sufficient to call into doubt the applicability of Mauss's ideas to the entire period. Camille Tarot notes, "Christian grace contradicts the very foundations of the Maussian gift, and vice versa, even more by the fact that the obligation to give does not apply to God, than by the impossibility of reciprocity and reversibility, which obviously do not apply to the relation between God and man."[42] For all Mauss's efforts to explain religion, he succeeds only in explaining away the generosity central to many of its expressions. Mauss's argument is not only universalizing but also secularizing.

Parry interprets Mauss as not conflating the gift and economics but merely restoring their original unity. Parry can therefore dismiss the pure gift as a recent construct, deeming it an ideology produced by a commitment to the capitalist market: "The ideology of a disinterested gift emerges in parallel with an ideology of a purely interested exchange." He insists that "while Mauss is generally represented as telling us how *in fact* the gift is *never* free, what I think he is really telling us is how *we* have acquired a *theory* that it should be." Our society makes a radical distinction between interested exchanges and disinterested gifts, in order to produce a market ideology in which transactions are self-cancelling, according to Parry, because the object received is paid for and there is no surplus of indebtedness. The free gift enslaves, Parry argues, because it "denies obligation and replaces the reciprocal interdependence on which society is founded with an asymmetrical dependence." Parry's reading still relies on the assumption that gifts impose obligations, only adding that these obligations do not normally cancel themselves out in the manner of commercial transactions. He claims that Mauss's "moral conclusion" was "that the combination of interest and disinterest in exchange is preferable to their separation."[43] However, such a combination still threatens the gift with annihilation, because interested gifts are easily and almost reflexively assimilated into commercial exchange, as Parry himself shows in his summary of the reception of Mauss, as Mauss shows in his choice of metaphors, and as Peperzak complains in his description of postmodern thinkers. Parry claims that the market generates the gift as its necessary corollary in "state societies with an advanced division of labour and a significant commercial sector,"[44] but the logic of the market seems more likely to assimilate and thereby extinguish the gift. Mauss's conflation of gift and economics threatens to obscure any vision of generosity at all, as every imaginable donation is categorized as an exchange. In order to comprehend ourselves as anything but participants in reciprocal trades, we must allow for the possibility of a pure gift, if only as a trace in quotidian exchanges. Otherwise, Mauss's call to generosity would enunciate nothing more than a desire to delude ourselves, obfuscating our own aggression, the better to indulge it.

The Claim of the Other in Continental Philosophy

Mauss's efforts to defend generosity by extending it into an all-powerful and ubiquitous social phenomenon has a perverse effect, because it incorporates and ultimately disqualifies the other person who might serve as the recipient of a gift. Specifically, what is required is a break with the all-encompassing social, so that one can imagine facing another person as a true interlocutor, not as a fellow subject of a sovereign system of exchange. Both Arnsperger and Paul Ricoeur attempt to salvage Mauss's theory of the gift from becoming merely another economy, one whose veiling compounds with bad faith all the evils of greed. Both do so by reference to the work of Levinas, the continental philosopher most closely associated with ethics and alterity.

Mauss's world has no true Other, in the sense used by Levinas, standing over and against me and demanding my aid by her or his very helplessness. Mauss argues that potlatch establishes and can destroy "face": "It is in fact the 'face', the dancing mask, the right to incarnate a spirit, to wear a coat of arms, a totem, it is really the *persona*—that are called into question...and that are lost at the potlatch, at the game of gifts, just as they can be lost in war, or through a mistake in ritual."[45] Where "face" for Mauss measures social respect won by exchanges, Levinas opposes face to social identity: "Ordinarily one is a 'character': a professor at the Sorbonne, a Supreme Court justice, son of so-and-so, everything that is in one's passport, the manner of dressing, of presenting oneself. And all signification in the usual sense of the term is relative to such a context: the meaning of something is in its relation to another thing. Here, to the contrary, the face is meaning all by itself."[46] Levinas treats the phenomenon of the face as the irreducible basis of all social relationships: "Like a shunt every social relation leads back to the presentation of the other to the same without the intermediary of any image or sign, solely by the expression of the face."[47] Specifically, the face makes an ethical summons, which Levinas reads through his Jewish heritage: "the relation to the face is straightaway ethical. The face is what one cannot kill, or at least it is that whose meaning consists in saying: 'thou shalt not kill.'" The face functions as a summons but achieves this summons in language: "The face speaks. It speaks, it is in this that it renders possible and begins all discourse."[48] Levinas refuses to reconcile self and Other within a language. On the contrary, he insists, "Language is a relation between separated terms."[49] He designates by the term "language," neither an impersonal structure standing over and above its speakers, as structuralism has taught literary critics to do, nor the apparent contrary of this structure, an authentic and independent expression by the individual. Instead, he takes language to mean the appeal of the Other, relationship and the interpersonal. Nor does Levinas consider self and Other to be united by society. Instead, their separation constitutes the social: "The idea of infinity is produced in the opposition of conversation, in sociology."[50] Where Mauss places individuals within systems of exchange to be described with the tools of ethnology, Levinas defines sociology by the confrontation between self and Other, who remain radically distinct.

Generosity characterizes the relationship with the Other, according to Levinas. To separate oneself from unconscious absorption in the elemental world, he claims, "I must know how to give what I possess. Only thus could I situate myself absolutely above my engagement in the non-I. But for this I must encounter the indiscreet face of the Other that calls me into question." One does not give to the Other to assert oneself; on the contrary, the Other's call to generosity allows the self to achieve self-awareness initially. The relationship with the Other does not take place outside economic life, however. There is no outside the economy, not because it already accounts for everything imaginable, but because "no face can be approached with empty hands and closed home." The self welcomes the Other "with all the resources of its egoism: economically." The encounter with the Other, and therefore generosity, calls us to participate in a material economy, rather than the exigencies of a material economy demanding gift exchange. For this reason, "No human or interhuman relationship can be enacted outside of economy."[51] Where Mauss describes social relations transcending and constructing the individual, Levinas places the ethical encounter of self and Other prior to an economy, even the gift economy that Mauss turns into a description of all societies. He therefore precisely opposes Mauss's views.

Levinas's understanding of economics as arising from the encounter with an Other becomes most overt in an essay titled "Meaning and Sense," which incorporates an earlier paper, "The

Trace of the Other." Levinas distinguishes his views from both phenomenology and ethnography. "Every human need is from the first already interpreted culturally," Levinas writes, which frustrates efforts to ground thought in a material economy. Ethnography, however, also fails to provide meaning. "The most recent, boldest, and most influential ethnography maintains the multiple cultures on the same plane," he declares. Such diversity produces not a welcome pluralism but a failure of meaning itself: "Absurdity consists not in non-sense but in the isolation of innumerable meanings, in the absence of a sense that orients them."[52] Rather than finding such an orienting sense in the superiority of one culture, the universality of economics, or the authority of a god, Levinas finds it in an orientation toward the Other, which he names "Work": "An orientation which goes *freely* from the Same to the Other is a Work."[53] Where work usually means submitting oneself to an economic system out of self-interest (say, in order to buy food), Levinas uses the same term for a generosity that violates self-interest. In fact, he insists upon asymmetrical generosity: "Now *the Work conceived radically is a movement of the Same toward the Other which never returns to the Same. The Work thought through all the way requires a radical generosity of the movement which in the Same goes toward the Other. It consequently requires an ingratitude of the Other; gratitude would be the return of the movement to its origin.*"[54] Levinas rules out gratitude in order to preserve the generosity of Work, which would otherwise become self-serving. In so doing, he makes a claim for a generosity so radically removed from exchange that it does not even find a recompense in thanks.

Peperzak declares that Levinas's statement "must be understood as an exaggerated expression of the radical independence that separates an authentic gift from the thanks it might yield." Peperzak proceeds to argue against the inverse claim by "some post-Levinasian philosophers" that "donation is inevitably trapped in the economy of mutually useful exchanges." Against such suspicion, he notes that absolute generosity need not occur in a pure state but instead might be found in "only contaminated or mixed realizations." While he insists that gratitude does not destroy generosity, he also insists that it cannot be necessary to any true gift: "If the expectation of gratitude motivates the 'giving,' this is indeed a veiled barter." Nevertheless, he dismisses with a rhetorical question the notion that the only true generosity would have to be so completely unselfish that the donor would not experience joy in giving: "What sort of puritanism or morbidity lurks here?"[55] While arguing in favor of the possibility of generosity, Peperzak also argues against the tendency to reduce the distinction between true generosity and barter to an absolute dichotomy.

If Levinas exaggerates, as Peperzak claims and as Levinas himself seems later to indicate, he nevertheless makes a valuable contribution by reversing the tendency of western thought to begin always with the self and its interests, which Peperzak recognizes.[56] In the original context of "Meaning and Sense," he also and more specifically breaks with the tendency of ethnography to understand all gifts as demanding repayment. Though this tendency finds strong expression in the works of Mauss, it also finds weak expression as a mere habit of thought, which reflexively assumes that all gifts seek recompense. This tendency manifests itself not only in the social sciences but also in the humanities and specifically criticism of early modern drama.

Derrida brings together Levinas's and Mauss's divergent views in his *Given Time*. Mauss's rejection of the gift as ever truly generous justifies Derrida's observation that Mauss's essay "speaks of everything but the gift." In contrast, Derrida claims to depart from a traditional anthropology in which, starting from Mauss, all gifts are returned. In fact, he treats Mauss's study as an example of how any "consistent discussion of the gift becomes impossible: It misses its object and always speaks, finally, of something else."[57] In conscious opposition to Mauss, Derrida defines the gift as an extreme instance of nonreciprocity. Derrida seems to assume, along with the "postmodern authors" whom Peperzak censures, that "appreciation, as such, destroys the very essence or structure of the appreciatable. Even simple awareness—if one perceives the generosity of giving—would annul its existence."[58] In keeping with Derrida's definition, to repay or even owe a gift annuls it. Mere recognition, Derrida argues, provides a symbolic equivalent to the gift as payment in exchange and therefore has the same effect. Acceptance already repays, he argues, at least to a sufficient extent as to annul the gift: "As soon as the other accepts, as soon as he or she takes, there is no more gift." If one allows for unconscious recognition or response, then every gift can become merely "the phenomenon of a calculation and the ruse of an economy." Pure gifts seem, under Derrida's rigorously suspicious gaze, to melt into impossibility. In fact, Derrida declares the gift to be not only impossible in practice but "*the* impossible. The very figure of the impossible. It announces itself, gives itself to be thought as the impossible." Derrida would seem to agree with Mauss in rejecting pure generosity. Derrida adds, however, that "we do not mean to say that *there is no* exchanged gift. One cannot deny the *phenomenon*."[59] The gift is and moreover remains in the presence of exchange, regardless of what its definition would seem to permit.

If the gift proves recalcitrant to thought, this may simply indicate the limits of thought itself, or at least of a way of thinking. Robert Bernasconi reads Derrida as presenting "the aporia of the gift," and argues that Derrida only expresses in more dramatic terms a notion he derives from Levinas's "The Trace of the Other": "the gift is impossible within the order of being and occurs only as an 'interruption' of that order."[60] Derrida concludes a dense passage, which begins with his observation that a description of the gift seems to violate language, by turning language itself into a gift, the origin of which must be investigated: "What is given by the language or the language as given, as a given language, in other words, two ways of determining the gift of the language said to be maternal or natural." Rather than submitting the possibility of a gift to the judgment of language, which seems to collapse into madness in contemplating it, Derrida suggests that one might view language itself as reliant upon the figure of the gift, "as if thinking, the word *thinking,* found its fit only in this disproportion of the impossible, even announcing itself—as thought irreducible to intuition, irreducible also to perception, judgement, experience, science, faith only on the basis of *this* figure of the impossible, on the basis of the impossible *in the figure of the gift?*" In the previous paragraph, he relates the possibility of thinking the gift to "a dimension...wherein *there is* gift—and even where *there is* period, for example time, where *it gives* being and time."[61] Rather than submitting the gift to examination by an economic reason governed by reciprocal exchanges, Derrida implies that the language in which we think the problem should itself be understood as a gift.

Explaining what he means by economy, Derrida emphasizes the importance of circulation. "The figure of the circle," he declares sweepingly, "stands at the center of any problematic of *oikonomia,* as it does of any economic field: circular exchange, circulation of goods, products, monetary signs or merchandise, amortization of expenditures, revenues, substitution of use values and exchange values."[62] This might recall the confidence with which Mauss declares that the word *kula* translates as "circle," which Derrida indeed cites, albeit later. Derrida's immediate metaphor is, however, quite different. "*Oikonomia,*" he declares, "would always follow the path of Ulysses."[63] Derrida borrows this image of circular motion from Levinas, who uses it to contrast with a movement to the Other: "To the myth of Ulysses returning to Ithaca, we wish to oppose the story of Abraham who leaves his fatherland forever for a yet unknown land, and forbids his servants to even bring back his son to the point of departure."[64] This metaphor appears near the description of Work as a movement to the Other, a movement which is not, Levinas insists, circular. Rather than maintaining the circulation of *oikonomia,* the Other interrupts it. In thinking about the gift, therefore, Derrida essays the possibility or impossibility of a Levinasian relationship with alterity.

By bringing Mauss and Levinas into contact, Derrida places two radically different understandings of the gift into debate.

Ricoeur and Arnsperger, on the other hand, combine the two views of the gift. In their argument, the gift remains, as Mauss sought, a basis of social solidarity but only because they insistently replace his economic view of the gift with an understanding of the gift as an ethical act. In one of his last public presentations, delivered by webcam less than half a year before his death, Ricoeur argues that in social contract theory, "[t]he myth of the state of nature accords to competition, to defiance, to the arrogant affirmation of solitary glory, the role of foundation and of origin. In this war of all against all, the fear of violent death would reign supreme." Against such a theory of society founded upon fear and violence, Ricoeur proposes, "we experience actual recognition in a peaceful mode. The model is found in the ceremonial exchange of gifts in traditional societies." Briefly touching upon explanations offered by "sociologists," Ricoeur favors those who find "in the exchange of gifts a recognition of each by the other, a recognition unaware of itself as such, and symbolized in the thing exchanged which becomes its pledge. This indirect recognition would be the peaceful counterpart to the struggle for recognition. In it, the mutuality of the social bond would find its expression. Not that the obligation to give back creates a dependence of the receiver with regard to the giver, but the gesture of giving would be the invitation to a similar generosity."[65] Ricoeur seeks to understand the desire to reciprocate a gift not as a gesture in a power struggle—as it is in much of *The Merchant of Venice*—but as itself an act of generosity. His alteration of Mauss's theory of the gift is subtle but absolute. Rather than conflating the socially productive ceremonies of generosity with the bad faith of aggressive gift exchange practices, Ricoeur separates them.

Ricoeur explicates his reading of gift exchange at greater length in *The Course of Recognition*, published in the same year that his webcast appeared. Ricoeur notes, "Mauss places the gift within the general category of exchanges, on the same level as commercial

exchange, of which he takes it to be the archaic form." Here, as in
many of his books, Ricoeur generously acknowledges the ideas of
others. Specifically, he summarizes the work of Marcel Hénaff as a
challenge to the equivalence of gift and commerce: "The ceremonial reciprocal gift is neither an ancestor nor a competitor of — nor
a substitute for — such commercial exchanges. It is situated on
another plane, that precisely of what is without price." Denying
that the gift forms a more or less covert exchange, Ricoeur finds in
it a moment of recognition. In the words of Claude Lefort, whom
Ricoeur also follows, "Human beings...confirm to one another
that they are not things." The historiography of Natalie Zemon
Davis directs Ricoeur to the early modern world and to the question of how gifts "can go wrong," decaying into mere exchanges.
In response to this challenge, Ricoeur overcomes the seeming
inevitability of reciprocal exchange by reference to the first gift,
that which starts the cycle and is not offered in response to anything else. Such a gift, he argues, does not call for "restitution,
which would, properly speaking, mean annulling the first gift,
but for something like a response to the offer." He concludes by
dismissing "the obligation to give in return" as "largely a weak
construction when considered phenomenologically." "Instead of
the obligation to give in return," he proceeds, "it would be better...to speak of a response to a call coming from the generosity
of the first gift." Gratitude, he concludes, stands as the mark that
distinguishes between gifts, which need recognition, and items
exchanged in commerce: "A *good receiving* depends on gratitude,
which is the soul of the division between good and bad reciprocity." The gift never becomes, for Ricoeur, an impersonal social
structure commanding the actions of individual agents. On the
contrary, as Ricoeur writes with elegant concision, "The one is
not the other. We exchange gifts, but not places." Generosity
remains always interpersonal. The obligation to return, he insists,
does not take place "at a transcendent level in relation to the
transactions between those who give and those who receive."[66]
Gift exchange does not stand over and above its participants or

render them interchangeable. The participants in gift exchange acknowledge each other as interlocutors, rather than merely submitting to social or cultural structure or practice. A gift elicits a response, according to Ricoeur, but because it makes an ethical appeal, rather than a social demand.

By referring to the appeal of an Other, Ricoeur recalls the work of Levinas, whom he discusses[67] and who insists that the face of the Other imposes an ethical obligation, prior and foundational to social norms. Arnsperger also draws upon Levinas in order to explore, as he emphasizes, *"the conditions under which the practice of gift-giving can be seen as foundational for the social link."* He presents his reading of Levinas in the context of an effort to redeem Mauss from serving as "the apostle of the purely agonistic gift (as he presents himself at various points in the *Essai*)." On the contrary, Arnsperger declares, Mauss's call for social solidarity "means much more than giving in order to affirm one's superiority to others—and Mauss himself shows at various points that he intuits precisely this, but he fails to make it nearly explicit enough."[68] Elsewhere, Arnsperger argues that Mauss "has uncovered nothing but another version of the Hobbesian-Lockean vision of society as a mutually beneficial social construct,"[69] albeit a more sophisticated version. In Levinas's claim that "pure altruism" precedes "any moment where, precisely, reciprocity comes in," Arnsperger finds an alternative social foundation to self-interest.[70] A theory of the gift that refuses to reduce it to an obtuse form of aggression not only better describes human life and experience but also rescues Mauss's own vision of the gift as the basis of solidarity from incoherence.

Levinas and Literature

Jill Robbins and Robert Eaglestone, the foremost theorists of Levinas and the literary in the Anglophone world, both construct their readings against the background of embarrassment in the face of Levinas's overt dismissal of the aesthetic in general and the literary in particular. In "Reality and Its Shadow," an essay published in the 1948 volume of *Les Temps Modernes*, Levinas sharply distinguishes between the relationship of a viewer toward a work of art and of the self toward an appellant Other. The artwork remains in an eternal present, whereas in *Time and the Other*, published the previous year, Levinas claims, "The situation of the face-to-face would be the very accomplishment of time."[71] Where the Other confronts, face-to-face, the artwork possesses only an "aspiration to life." Levinas refers to Pygmalion, though he might refer to any number of the Ovidian transformations to which Shakespeare alludes in *Titus Andronicus, The Winter's Tale, Venus and Adonis*, and elsewhere. This "aspiration to life," always fails, however, because "the life of an artwork does not go beyond the limit of an instant." Not only does the artwork take the paradigmatic form of a statue, frozen into timelessness, but also threatens to bewitch the appreciative viewer in an irresponsible participation. With implicit reference to Friedrich Nietzsche's understanding of tragedy, Levinas claims that the artwork possesses a "rhythm," which he defines as "a unique situation where we cannot speak of consent, assumption, initiative or freedom, because the subject is caught up and carried away with it." For Levinas, aesthetics therefore resembles a surrender to myth. "This is not the disinterestedness of contemplation," he declares, "but of irresponsibility." He even goes so far as to declare: "There is something wicked and egoist and cowardly in artistic enjoyment. There are times when one can be ashamed of it, as of feasting during a plague."[72] Robbins concludes that Levinas "is a philosopher who is at pains to exclude the aesthetic,"[73] while Eaglestone asserts, "The essay begs the question of why anybody should be concerned with art at all. The first ethical duty of the critic would appear to be to exile art altogether, thus depriving him or herself of a profession."[74] Eaglestone exaggerates. Levinas does not declare that one should be always and everywhere ashamed of art, only that it should not be identified with "the spiritual life." Only a few sentences later, he claims that "one cannot contest" artistic pleasure "without being ridiculous."[75] In any case, both critics find themselves confronting the embarrassing fact that Levinas's explicit views toward literature and aesthetic objects in general are, at best, ambivalent.

In response to this challenge, both critics build an ethics of critical interruption. Robbins argues that while a text does not interrupt like a person interrupts, reading can interrupt the economy of the same.[76] Eaglestone makes a similar argument, quoting Terence Hawkes's call for "hooligan criticism," meaning criticism that frequently indulges in interruption. Such interruption, he argues, reveals the "Saying" that Levinas describes as an address prior to linguistic systems. Eaglestone places great importance on Levinas's claim in *Otherwise than Being* that books "are interrupted, and call for other books and in the end are interpreted in a saying distinct from the said." Eaglestone finds in such interpretive interruption a constitutive element of contemporary literary theory as a whole: "currently, the various different strands of 'theory' are perhaps the clearest examples of the saying in criticism."[77] Eaglestone published his work in 1997, only a year after Graham Good dismissed Theory as a new orthodoxy, indeed a "hegemony" boasting "cardinal doctrines."[78] The mere practice of seeking fissures, gaps, interrogations, moments of undecidability, or Derridean *aporiai* does not save Theory from becoming its own belief system. More seriously, while Eaglestone entertains to dismiss the possibility that interruption might open not to the face of the Other but to the night of anonymous Being—prior to both the self and ethical responsibility that Levinas describes in his early works[79]—he does not consider that interruptions might open to nothingness itself or simply to nothing in particular.

Levinas does consider these things in a response to Derrida. After an appreciative summation of "the primordial importance of the questions raised by Derrida," Levinas poses a rhetorical question that he proceeds to answer: "Whence the sign from which the presence that is lacking to itself is made, or the inassemblable diachrony from which creatureliness is made? It does not begin (if it does begin, if it is not anarchy through and through) as a Said." This allows him to argue that deconstruction should not be seen as opening only to "*surplus*" but potentially to "the ethics of before being or the Good beyond Being."[80] However, Levinas suggests a contrary possibility in his parenthetical addition: the play of signs might not open to anything. He expands on this possibility in a paper presented at the University of Ottawa, at a conference in honor of Ricoeur. Here, Levinas demonstrates how interruption fails to threaten a philosophy that reduces all Other to the Same and moreover, how the recourse of thought to linguistic signs does not break this pattern. On the contrary, "That one cannot have thought without language, without recourse to verbal signs, would not then attest to any definitive rupture in the egological order of presence.... Finite thought is split in order to interrogate and answer itself, but the thread is retied. Thought reflects on itself in interrupting its continuity of synthetic apperception, but still proceeds from the same 'I think' and returns to it." Within a few pages, Levinas identifies the Said with "all that can be written." Levinas's friendship with Derrida notwithstanding, the mere fact that language is made of signs, or even that signs can be deconstructed, need not produce the sort of interruption that opens to the face of the Other. Over and against the Said, Levinas places "the sociality of the *saying*, in responsibility to the Other who commands the questions and the answers of the saying." Levinas overtly links this responsibility with gratuity: "*From the first*, that is, the ego answers 'gratuitously,' without worrying about reciprocity."[81] Elsewhere, and in another nod to *Macbeth*, he contrasts language as response with the anti-language of "those derisive beings communicating across a labyrinth of innuendos which Shakespeare and Goethe have appear in their scenes of sorcerers."[82] One might contrast the understanding of language as a semiotic system, a social convention, an economy and even a source of critical ambiguity, with language defined by sociality. The former would correspond to the Said and the latter to the Saying. That both can be referred to as *language* is not merely a source of confusion—though it certainly is that—but an indication that they occur simultaneously. In a conversation with Philippe Nemo, Levinas describes the Saying by observing, "It is difficult to be silent in someone's presence; this difficulty has its ultimate foundation in this signification proper to the saying, whatever is the said. It is necessary to speak of something, of the rain and fine weather, no matter what, but to speak, to respond to him and already to answer for him."[83] Of course, one can understand that recourse to the weather as a neutral subject of discussion is a social convention, just as one can analyze or even deconstruct the precise wording of the conversation. None of this, however, would explain the ethical imperative to speak at all, to treat the other person as an interlocutor. Saying explains why there is something and not nothing linguistic. One might draw a parallel between this initial call to language and Ricoeur's "first gift," which starts the pattern of exchanges and cannot be understood as a repayment. The generosity at the heart of language, understood as Saying, is not reducible to the social conventions and semiotic structures that constitute the Said.[84]

Robbins makes the relationship of Saying and the gift particularly clear. She explains: "Generosity and language are the only *non*totalizing modes of relating to the other that are suggested in *Totality and Infinity*." On the next page, she argues that Levinas conceives of language itself as a gift. Specifically, what characterizes both language and gift is non-reciprocity. "Generosity preserves, for Levinas, the radical and absolute asymmetry between myself and another." This primary discourse would be presemiotic, "prior to language conceived of as a system of signs."[85] Robbins rightly and even eloquently argues that language in the sense of Saying shares with the gift a primary importance in Levinas's work. As early as her introduction, Robbins argues that the interruption of the totality should be understood as a gift, coming from without.[86]

I would quibble with both Robbins and Eaglestone, however, by noting that not every interruption can be identified with an ethical response to the Other. Some might even silence the Other, as would interrupting someone begging for mercy by killing him. Chiron's interruption of Lavinia's curse toward him in *Titus Andronicus* furnishes a Shakespearean example.[87] Lavinia's father and uncle seek in vain to find her meaning in her silence, facing a sheer demand. Chiron, by contrast, attempts to silence Lavinia's appeal. One occasionally finds a similar, if considerably less violent, effort at silencing in postmodern theory, driven by a hermeneutic of suspicion to ignore the interlocutor in favor of the subconscious or ideological or bad faith motives ascribed to her or him. The postmodern suspicion of the gift, about which Peperzak complains, is also a suspicion of the Saying. The interruption of the Said is not generous in itself but only when it opens to Saying.

Like Eaglestone, Robbins attempts to discover the ethical in literature and its criticism, though she acknowledges that, as she describes, "it is no more clear that one can ever claim to be exemplifying this ethical language than that one can be in the presence of the saying."[88] Nevertheless, she asks how, for instance, Levinas's own language can achieve what he claims ought to be done by language, when he describes language as originating in responsibility and response to the Other.[89] Levinas never, however, claims that his books constitute pure Saying. On the contrary, Saying always surrenders itself to the Said in order to achieve manifestation. In "Diachrony and Representation," he identifies the Said not only with "all that can be written," but with "the presence of a book—something between bindings—or the presence of a library united between bookshelves."[90] In asking that Levinas's books rise to the achievements he ascribes to language, Robbins seems to confuse language as necessarily relational (the Saying), with language as what can be rendered a written text (the Said). Levinas's hostility toward artwork can be explained by considering that a work of art as such, an aesthetic object, is, like the book, a Said. This does not mean, of course, that it cannot also be a Saying, offered generously to another. One might, for instance, give a book as a gift. For that matter, one might use a quotation from Shakespeare or Marlowe in conversation or even offer it to a lover as a verbal caress. Moreover, the status of artwork as Said in no way contradicts the claim that the language in which the book is written or the aesthetic language in which a painting is executed ultimately derives from the primordial sociality of the face-to-face relation. It merely indicates that the Saying and the Said, though simultaneous, are nevertheless distinguishable. As long as an address takes the form of words, it constitutes both. The difference is not between classes of objects, gestures, words or sentiments, some Saying and some Said, but between the same objects, gestures, words or sentiments, whether understood as addresses by an Other or as impersonal social or linguistic arti-facts. Reference to literary theory is liable to confuse the issue, in fact. Since structuralism, theory has usually labeled a text as "language" in its impersonal aspect, whereas since romanticism, we have thought of art as expressive. Levinas uses these terms in almost the precise reverse of what literary criticism has made customary. In "Reality and Its Shadow," he describes the work of art not as an authentic product of the self or even of the Other but by reference to the idolatry denounced in the Hebrew scriptures.[91] By "language," on the other hand, he usually means the inter-personal, as in the examples offered previously. The aesthetic relationship is with an object, whereas the ethical relationship is with an Other, and Levinas's apparent dismissal of aesthetic objects insists upon the distinction.

While both Robbins and Eaglestone eloquently distinguish between Saying and Said, they seem to wish to blur this distinc-tion, as when Eaglestone appears to argue that interruption turns aesthetic objects into ethical relationships, or when Robbins argues that a mask and a face can be confused and that there is "a certain intercontamination of the governing oppositions in Levinas's discourse."[92] Here, Robbins comes dangerously close to deconstructing or at least denying the distinction of Saying and Said, thereby evading an important part of Levinas's argument.

An attempt to justify criticism leads both Robbins and Eaglestone to take serious risks.

This is not to rule out the possibility of either the literary text or the stage functioning as a Saying, appealing to us directly. The character's gaze toward the audience is simultaneously the actor's, and we remain aware of both. If one does wish to seek interruptions, one might note that dramatic literature is always made up of dialogue between characters, so the viewpoint of an omniscient narrator never simply bewitches the reader of early modern drama. I am principally concerned, however, with how the ethical emerges between the characters for the characters themselves. As readers or audience members, we observe it secondhand and therefore already in the Said. For instance, while Cornwall is threatened by the appeal of Gloucester's defenseless eyes and responds by tearing them out, we feel no such violent anxiety. We might feel something of the appeal, which calls Cornwall's servant to turn upon and indeed slay his master, but we do not lend our hands to their mutual slaughter.[93]

Our judgment and analysis of Gloucester's desperate appeal, Cornwall's cold rage, and the servant's courageous defiance, however, will be colored inevitably by our view of our own world, which is in turn informed by the play. When Levinas declares that "the whole of philosophy is only a meditation of Shakespeare," he does not say that philosophy consists in an experience of Shakespeare, a manner of reading Shakespeare, or an interruption of Shakespeare. On the contrary, in the paragraph in which Levinas's extraordinary statement occurs, he turns to a highly original reading of *Macbeth* to understand the tragedy of existence.[94] Cohen explains the extraordinary importance Levinas ascribes to Shakespeare by arguing that Levinas finds that literature "is thicker, closer, 'truer,' to the ethical exigencies, to the obligations and responsibilities, the imperatives of social life, than is philosophy." In literature, rather than philosophy, one finds "that fundamental moral exigency that constitutes the very humanity of the human."[95] Shakespeare's plays and other literary texts from throughout the Western tradition offer Levinas models for seeing the world and our place in it that are in some ways superior to those offered by philosophy. Where literature informs Levinas's philosophy, Levinas's philosophy offers new readings of literature.

Rather than running the risk of idolatry by trying to turn the relationship with either the plays as performed or their scripts as texts into an ethical relationship, I am content to show how the texts themselves meditate on ethical relationships by presenting ethical relationships between the characters on stage. Of course, early modern plays neither are reducible to morals nor depict only ethical acts. Literature, as Cohen and Levinas recognize, depicts a world, like our own, characterized by ethical exigency. For the most part, our relationship with literature and even theater remains in the Said; it is an intellectual relationship with an object that can be studied. Moreover, an intellectual engagement with the work of literature is not merely a matter of pleasure. It moves us, as Levinas desires, into "full self-possession, . . . through concepts, which are like the muscles of the mind."[96] My goal (and perhaps that of criticism in general) is not to transform plays or their scripts from Saids to Sayings but to treat them as objects of thought. "Nothing can be seen without thematization," Levinas observes in his appreciation of Derrida, "or without the oblique rays reflected by it, even in the case of the non-thematizable."[97] The plays remain in the Said but in a Said that can thematize and be cognizant of love, ethics, generosity and the Saying.

We need not experience or receive the plays as gifts any more than we need take Levinas's own work as a gift. Nevertheless, our understanding of both Levinas's works and those of Shakespeare and Marlowe, and indeed our understanding of our world itself, will be strengthened if we can overcome our suspicion and accept the reality of gifts. For one thing, such a process would allow us to recognize that the suspicion and anxiety various characters exhibit toward the gift reveals a weakness in themselves and in their fictive societies. We can also better understand the action of *Edward II* by acknowledging the possibility of generous love or that of *The Tempest* by recognizing forgiveness. To instead indulge our suspicion of the gift, denying or merely ignoring generous acts and gestures, renders the plays truly mysterious to us. Worse, it renders us mysterious to ourselves, unable to acknowledge our own acts of generosity or those of our neighbors.

New Historicism and Circulation

Mauss's *a priori* assumption dominates criticism of early modern drama. Alan Jacobs parenthetically notes, "The prominence of the terms *exchange* and *negotiation* in the vocabulary of the New Historicism, especially in Stephen Greenblatt's work, is an inheritance from Mauss."[98] Greenblatt's reading of circulation goes well beyond a naive fascination with the circulation of material goods. Whereas Mauss extends "the circulation of goods" to "men, women, and children,...feasts, rituals, ceremonies," Greenblatt extends the objects of his study even further. "What then is the social energy being circulated?" he asks. "Power, charisma, sexual excitement, collective dreams, wonder, desire, anxiety, religious awe, free-floating intensities of experience: in a sense the question is absurd, for everything produced by the society can circulate unless it is deliberately excluded from circulation."[99] Greenblatt does not reduce circulation to goods, but he does reduce social life to circulation, albeit of a broadly defined "social energy." Ricoeur insists that "it is the spirit of the gift that provokes a rupture within the category of goods, consistent with an overall interpretation of sociability as one vast system of distribution."[100] Mauss treats gifts as part of an economic order, but Ricoeur treats the gift as an exception to the economic, which allows an understanding of the social beyond Mauss's treatment of all societies as networks of exchange. While avoiding a crass materialism, Greenblatt nevertheless refuses "a rupture within the category of goods," instead extending the category of goods to cover the most abstract things, in keeping with his understanding of society as a circulation.

While Greenblatt's assumptions handicap criticism, they have enabled brilliant readings of a wide range of texts, not only by Greenblatt himself, but indeed by an entire generation of critics. Greenblatt's abjuration, as he puts it in the first pages of *Shakespearean Negotiations*, of even the possibility of "spontaneous generation of social energy"[101] leads him to discover fascinating lines of influence between far-removed aspects of Renaissance culture, achieving original descriptions not only of Renaissance drama or even literature but of the period as a whole. Douglas confidently declares that in anthropology, "Nothing has been the same since" Mauss's ground-breaking publication,[102] and Greenblatt's work marks a similar watershed in the criticism of early modern drama. We should not, however, consider either Mauss's or Greenblatt's premises binding outside the fields that they serve to create. Mauss defines ethnology, not life itself, and Greenblatt defines his own method of New Historicism rather than drawing impassable frontiers around literary criticism.

Specifically, Greenblatt's methodology seems to share the limit of King Lear's mind. "I believe that nothing comes of nothing," writes Greenblatt in the introduction to *Hamlet in Purgatory*, "even in Shakespeare."[103] With these words, he echoes Lear's "nothing will come of nothing" and "nothing can be made out of nothing."[104] Lear's unwillingness to accept something coming from nothing forces him to understand love as an exchange, thereby bringing about his tragedy. Ironically, Greenblatt's declaration follows closely on his complaint that "my profession has become so oddly diffident and even phobic about literary power, so suspicious and so tense."[105] In his insistence that literary power always has a knowable source, he seems to indulge in the very suspicion of literary power that he claims to diagnose. His assumption allows him to understand early modern drama as a sort of vast recycling depot crammed with the obsolete but still potent anxieties and social energies of its age. He follows John Foxe, for instance, in showing how doctrines of Purgatory become available for fiction by being impugned.[106] The self-imposed limitations on Greenblatt's reading are, however productive, limitations nevertheless.

In *Shakespearean Negotiations*, Greenblatt claims he finds, in place of "an originary moment," only "a subtle, elusive set of exchanges, a network of trades and trade-offs, a jostling of competing representations, a negotiation between joint-stock companies."[107] By *Hamlet in Purgatory*, however, he finds himself arguing that the exchanges that he describes should be understood as individual ones, or at least ones that are motivated by individual concerns. Describing one of the earliest artistic representations of Purgatory, Greenblatt points out that the donor wishes masses to be sung for himself and his family, "for their individual benefit and not for a general communal purpose."[108] If doctrines of Purgatory express a desire to succor the dead, Greenblatt explains this not in terms of how, according to Levinas, one can orient oneself to "a time without me, . . . in an eschatology without hope for oneself,"[109] but in terms of self-interest. Greenblatt considers a foundation in fear, borrowing from Giambattista Vico, and also the mercenary motive that Protestants ascribed to Roman Catholicism, before reaching the more or less ethnological explanation that such doctrines build social solidarity.[110] In this case, he finds only self-interested or socially interested motives for a belief in Purgatory.

Greenblatt later acknowledges concern for an Other in summaries of the texts he analyses, but he gradually detracts from such concern in his expositions. For instance, in summarizing *The Gast of Gy*, he declares, "The loss of all [Gy's] worldly possessions, the crossing of the boundary between life and death, the encounter with vengeful fiends, the dismaying recognition of the sins of the flesh, the commencement of unspeakable torments—none of these ghastly experiences has severed his deepest mortal passion." The ghost returns not only in order to seek prayers that might reduce his own torments but also and primarily in order to warn his wife of what might await her, urging her to seek forgiveness before death. Rather than acknowledging that the doctrine of Purgatory arises from a generous love, distinguishable from self-interest and surviving even death, however, Greenblatt carefully notes that the ghost also wishes to escape his own torments. Ultimately, he dissipates the sources of the doctrine of Purgatory into "a tangle of intense, intimate feelings in the wake of a loved one's death."[111] In his summary of Thomas More's *The Supplication of Souls*, Greenblatt begins by noting that the ghosts in whose voice More writes "do not speak about sin; they speak about connectedness," recalling relationships and promises made while living. His account of this connectedness, however, ends in reciprocity and therefore in self-interest on the part of the person being solicited for prayers: "Not only are the living helping their loved ones; they are also helping themselves."[112] Within a few pages, he describes the appeal of the souls in Purgatory "as if their supplication were an investment prospectus."[113] While Greenblatt acknowledges a charitable impulse underlying prayers for the dead, he tends to side with the Protestant polemicists whom he quotes in viewing the interest in Purgatory as a form of self-interest, fueled by fear of punishment. Like them, he focuses on the material cost of chantry masses and offerings. He quotes William Tyndale, for instance, denouncing the purchase of indulgences as a scam, not truly aiding anyone but the Pope.[114] Instead of recognizing generosity in the purchase of indulgences or the offering of prayers for others, Greenblatt roots such practices in fear for the self, fueled by highly theatrical images of torment. While Peperzak argues that generosity may only be found in "contaminated or mixed realizations,"[115] Greenblatt follows Mauss in minimizing the radical claims of generosity in favor of structures of exchange.

Greenblatt acknowledges that the doctrine of Purgatory relies upon generosity but then finds other explanations for its power. He also acknowledges but marginalizes how the Protestant denunciation of the economy of salvation derives its force from a doctrine of salvation by grace. Catholic doctrines of Purgatory grow from a love for the dead; Protestant rejection of this doctrine grows from a belief in the gratuity of grace. Peperzak argues: "Together with generosity, gratuitous benevolence, goodness, love, and superabundance, giving has formed an all-encompassing horizon for Jewish and Christian theologians, from the time of Philo and Origen to today."[116] Both the contending parties in the great debates about the status of Purgatory derived their positions from a commitment to generosity, whether God's or man's,[117] whereas Greenblatt's criticism relies on an unending circulation of social energy.

A quarter century before writing *Hamlet in Purgatory*, Greenblatt examined Tyndale and More's polemical duel in *Renaissance Self-Fashioning*. In Tyndale's "nothing bringeth the wrath of God so soon and so sore on a man, as the idolatry of his own imagination," Greenblatt reads a confession of the weakness of the entire doctrinal structure of Christianity, arguing, "To a reader who believes, as I do, that all religious practices and beliefs are the product of the human imagination, these charges have a melancholy and desperate sound. It is as if the great crisis in the Church had forced into the consciousness of Catholics and Protestants alike the wrenching possibility that their theological system was a fictional construction; that the whole, vast edifice of church and state rested on certain imaginary postulates; that social hierarchy, the distribution of property, sexual and political order bore no guaranteed correspondence to the actual structure of the cosmos."[118] This has obvious importance for Greenblatt's reading of religion in the early modern world. Denounced as imaginary, social energies hitherto associated with religion became liberated to play a role as overt imaginary constructs, converting their charisma into the power of Elizabethan and later Jacobean theatre and poetry. It is typical of Greenblatt that his strongest argument reduces the importance of religion to providing a metaphysical justification for social arrangements. More importantly for his response to Tyndale, he also reduces religion to a product of the imagination. His argument treats religious belief as nothing but what comes from within. Religion and religious worship cease to be relationships with an Other in Greenblatt's description. In fact, later in the same paragraph, he reduces alterity to a product of the demonization of an opponent, in order to "assure the absolute reality and necessity of the order to which one has submitted oneself."[119] It is hardly surprising to find a secular thinker denying revelation, of course, but Greenblatt bases much of his criticism on this denial, extending it to an implicit denial of alterity as radically exterior to the self and society. This denial allows him to examine all of early modern society as a ceaseless web of circulations, exchanges, and negotiations, which seems profoundly at odds with the religious character of early modern thought.

Greenblatt's assumptions impose limits not only on readings of early modern drama, but also on our understanding of our own world.[120] The assumption that all gifts call for return, which Mauss enunciates in ethnology, leads critics to ignore or explain away acts of generosity. While Peperzak rightly notes that the gift might never exist in a pure state in nature, the hyperbolic claim of Levinas's ethics must nevertheless be heard, lest we forget that the gift exists at all. Only by recognizing a radical generosity can we avoid the tendency to think of dramatic characters as nothing but participants in exchanges. Questioning the assumptions of critics regarding the fictive worlds in which the characters of Elizabethan and Jacobean drama find themselves allows me to question our assumptions about our own world and about whether we are condemned to view each other exclusively or merely primarily as participants in exchanges.

The powerful utility of Mauss's belief in reciprocal exchange can be applied to *The Merchant of Venice*, Shakespeare's most extended meditation on debt and obligation. A charming but strictly internal generosity characterizes this fictive society at the cost of excluding aliens and denying the extraordinary claim of the Other. The fictive Christian society of Venice also evades the possibility of gratuitous salvation, central to Protestant soteriology from Luther onward. This exclusion of grace and of the gift more generally dramatizes the difficulty of reconciling a culture understood in Maussian terms with a belief in true generosity. Early modern drama questions an absolute belief in exchange. In the characters of Lear and Faustus, such a belief in exchange approaches the fatality of a tragic flaw, and in *King Lear*, the tragedy proceeds from an unwillingness to make a gift as anything other than an exchange. Lear's moral transformation takes the form of a new openness toward generosity. The denial of the gift is tragic for characters and debilitating for critics.

As in *King Lear*, the effort in *Merchant* to speak love opens it to betrayal. Antonio's offer of "my purse, my person, my extremest means"[121] to Bassanio expresses his love but leads him into competition with Portia, transforming his failed attempt at self-sacrifice from an act of generosity to the imposition of an obligation. The king's love for Gaveston in Marlowe's *Edward II*, initially almost absurdly nonreciprocal, becomes assimilated into political structures, and the participants in those structures understand love as little more than another form of alliance. An initially generous and nonreciprocal love betrays itself by taking expression.

The movement from radical generosity to reciprocal exchange mimics the movement from the Saying to the Said in Levinas's theory of language. In *Titus Andronicus*, Lavinia initially appears as little more than an object exchanged between men: rape and mutilation brutally erase her value in exchange. Rather than being immediately rejected as worthless, however, she commands a new interest from Titus, Marcus, and the other men of her family. These men replace their view of Lavinia as a guarantor of dynastic alliances with a heartbreakingly unrealizable but nevertheless generous concern to hear her voice. Prospero in *The Tempest* shows a similar love for his daughter Miranda when he abandons absolute power on the island for death in Milan. Like Titus surrendering his hand for his sons, Prospero ransoms his own power for Miranda's future. Like Edward II, he makes his sacrifice by entering into the political world. Unlike Antonio attempting to suffer death to express his love for Bassanio, moreover, he makes his sacrifice anonymously, because Miranda never learns what he has done. Political engagement, in this last play, realizes sacrifice rather than self-aggrandizement.

On the early modern stage, both language and politics arise from an originary generosity. Edward only wields political power for the sake of Gaveston, whom he loves; similarly, Prospero only returns to the dukedom of Milan for the sake of Miranda, whom he also loves. Antonio becomes indebted to Shylock and enters into the entire web of obligations and debts out of a love for Bassanio that initially seems barely to enter his consciousness, much less overtly drive his decisions. It is a habit of criticism to attempt to explain characters' actions in terms either of self-interest or manipulation (by others or by power or by society in general). However, in these plays, generosity does not reveal itself as a ruse of economics, a polite fiction driven by self-interest, or an instrument of social organization. Rather, a primary generosity inspires politics and even language.

ONE

The Venice of Merchants

In his moment of triumph, immediately after choosing the correct casket, Bassanio turns to Portia: "Fair lady," he defers to her, "by your leave, / I come by note, to give and to receive." He refuses to believe his good luck "Until confirmed, signed, ratified by you" (3.2.139–48). The scroll instructs him to "claim her with a loving kiss," so he will presumably give and receive a kiss, as John Cunningham and Stephen Slimp note.[1] More broadly, however, he receives what he came for, Portia's fortune and person. What he gives may strike us as trivial—his blood as a gentleman (3.2.250–53)—but he nevertheless feels a need to give something and describes the transaction as governed by a written note and requiring a seal, signature, and ratification. Bassanio declares love in commercial terms, and belief in the reciprocity of giving and receiving informs his language. He chooses the lead casket, which requires him to "give and hazard all he hath" (2.7.16; 2.9.20), or, as he says, "Which rather threaten'st than dost promise aught" (3.2.105). Morocco and Arragon reject the notion of giving without recompense. "Hazard for lead?" Morocco asks, incredulously (2.7.17), while Arragon dismisses the lead casket with an apostrophe: "You shall look fairer ere I give or hazard" (2.9.21). No suitor wishes to give freely, but Bassanio's success endorses the belief that giving elicits recompense. "To give and to receive" are intimately bound together in this play, making the inscription that appears threatening also, paradoxically, promising.

In their exchanges of reciprocal favors, gifts, and donations, the characters anticipate Maussian ethnology, in which, according to Douglas, "The whole society can be described by the catalogue of transfers that map all the obligations between its members. The cycling gift system is the society."[2] *The Merchant of Venice*, rather than demonstrating Mauss's thesis, explores what the world would be like if Mauss were right, that is, if all gifts really were aggressive acts. While Faustus refuses to recognize a gift in the form of grace, Venice's entire fictive society bases its internal order on the rejection of pure generosity. Such a constriction of thought need not necessarily be conscious on the characters' parts, or even on the author's part. In their expectations of payment, the characters merely reflect the norms of their society. The author, similarly, depicts a society with certain norms, then creates consistency based on those norms. The play depicts the tendency of commercial societies to view people as little more than agents in agonistic exchanges. It therefore illustrates the cost of a model of social life in which love becomes competition and mercy is traded for money. If we do not always notice how strange such a world is, this is because we, too, are bewitched by exchange.

This is not to say that the play is a satire. It does not depict the characters abandoning love for the sake of gain, for instance, nor merely obfuscating commercial transactions under the guise of love. Audiences and readers generally react to *The Merchant of Venice* with vague discomfort, not disgust at the Christian characters, as they would were it a straightforward social satire. Nor does my reading of the play undertake the sort of "phenomenology of unveiling"[3] by which an apparently generous society reveals how it truly operates. Though the characters show themselves to be more self-seeking than they admit, their actions proceed from the premises of their society. René Girard reads the play as a damning satire, but even he must argue that the satire is covert, cleverly hidden under a comic structure from "those fools" who do not notice it.[4] In doing so, Girard acknowledges, however reluctantly, the charm of the play and its depiction of a society structured by gift exchange. The belief that every donation stakes a claim constricts the characters' understanding of love and everything else, as though they have already read Mauss and then built their own community around what is both his descriptive claim about how societies actually function and his prescriptive demand for the social solidarity created by reciprocal gift giving. This solidarity of the fictive Christian community comes at the cost of a denial of true generosity, however. The limitations of its worldview explains why this society needs Shylock as a scapegoat as well as why it practices slavery. Rather than unveiling how society really works, the play unveils the openness of a belief about how society really works. Mauss's *a priori* claim that all gifts stake claims constricts any society that adopts it.

The play's world can be mapped in terms of obligations created by donations, in keeping with Mauss's ethnology. "The play" as Gabriel Egan notes, "is set in a city utterly dependent on exchange."[5] Whereas Shylock charges "[d]irectly int'rest" (1.3.74), the Christian Venetians obtain a more tacit recompense. "To you, Antonio," says Bassanio, "I owe the most in money and in love" (1.1.130–31). Marc Shell calls such indebtedness "spiritual usury," which he claims was condemned by "the church fathers." Such rarefied banking "refers to hoping for gratitude, or some other kind of binding obligation, in return for giving a loan that is otherwise given gratis. Perhaps Antonio's loan of his body for Bassanio's wealth not only bound, but was also made with the intention of binding, Bassanio to him."[6] In this case, as throughout the play, a favor precedes and imposes an obligation. Girard describes these exchanges as "a new form of vassality" that is "grounded no longer in strict territorial borders but in vague financial terms."[7] Even Old Gobbo offers a dish of doves in exchange for his son's position (2.2.129–30).[8] Given the ubiquity of exchanges, any apparent gesture of goodwill is immediately dismissed—by critics and usually by characters—as an effort to impose an obligation. Indeed, it seems intended to impose an obligation, leaving a truly generous gift almost unthinkable.

That commercial models extend into all spheres of Venetian life has become a critical commonplace. Lars Engle observes that *The Merchant of Venice* "is unusual," among Shakespearean plays, "in that hardly any relationship between two characters is left as solely emotional or erotic: all have some explicit economic or legal analogue," and concludes that "the pattern of credit and debit, payment and profit, is drawn in this play with nearly the precision of an auditor's report."[9] The tendency to understand human relations in commercial terms spreads like a contagion. The seemingly discrete worlds of Belmont, Venice, and its ghetto are, Tony Tanner observes, "inter-involved" by ties of credit and cash flows.[10] Antonio sends ships to participate in distant commerce and he borrows against their return in order to finance Bassanio's journey to Belmont. For all the rhetoric of cultural difference between Jew and Christian, all the characters submit themselves to what Geoff Baker calls "the market politics that transform everyone involved into a pure other-denying investor."[11] Richard Henze declares that all of the characters are merchants: "First there is the title, *The Merchant of Venice,* which applies to Antonio with his ships, then to Bassanio with his hopeful voyage toward Belmont, love, and profit, then to Shylock and his breeding of money, then to Portia and her dear buying of Bassanio. Portia's questions, " 'Which is the merchant here? And which the Jew?' (IV, i, 174) come later, in the trial scene, but the audience may well inquire earlier, for each of the leading characters is indeed a merchant."[12] Henze's observation threatens to become a platitude, in fact. At least five articles have used Portia's questions as their title, starting with Henze's own in 1974.[13] A reading of the play as a satire implies an unveiling of the commercial basis of the play's society and perhaps even Shakespeare's own, but it does not question Mauss's central thesis. On the contrary, such a reading exploits Mauss's strategy of unveiling and endorses his *a priori* assumption that all gifts are self-interested.

Rather than revealing how the world operates in general, an exploration of the ubiquity of reciprocal exchange in this play reveals the horizons of this society in particular, and why it seems in many ways a strange and even self-contradictory world. Rejecting bonds seems almost literally unthinkable to most of the characters. Hence, Portia's legal quibble appears obvious but only in retrospect. At least the second half of her argument, that attempted murder of Venetians by aliens is illegal, albeit governed by xenophobic laws, should have been apparent to the duke and everybody else. It needs no cross-dressed and counterfeit doctor come from Padua to tell us this. Shakespeare appears to have added the injunction against murder, which John Russell Brown claims is not found in any of his sources.[14] His addition of the murder law renders obvious the case against Shylock. One may certainly join John Velz in admiring Portia's legal shrewdness[15] but may also wonder if it is not rather her naivety that allows her to notice the loophole hidden in plain sight. Fidelity to the interlocked notions of commercial contract, reciprocal agreement, and the integrity of the state blinds everyone else. Even Portia over-enforces the bond rather than overturning it. Shylock is, as Hugh Short terms it, "maddeningly literalist,"[16] but Portia adopts and extends his hermeneutics, interpreting the bond in a way that Richard Weisberg describes as "so narrowly, so literally, that it cannot be enforced on its terms."[17] Portia reads the bond with malevolent precision: "He shall have nothing but the penalty" (4.1.318). Her insistence on fastidiously weighing the pound of flesh would render almost any contract illegitimate:

> But just a pound of flesh. If thou tak'st more
> Or less than a just pound, be it but so much
> As makes it light or heavy in the substance
> Or the division of the twentieth part

> Of one poor scruple—nay, if the scale do turn
> But in the estimation of a hair,
> Thou diest, and all thy goods are confiscate.   (4.1.322–28)

In the world of this play, bonds cannot be rejected; they can only be enforced.

The tendency of each character to become, as Baker writes, "pure other-denying investor," and of critics to understand their relationships in commercial terms, follows from the fictional society's rejection of pure generosity. Lear's (and Greenblatt's) claim that "nothing will come of nothing" could serve as the motto of the Venetian republic.[18] Not all exchanges are overtly commercial or take legal form like Shylock's bond, but all express the same assumption that obliges Bassanio to send "[g]ifts of rich value" (2.9.90) to Belmont and therefore to borrow from Antonio. As Lawrence Hyman notes, "In a purely literal sense there is no good reason for Bassanio's wanting a large sum of money to carry on his suit."[19] Bassanio begs "the means / To hold a rival place" (1.1.173–74) but he has no rivals, because Portia, as she complains, "may neither choose who I would, nor refuse who I dislike" (1.2.20–21). Moreover, Bassanio soon abandons his pretense of affluence, as he shows by recalling that he "freely told" Portia that "all the wealth I had / Ran in my veins: I was a gentleman" (3.2.250–53). In his over-elaborate metaphor to loans as arrows, he seems to promise not to spend Antonio's money, offering "to find both / Or bring your latter hazard back again" (1.1.150–51). Hyman argues that the loan establishes a symmetry between Portia and Antonio as rival donors to Bassanio, allowing Antonio to make a claim on him, but this is Antonio's reason to offer, not Bassanio's reason to ask.[20] Bassanio borrows the three thousand ducats simply because he cannot imagine approaching Belmont empty handed.

Similarly, Jessica furnishes herself with wealth when escaping into Lorenzo's grasping arms, as though providing herself with a dowry. Ironically, Lorenzo takes her theft as evidence that "true she is, as she hath proved herself" (2.6.52–57). In a world in which exchange is so important, Jessica's gift allows her to enter the marriage as a bargain, to provide a reciprocal exchange for her new Christian identity and even for her salvation because, as she later argues with Lancelot, her husband "hath made me a Christian" (3.5.17–18). Lorenzo's declaration of Jessica's truth might actually follow from the fact that she prefers to purchase and thereby participate in her new society's values. To exchange is to be "true," in this society built upon exchange.

Various readings, and certainly the characters themselves, insistently distinguish between Shylock's contract and the relationships of the Christian characters. These same characters, however, recognize the legitimacy of Shylock's bond. Nevill Coghill seems to have been the first critic to treat the play as an allegorical battle of "Justice and Mercy, of the Old Law and the New,"[21] and a whole spectrum of interpretations have relied upon "a contrast between Portia and Shylock, Belmont and Venice, love and hatred, or mercy and strict justice."[22] Whether the victory is interpreted as one of mercy or love or Belmont, the bond is nevertheless enforced. The law, Portia makes clear, is unalterable: "'Twill be recorded for a precedent, / And many an error by the same example / Will rush into the state. It cannot be" (4.1.215–19). Shylock declares, "If you deny me, fie upon your law! / There is no force in the decrees of Venice" (4.1.100–01). Oddly, Antonio agrees with him, claiming that denying the bond would "much impeach the justice of the state" (3.3.29). Not even Antonio suggests that the bond is simply illegitimate. Later, he refuses to seek his own life and asks that nobody else intercede for him, either:

> I do beseech you,
> Make no more offers, use no farther means,
> But with all brief and plain conveniency
> Let me have judgement and the Jew his will.   (4.1.79–82)

As Cynthia Lewis argues, Antonio embraces his fate because by dying he makes another gift to Bassanio, one sealed by death, and thereby wins forever the contest of patronage with Portia.[23] The desire to place Bassanio under a debt drives him to accept Shylock's bond in all its mortal consequences. The Christian characters accept the bond because they accept the wider assumption that donations stake claims. In particular, the logic of exchange has a death grip on Antonio's mind.

All the play's major characters seek the dignity of active agents in reciprocal exchanges. To do otherwise would be to become a thief, like Lorenzo,[24] or a beggar, as Antonio briefly is, imploring Shylock merely to listen to his pleas for life. His claim, "Fortune shows herself more kind / Than is her custom," because she spares him having to "outlive his wealth" (4.1.264–66) should not be dismissed as the stoicism of a man facing a firing squad, or, in Antonio's case, a knife-wielding banker. Antonio earlier illustrates his willingness to die rather than beg when he abandons the effort to implore Shylock for his life: "I'll follow him no more with bootless prayers" (3.3.20). His interview asking for the loan is a study in embarrassment. Antonio opens with an apology for his hypocrisy: "[A]lbeit I neither lend nor borrow / By taking nor by giving of excess, / Yet to supply the ripe wants of my friend / I'll break a custom" (1.3.58–61). Shylock, for his part, does not neglect the opportunity to rub it in: "Methoughts you said you neither lend nor borrow / Upon advantage" (1.3.66–67). A few lines later, he makes Antonio's reliance upon him explicit: "Well then, it now appears you need my help" (1.3.111). Rather than being "beholden" to Shylock (1.3.102), even for the friendship expressed by a loan, Antonio prefers to pay a usurer: "[L]end it rather to thine enemy / Who, if he break, thou mayst with better face / Exact the penalty" (1.3.131–33). Shell suggests that the pound of flesh is added in order to allow for an interest-free loan, but he admits that it does, in fact, constitute a sort of interest, a penalty for nonperformance such as the "mortgages and bonds" that Francis Bacon viewed as more extortionate than usury itself.[25] More generally, the pound of flesh allows the bond to be reciprocal, an exchange rather than a favor, for which Antonio would be "beholden."

Not only do all characters share the *a priori* assumption that gifts create obligations, but also the plot itself relies upon it. For instance, Bassanio becomes indebted to Antonio for his wealth and nearly placed under a crushing debt by watching Antonio die for him. Bassanio is "much bound" to Antonio, as Portia observes (5.1.136). The narrative would fail if an act of true mercy or a true gift were to violate the reciprocity of exchange, if Shylock were to tear the bond, for instance, or if Antonio were to tell Bassanio literally to forget all about repaying, even with memory. Even the last act would be dramatically foreshortened were Portia to shrug off Bassanio's decision to give away her ring. Antonio seems troubled by his own logic in describing why the state must grant Shylock's suit. Lewis notes that his lines are "rendered nearly impenetrable by" his "tortuous language" and takes this as "evidence of his maladjustment to the material world."[26] However, his syntax could just as easily betray the difficulty of forcing himself to subscribe to an irrational belief, albeit one in which, according to Edward Andrew, he "anticipates the great founders of rights-doctrines in the century following Shakespeare."[27] Even if we accept the legitimacy of Shylock's bond, however, other questions present themselves, some proposed by Moody E. Prior: "And why does Antonio have to default? Where are those many whom he had saved from Shylock's clutches? Was there no one to save a respected citizen from the humiliation of becoming prey to a despised usurer?"[28] Shell asks why Antonio fails to insure his argosies and concludes that his rejection of usury must amount to a sort of fanaticism.[29] As Brown notes, Shakespeare seems to have exaggerated some of the improbabilities in his sources, multiplying Antonio's lost ships from one to six, for instance.[30] Shakespeare seems determined to test the limits of probability, as if to emphasize the strangeness of the world he has created. The principle of reciprocal exchange becomes extended to absurd lengths, constraining not only the characters' minds but also the plot in which they find themselves.

The logic of exchange also constrains love, as Portia's scrupulous adherence to her father's will illustrates. The lovers in two of Shakespeare's sources for the plot of *The Merchant of Venice* receive assistance[31] but Portia considers cheating only to reject the very notion with a tautology: "I could teach you / How to choose right, but then I am forsworn" (3.2.10–11). In fact, Portia does not even reveal the right casket once Bassanio has already chosen it, instead urging her love to "be moderate! Allay thy ecstasy, / In measure rain thy joy, scant this excess!" (3.2.111–12). Her denials, Harry Berger notes, present hints that she might surrender to the temptation to reveal the correct chest. Portia's and Bassanio's desire to cheat is never explicit and perhaps never rises to consciousness.[32] Their reluctance shows that the characters remain slavishly faithful to whatever bonds have been placed upon them, even unenforceable ones; it also shows that an admission of their desire would constitute an admission of love, something that they flirtatiously approach but always try to control. Such flirtation manifests itself in their playful inquisition, or what Bassanio calls a "happy torment, when my torturer / Doth teach me answers for deliverance!" (3.2.37–38). As Lewis notes, Portia shows her first instance of concern for anyone other than herself during her interview with Bassanio.[33] The incident seems to disturb her. When Nerissa first mentions Bassanio, Portia responds eagerly and then implies that she has nearly forgotten him: "Yes, yes, it was Bassanio—as I think, so was he called" (1.2.112–13). Later, she denies an amatory motive: "There's something tells me," she says, "but it is not love— / I would not lose you" (3.2.4–5). Bassanio finds himself "Giddy in spirit" at his triumph (3.2.144) and must reduce the situation into the terms of commercial exchange to regain his balance, as it were. Portia's confession of love is also couched in the language of commerce but strains it to the breaking point. She wishes "That only to stand high in your account / I might in virtues, beauties, livings, friends / Exceed account" (3.2.155–57). The "credit and debit, payment and profit," of which Engle writes nearly overwhelm the "auditor's report" in which he contextualizes them.[34] Love threatens to violate the exchange mechanisms by which the characters, and for that matter critics, understand the fictive world. Portia risks giving herself absolutely and without recompense:

> Myself and what is mine to you and yours
> Is now converted. But now I was the lord
> Of this fair mansion, master of my servants,
> Queen o'er myself; and even now, but now,
> This house, these servants, and this same myself
> Are yours, my lord's.   (3.2.166–71)

Portia's love threatens her with subjugation; moreover, it threatens the system of exchanges that organize her society and the action of the play. In George Granville's eighteenth-century adaptation, Bassanio "immediately gives it all back in a flood of gratitude."[35] In Shakespeare's play, on the other hand, Portia salvages her dignity by adding, "I give them with this ring" (3.2.171). The ring and Portia's florid self-surrender impose reciprocal bonds of loyalty and debt. Briefly, however, the best-laid plans of Mauss and men threaten to go astray. The love of Portia and Bassanio is not simply false, as it would be in a satire, but constrained by a society constructed upon Maussian lines.

Relations between Christians and Jews distinguish themselves from those internal to the Christian community in a straightforward way. This sectarian distinction follows that between an explicit economy, driven by money, and an implicit economy, expressed in reciprocated acts of generosity. Whereas the exchanges between Christian characters include all the social obligations of friendship and kindness, indifference and even hostility mark those with Jewish characters. The duke judges Shylock in advance of the trial, calling him "an inhuman wretch / Uncapable of pity, void and empty / From any dram of mercy" (4.1.3–5). Shylock certainly seems to merit such a description, but the Christians act cruelly toward him in turn, or rather preemptively. Antonio leads the play's anti-Semitism but his hatred exemplifies that of all the Christian characters and is not merely an idiosyncratically malevolent quirk. Salerio and Salarino, two nearly choric characters, announce Shylock's heartbreak at Jessica's abandonment of him by parodying his "passion so confused, / So strange, outrageous, and so variable," and describing how "all the boys in Venice follow him, / Crying, 'His stones, his daughter, and his ducats!'" (2.8.12–13; 2.8.23–24). They frankly admit their role in the plot, as Salerio confesses, or rather boasts, "I for my part knew the tailor that made the wings she flew withal" (3.1.25–26). This may be more than a metaphor, because Jessica disguises herself in "the lowly garnish of a boy" (2.6.45) and must obtain the costume somewhere. A small detail from Antonio's interview with Shylock seeking the loan is perhaps more indicative of the vast gap between the religious communities than the wide-ranging conspiracy at which Salerio hints. Though Antonio admits spitting on Shylock, he nevertheless has to be introduced to him, as though they have never before acknowledged one another (1.3.37–38). The two communities share an intimacy marked by enmity, which individual acts of hate exemplify rather than explain.

Neither Mauss's unveiling of self-interest under the cloak of generosity nor his praise of social solidarity constructed and reinforced by gift-exchange fully explain the play. The Christian community finds its definition in acts of intracommunal generosity, but these acts not only construct their community but also measure its limits. In one of his earliest statements of the radically nonreciprocal relationship with the Other, Levinas uses the figure of the stranger.[36] Because reciprocal exchanges of gifts both construct and measure the limit of the fictive Christian community of Venice, the stranger is necessarily excluded. Throughout the play, generous acts are almost strictly intracommunal, and the rare exceptions, such as Shylock's supposedly "kind" offer, merely illustrate the rule. Lester G. Crocker opposes the tendency to read the Christian characters as malicious by observing, "The Christians are condemned only through Jewish eyes, and those words are turned to mockery and villainy."[37] Alan Holaday also observes Antonio's many virtues but adds that "what one dare not overlook in one's admiration for these virtues is his cruelty to the Jew."[38] Both critics are correct, because Antonio's virtues and cruelty show, respectively, the solidarity of a society based on gift exchange and its cruelty to the alien outside it. His virtues are shown only toward his own community: "he loves and forgives Bassanio beyond all measure, but hates and reviles Shylock."[39] Although Antonio initially refuses a bond from Shylock that would imply friendship, he tells Bassanio to "but say to me what I should do / That in your knowledge may by me be done, / And I am pressed unto it" (1.1.158–60). Similarly, even before learning what Gratiano's suit is, Bassanio assures him, "You have obtained it" (2.2.170). The Christian characters exchange favors with all the spontaneity of friendship but deal with the Jewish characters only by way of contract and as enemies. The Christians insist on the distinction between the friendship enjoyed within their own community and the enmity that marks its relations with outsiders. Shylock, for his part, shows no compunction to even feed his Christian servant well, or at least so Lancelot claims in his incoherent manner: "you may tell every finger I have with my ribs" (2.2.102). Rather than serve him, Lancelot redirects his father's gift to Bassanio, "who indeed gives rare new liveries" (2.2.104–05) entering into a gift exchange with a potential master in the Christian community. The circulation of gifts constitutes the Christian community in Shakespeare's fictive Venice, and gift exchange also measures the limits of this community, which excludes aliens, treating them not as partners but as enemies.

The *Oxford English Dictionary* lists two groups of definitions for the word "kind" as an adjective. The more common meaning, at least now, is "Naturally well-disposed; having a gentle, sympathetic, or benevolent nature; ready to assist, or show consideration for, others."[40] An older definition—denoting a natural condition, or even kinship—was still active in the late sixteenth century,[41] and both definitions resonate in the play, where being "kind" implies both social decency and blood relationship. Shylock calls breeding "the deed of kind" (1.3.82), then later describes Lancelot as "kind enough, but a huge feeder" (2.5.45–47). Bassanio conflates both definitions when he calls Antonio:

> The dearest friend to me, the kindest man,
> The best-conditioned and unwearied spirit
> In doing courtesies, and one in whom
> The ancient Roman honour more appears
> Than any that draws breath in Italy.   (3.2.290–94)

In being kind, in the sense of well-disposed, Antonio shows himself a member of his kind, an Italian and the inheritor of ancient Romans virtues. When Salerio says, "A kinder gentleman treads not the earth" (2.8.35), he makes a similar conflation between Antonio's benevolent disposition and his membership in a community. Shylock makes a bid for membership within the Christian community by entering into the noncommercial exchanges that constitute it, declaring, "This is kind I offer" (1.3.138). Bassanio distrusts him, rhyming "kind" with "villain's mind" (1.3.176), but Antonio accepts Shylock's bid for membership in the community, observing, "The Hebrew will turn Christian: he grows kind" (1.3.175). In the previous line, he calls Shylock "gentle," punning on "gentile" (1.3.174). The Christian characters reflexively understand kindness as membership in their own community. Even following her baptism, Jessica is referred to as Lorenzo's "infidel" (3.2.216). Bassanio greets her husband but not her, while Portia delegates the job of greeting her to Nerissa (3.2.235). The play as a whole portrays a Christian community defined by reciprocal acts of kindness, reflecting the common racial kind of its members, and sharply distinguishing itself from the non-Christians with whom they have strictly business dealings.

The Venetian Christian community enjoys a gift economy like those Mauss finds in many of the world's cultures, but deals with aliens using an explicitly legal economy. In fact, the Venetian Christian community appears to be constituted by exchange, with reciprocal acts of kindness building social solidarity, as Mauss insists ought to happen. The Christian society can be described nearly exhaustively by relationships based on gift exchange and incorporating even the Gobbos. In this case, "The cycling gift system is the society," indeed.[42] On the other hand, Shylock stands outside such a gift system. Other than a dinner he attends reluctantly (2.5.12–14), nobody gives him anything in the way of a gift. Mauss appears to join the Christians of the play in taking Shylock to epitomize a life outside a community based on gift exchange when he claims, "The life of a monk and the life of a Shylock are both equally to be shunned."[43]

Both the Christian characters and Mauss are wrong, however, to see Shylock's business dealings as opposed to a gift economy. On the contrary, the gift economy does not stand over and against economic reason but extends it. Shylock's bond renders the tacit obligations that constitute the Christian community not only written and legal but also explicit. "So says the bond; doth it not, noble judge?" he asks rhetorically but eagerly, citing "the very words" (4.1.250–51). Like social contract theorists, Shylock insists upon the importance of contractual bonds. "Hobbes," writes Andrew, "enunciated philosophically Shylock's emphasis on fidelity." To Hobbes, "the violation of faith, the failure to keep promises" appears only "as absurdity, logical contradiction, or insignificant speech."[44] Shylock seems to make a similar elision between covenant keeping and reason. "Repair thy wit, good youth," he advises Graziano, "or it will fall / To cureless ruin. I stand here for law" (4.1.140–41). Earlier, he claims that he would be "a soft and dull-eyed fool" to relent (3.3.14). Like Hobbes, Shylock views fidelity to contractual bonds as absolute. Despite the similarity of their ideas, however, Shylock only partially anticipates Hobbes. Shylock's bond limits charity, not the tendency toward anarchy that Hobbes wished to avoid. When told that he should provide a doctor "for charity," Shylock objects: "I cannot find it; 'tis not in the bond" (4.1.258–59). Shylock's obsessive reference to his bond exemplifies the tendency of all characters to reduce human obligations to those imposed by reciprocity.

The Christians express little more belief in grace than Shylock does, so belief fails to distinguish the Christian and Jewish communities of Venice. Precisely because the distinction between Jew and Christian is minor, however, its expression rises to virulence. Antonio leads the chorus of anti-Semitism, as Shylock complains: "You call me misbeliever, cut-throat, dog" (1.3.108). He also resembles Shylock more than any other character, since he lends money, albeit "for a Christian courtesy" and cuts a figure on the Rialto (3.1.45–46; 3.1.43–44). Shylock recognizes him as a competitor, complaining that Antonio "brings down / The rate of usance here with us in Venice" (1.3.41–42), then gloating to Tubal that "were he out of Venice I can make what merchandise I will" (3.1.120–21). During the court scene, in Portia's famous question, Antonio also becomes the only character mistaken for Shylock. Both Girard and Ralph Berry point out that the two characters must be practically identical in costume.[45] Characters distinguish themselves from Shylock so bitterly because their difference from him is so small; Antonio, the character most easily confused with Shylock, shows the greatest anxiety and therefore hate.

Such an anxious distinction recalls the criticism of Girard, in particular, who argues that a series of binaries structure the play, starting with the stereotype of the Jewish usurer: "First comes the opposition between Jewish greed and Christian generosity, between revenge and compassion, between the crankiness of old age and the charm of youth, between the dark and the luminous, the beautiful and the ugly, the gentle and the harsh, the musical and the unmusical, and so on."[46] The binaries, he argues, are constructed by scapegoating Shylock. Although the term "scapegoat" has become so closely associated with the work of Girard as to seem inseparable from it, Girard in this instance participates in a whole tradition of criticism of *The Merchant of Venice*. Psychoanalytic critics take a particular interest in reading Shylock as a convenient object for the projection of communal guilt.[47] Some critics read Shylock specifically as a scapegoat for his society's commercialism. Patrick Grant declares that the binary of charity and usury obfuscates "a wilderness of evasive behaviours and sharp practices,"[48] and Andrew observes, "The noble aspects of commercial enterprise are embodied in the Christians, the base aspects in the Jew."[49] Shylock himself anticipates such critics, recognizing that Antonio's hatred embraces his race, self, and usurious practices, conflating them into a single figure:

> He hates our sacred nation, and he rails,
> Even there where merchants most do congregate,
> On me, my bargains, and my well-won thrift,
> Which he calls interest.   (1.3.45–48)

Many critics and even Shylock himself recognize scapegoating as an effort by the Christian characters to deny their own commercialism.

An equally large number of critics follow or even anticipate Girard in seeing such scapegoating as ironic, revealing the proximity of the Christian characters to Shylock, even while appearing to measure their distance.[50] Girard makes the heavy-handed claim that Shakespeare wrote for two audiences because "he could not attack openly" the sensitive themes he raised. The playwright therefore made "an indirect satire, highly effective with the knowledgeable few and completely invisible to the ignorant multitude, avid only to the gross catharsis Shakespeare never failed to provide." Earlier in the same essay, Girard argues that Shakespeare "was able to satisfy the most vulgar as well as the most refined audiences." If Shakespeare's anticipation of Girard's argument seems improbably adroit, Girard at least recognizes "something frightening in his efficiency."[51] The gap that the play presents between the characters' beliefs and actions seems so wide as to require two completely different readings of the play, one of which satirizes the other. One need not read the play as a satire, however, to understand that the similarity of Shylock to other characters necessitates his scapegoating. Because Maussian gift exchange generalizes an economy to the most intimate aspects of social life, Shylock's bond exemplifies all bonds in the play. The Christian community denies the ubiquity of gift exchange in order to maintain itself and therefore must victimize Shylock.[52]

A reader might be tempted to view Shylock's bond as a debenture, but that usage dates only from 1651. The word seems to have entered the language to denote a physical restraint, "a shackle, chain, fetter, manacle."[53] The term also denotes a state of servitude: "Base vassal, serf; one in bondage to a superior; a slave."[54] Shylock deploys this meaning when he describes an abject speech as "in a bondman's key" (1.3.120). Such darker meanings remained current in the sixteenth century; in fact, the strictly financial use had barely entered the language, and this play provides only the second instance recorded by the *Oxford English Dictionary*.[55] Shylock's bond is not merely a financial instrument but an intimate claim on the body of the signatory, applying to Antonio's flesh as well as goods. Antonio "courts risk" as Berry says, by embracing it.[56] He enters into the bond over Bassanio's objections (1.3.151–52) and also anticipates Bassanio's request by alliterating "My purse, my person" and placing both at Bassanio's service (1.1.138). Shylock alludes to the ancient association of cannibalism with usury when he promises to "feed fat the ancient grudge I bear" (1.3.44).[57] However, the desire for Antonio's flesh contradicts Shylock's habitual greed. He recognizes the worthlessness of the pound of flesh, though couching his recognition in anthropophagic imagery: "A pound of man's flesh taken from a man / Is not so estimable, profitable neither, / As flesh of muttons, beeves, or goats" (1.3.162–64). Even when determined to claim it, Shylock recognizes that it has no use other than "to bait fish withal" (3.1.48–51). The villain in one of Shakespeare's source texts suggests cutting off his debtor's testicles,[58] turning the competition over a pound of flesh into a sexual competition and thereby explaining it, if only to Freudians. Frustrating such arguments, however, Shylock wishes to cut the flesh from "Nearest his heart" (4.1.250–51). Antonio's flesh does not possess a value to motivate Shylock's claim, nor even a sexual symbolism. Rather than the claim being motivated by the value of the pound of flesh,

the price of Antonio's flesh is established by Shylock's willingness to forgo 36,000 ducats[59] in order to purchase it. The exchange
establishes value, even for human flesh. Shylock's bond unveils
the basis of the fictive society in self-interested exchanges; it also
shows how a dogged insistence on the ubiquity of exchange dehumanizes its participants.

Specifically, the bond offers Shylock a chance to enslave
Antonio, to treat him as a thing rather than a person. As in Mauss,
exchange extends with horrifying ramifications to the bodies of
persons. Shylock refuses to grant Antonio even the personhood
implied by a name, referring to him as "that bankrupt there"
(4.1.121), after making the metaphor to slavery explicit:

> You have among you many a purchased slave
> Which, like your asses and your dogs and mules,
> You use in abject and in slavish parts,
> Because you bought them.   (4.1.89–92)

Shylock is not denouncing the inhuman practices of his gentile
neighbors; on the contrary, he seeks to join them, at least in this.
Slavery shows that people can be property,[60] and Shylock wants
to treat Antonio as property: "The pound of flesh which I demand
of him / Is dearly bought: 'tis mine, and I will have it" (4.1.98–99).
His argument derives from Declaration 95 of Silvayn's *The Orator*,
translated into English in 1596.[61] Roman law allowed a debtor
to be executed, even for his body to be divided among his creditors.[62] Raising the threat from the physical to the metaphysical,
Satan claims possession of man in certain medieval versions of
the *Processus Belial*.[63] In any case, the metaphor of slavery allows
humans to become items of exchange.

The reciprocal bond and the institution of slavery both allow
people to be treated as objects of a claim rather than Others. The
fictive Venice constitutes a society in the Maussian sense, built on
reciprocal exchanges so ubiquitous that escape from them seems
literally unthinkable, but not a society in the Levinasian sense,
founded on the relationship with the Other. Rather than being,

as Camille Pierre Laurent says, "both valueless and priceless,"[64] human flesh becomes just one more item of gift or commercial exchange. "Mankind," Girard observes, "has become a commodity, an exchange value like any other." He points to Graziano's bet of a thousand ducats "on the first boy."[65] Grant argues, "It is another bargain, another bond, this time dealing with a few extra pounds of flesh, but never mind."[66] Shylock is not the only character to give monetary value to his offspring, in his famous conflation of his ducats and his daughter, though he first proposes "the work of generation" as a form of thrift, albeit a work of generation between "woolly breeders," not Italian aristocrats (1.3.73–87). The play relates the most intimate bodily contact to money, not only revealing the system of gift exchange at the base of this fictive society but also revealing the limits of such a society in its inability to recognize the extraordinary value of persons.

In particular, the value of women finds monetary expression in the play. The first reference to a woman is Gratiano's throwaway reference to "a maid not vendible" (1.1.111–12). Jessica feels a need to "gild myself / With some more ducats" before eloping with Lorenzo (2.6.49–50). In introducing his plan to free himself from debt, Bassanio first mentions Portia's wealth, then beauty, then "virtues" and finally availability (1.1.161–64). Numerous critics, Lewis among them, have pointed out that Bassanio's "language of financial speculation in 1.1 fits his professed love for Antonio and Portia only uncomfortably, if at all."[67] Sending Bassanio on his way, Antonio tells him to "Slubber not business for my sake," reducing whatever wooing the lottery of Portia's fate permits to "business" (2.8.39). Catherine Belsey opposes the tendency to see Bassanio as "no more than a fortune-hunter who desires Portia only, or primarily, for her money,"[68] arguing that the opposition between love and money dates from the Victorians. Belsey is wrong to blame the Victorians, however, because Alexander Pope declared unworthy of Shakespeare the coarse logic of Portia's declaration, "Since you are dear bought, I will love you dear" (3.2.311), and relegated it to a footnote in his own edition.[69] It is tempting to dismiss Bassanio as a mere fortune seeker, but the play does not set love and money in opposition as a satire would. On the contrary, Berry comments that "the worlds of commerce and love use each other's terms as a frame of reference."[70] Both are exchanges and they share a common language. Hence, John Russell Brown is right to argue, "*The Merchant of Venice* presents in human and dramatic terms Shakespeare's ideal of love's wealth, its abundant and sometimes embarrassing riches."[71] Girard, however, is also correct to note, "The symmetry between the explicit venality of Shylock and the implicit venality of the other Venetians."[72] As in the Polynesian cultures or the British Columbia First Nations that Mauss describes, in Shakespeare's Venice, amorous and financial economies are conflated into a single — Mauss would say total — system of exchanges.

Ubiquitous exchange dehumanizes its participants, as when Antonio becomes merely the bearer of a pound of flesh, or, conversely, when Shylock becomes wolfish in his claim (4.1.127–37). "Never did I know," says Salerio, "A creature that did bear the shape of man / So keen and greedy to confound a man" (3.2.272–74). While the bond provides a language in which love can express itself and be spoken, it also threatens with cruelty and even the silence of solipsism. "I will not hear thee speak," says Shylock, "I'll have my bond; and therefore speak no more" (3.3.12–13). The system of imposed debts and reciprocal exchanges provides Venice with a structure, even an epistemological framework, within which the characters find the world comprehensible. In the limits of exchange, however, they find the discomfiting limits of their world.

All too often, these are also the discomfiting limits of our criticism, which easily dismisses gestures of love or acts of worship as self-interested. *The Merchant of Venice* fascinates us, commending itself to our materialist age and its analytical tools, but it also disquiets us. Whereas the original audience may have viewed a play set in a vilified hyper-mercantile context with ironic detachment, as Karoline Szatek claims,[73] we find our own modern or postmodern assumptions about exchange reflected back to us and carried to a logical conclusion that is no more satisfying than the play's last act. A form of criticism that assumes the ubiquity of exchange can never do justice to those things that threaten the world of the play because they also threaten the premises of the criticism itself. Despite the references to cultural alterity in Shylock's dietary restrictions, there is no true Other in the play, not even the radical alterity of God. All of the characters are just more of the same, "pure other-denying investor." When the Other makes an extraordinary claim, as when love nearly overwhelms Portia and Bassanio, the characters assimilate the situation to terms borrowed from commerce. Extraordinary claims must be contained in order for the plot to take place and for Venetian society to maintain itself. Moreover, they must be contained in criticism so that our more or less anthropological models of exchange can continue to be applied, so that the critic can master the play by extending the circulations of social energy outward indefinitely. The analysis of reciprocal exchange offers us an understanding of the text, just as it offers the characters an understanding of their world. *The Merchant of Venice* reminds us, however, that our understanding of society and being-in-the-world, expressed in notions of reciprocity and reflected in our criticism, threatens to devolve into a dehumanizing trap. The characters live in a society that has, as Mauss urged, rediscovered "the joy of public giving; the pleasure in generous expenditure on the arts, in hospitality, and in the private and public festival."[74] Theirs is also, however, a society anxious in its need to obfuscate its own basis and unable to recognize a true Other, whether in the form of aliens who live in but are not members of their community, or in the form of persons with an extraordinary claim not to be treated as mere things.

Two

Romans and Venetians on Grace and Exchange

Few readers would dispute the importance of Christianity in *The Merchant of Venice*. Biblical references suffuse the play, providing Shylock with Old Testament citations and his Christian interlocutors with New Testament counterarguments. Critics may nevertheless be divided into two broad groups: those who read the play as an allegorical expression of Christian theology, and those who read the play as a criticism, even parody, of Christians who fail in their beliefs. *The Merchant of Venice* makes a sophisticated presentation of the difficulties involved in reconciling the radical commands of soteriology with the exigencies of social organization and thereby renders both readings possible. The play stages a conflict between the exigencies of social organization, analyzed by Mauss as a network of exchanges, and the radical commands of religious faith, which offers the subversive notion of a true gift. The characters call themselves Christians and are, in some sense, correct in their self-description, but the survival of the exchange networks that constitute their state and society demands that their commitment to grace be attenuated. If culture is based on reciprocal exchange, grace must appear countercultural. The radical choice in *Doctor Faustus* between belief in grace and in the diabolical pact finds quotidian expression in *The Merchant of Venice*, where grace and Christian universalism must be rejected, or at least diminished, in order that a society based on bonds, pacts, and reciprocal exchanges can maintain itself.

Shakespeare's Venetians build their society on the basis of distinctions that Saint Paul denies in his Epistle to the Romans. Sixteenth-century translations of and popular commentaries upon Paul's letter demonstrate the doctrine of salvation by faith. Reformation soteriology and its understanding of grace and gift furnish a contrast with the reciprocal generosity described in Mauss's *The Gift*. Two ideas of forgiveness, that of an exchange and that of a pure gift, collide in the play's trial scene, in which the burden of offering free mercy is first shifted onto Shylock's bending shoulders and then replaced by an exchange. In fact, the play is marked by an entire absence of Christian ceremony. Rather than the social order undergoing mystification as Christian ideology, it is presented most forcefully as independent of and even opposed to Reformation belief.

A number of critics consider not only the non-Jewish characters but also the play itself to be Christian, and to express themes of mercy and salvation. These include Barbara Lewalski, famously, as well as Frank Kermode.[1] Their argument enjoyed its fullest critical acceptance in the early second half of the twentieth century but continues to be made.[2] The contrary thesis, which declares the Christian characters unworthy of the name, is even more time-honored, beginning with William Hazlitt and Heinrich Heine in the nineteenth century,[3] and continuing with René Fortin and Crocker.[4] In the readings of several critics, the social and cultural mores of a community calling itself Christian sharply contrast with and even displace what ought to be a Christian ethics.

Neither position could command such wide support without textual evidence. While almost every character self-identifies as

Jewish or Christian, and even Morocco calls vaguely on "some god" before choosing a casket (2.7.13), not even Antonio, in what he believes to be the hour of his death, offers any sort of extended prayer. Two sacraments, Shylock's baptism and the marriage rite between Bassanio and Portia, are anticipated only to be deferred. More importantly, the play more than once presents Christian practice as a self-conscious pretense. Preparing to join Bassanio on his voyage to Belmont, Graziano assures his friend of his good behavior:

> If I do not put on a sober habit,
> Talk with respect, and swear but now and then,
> Wear prayer-books in my pocket, look demurely—
> Nay more, while grace is saying hood mine eyes
> Thus with my hat, and sigh, and say "Amen,"
> Use all the observance of civility,
> Like one well studied in a sad ostent
> To please his grandam—never trust me more.   (2.2.182–89)

Graziano reduces religion to a facade of respectability. Similarly, Portia defends her absence from Belmont with the promise "To live in prayer and contemplation" (3.4.28). After her return to Belmont, Stefano repeats her alibi, describing her praying at "holy crosses" and accompanied by "a holy hermit" (5.1.31–34), and then she does so herself, claiming to "have been praying" (5.1.114). Lancelot similarly renders religion dramaturgic, imagining himself tempted by the fiend and counseled by his conscience, each furnished with a suitable, though improvised, script (2.2.1–29). In doing so, he casts himself as the protagonist in what Horst Meller calls his "absurd *psychomachia* monologue as the main figure of a morality play."[5] Steven R. Mentz argues that Lancelot's choice "appears wholly arbitrary" because "Both the fiend and conscience 'counsel well,' and there is a devil on either side of the equation."[6] However, "the Jew," as Lancelot declares, is merely "the very devil incarnation" (2.2.25). Fortin argues that Lancelot's identification of Jew and devil betrays Lancelot's "unabashed and simple-minded contempt for Judaism."[7] Moreover, this identification of the Jew with the devil allows him to obey "the devil himself" (2.2.24). In Lancelot's mind, anti-Semitism justifies even the most spiritual of sins and unconscionable acts become possible under the pretense of a conscientious crisis. Throughout this scene, he, like Graziano and Portia, treats religion as a role to play for reasons of his own. Critics who consider the characters Christless Christians do not merely project their own assumptions about Christian dogma onto the world of the play. Nor, for that matter, are the characters necessarily hypocritical in their claims of religious identity. The characters' repeated pretenses of Christian practices nevertheless tend to reduce Christianity to a social convention, distinct from doctrine and even serving as a means of evading its demands. In *The Merchant of Venice*, Christianity becomes a culture and a community, amenable to Maussian analysis. It is threatened not by another culture but by the countercultural threat of absolute generosity, which finds doctrinal expression in Pauline soteriology.

A third group of critics, distinct from both those who discover Christian allegory and those who accuse the Christian characters of being false to their own beliefs, view the relationship between Christianity and anti-Semitism as causal rather than paradoxical. Catherine S. Cox, for instance, places "The Venetian Christians" on an "essentialist religious quest," albeit one which fails, to establish their identity vis-à-vis the Jewish Other.[8] Harry Berger argues that Portia gives gifts in a bid for power, one informed by her own Christian beliefs: "She is a Christian, and she knows the power of the charity that wounds."[9] If the characters treat gifts as exchanges, then in Berger's reading, they merely enact their religion. Engle implicitly follows Mauss in his reading of *The Merchant of Venice*, arguing that theological terms are "shown in the play to define a system of exchange or conversion."[10] Stephen Marx draws on Paul's Epistle to the Romans to argue that the play shows how Christian characters and, by extension, sixteenth-century Christianity in general, appropriate Jewish scriptures.[11] If those who call the characters "Christless Christians"[12] can be accused of ahistorically projecting their own Christian beliefs onto the world of the play, those who view the play's characters as typical Christians fail to distinguish between a Christian society as a set of social norms and Christian belief as a violation of social norms. The play, on the other hand, seems to dramatize this distinction, creating a Christian society apparently oblivious to the most central, and indeed the most subversive, doctrines of its time.

Specifically, the play seems to ignore notions of the gift associated with the Pauline doctrine of grace and with the doctrine of Christian universalism expressed in the Epistle to the Romans. Reformation thought rediscovered in Saint Paul's soteriology a theology of radical and unearned grace. The Christian characters may not break with the entire Christian tradition but do at least implicitly reject a fundamental element of Reformation thought. While drawing, like Marx, on contemporary readings of the Epistle to the Romans, my emphasis draws on Paul's earlier chapters, which insist on both the ubiquity of sin and the universal need for grace. The Venetian characters are conscious of the call to charity, as Portia's famous speech on "the quality of mercy" amply confirms. However, they face the difficulty of reconciling the radical claims of Reformation soteriology — and in particular its renewed sense of Pauline universalism — with the requirements of a commercial and law-bound society. The critical debate may be understood as a disagreement over whether they succeed, at least at the level of allegory, or betray their beliefs. More broadly, the play illustrates the conflict between a radical gift, in the form of grace, and the requirements of a Maussian ethnology, with its ubiquitous exchange. The characters choose to preserve their society, built as it is from reciprocal exchanges, like Faustus preserves his worldview, by obliviousness toward grace.

The problem of how to live in society need not be understood strictly as a delimiting of violence. Like Ricoeur, Levinas questions the validity of social contract theory, starting from the depiction of the state of nature by Hobbes. After the delivery of his paper "Ideology and Idealism" in 1972, Levinas responded to a question from the audience by inverting one of the premises of social contract theory: "But it is very important to know whether the state, society, law, and power are required because man is a beast to his neighbour (*homo homini lupus*) or because I am responsible for my fellow."[13] Levinas made the contrast with Hobbes overt later in his career, writing of "Hobbes's vision—in which the state emerges not from the limitation of charity, but from the limitation of violence" and juxtaposing it with one in which the call to charity founds and therefore delimits the state's power. In place of Hobbes's Leviathan, which ends the war of all against all by monopolizing violence, Levinas imagines instead a state that adjudicates between competing claims on our responsibility and therefore delimits it: "If there were no order of Justice, there would be no limit to my responsibility."[14] In Levinas's conception, responsibility potentially exceeds the measure and restraint of social order. Baker applies Levinas's understanding of alterity to *The Merchant of Venice* and notes, "Readers and reviewers of Levinas have not remained silent on the perceived 'Christianity' of this Jewish thinker's openly-giving, non-reciprocal relationships which must be maintained, even were it to cost one one's life."[15] *The Merchant of Venice* stages a conflict not between law and mercy but between a radical commandment and the legal, reciprocal, and ultimately commercial basis of the characters' society. If the characters appear less than perfectly merciful, in fact less than Christian, this may simply illustrate the need to limit generosity in order to construct and govern any society, even one overt in its allegiance to the Christian faith.

A few years after his famous essay on *The Merchant of Venice*, Girard justified his criticism of historical Christianity by claiming, "I am just repeating what Paul says about all of us being guilty so that God can save us all."[16] While Girard concentrates most of his energy on showing how the play reveals and therefore demystifies the scapegoat mechanism, his reference to Saint

Paul suggests a particularly useful intertext to *The Merchant of Venice*. Writing to the polyglot Christian community in the imperial capital, composed both of Jews and gentiles, Paul stresses the equality of both communities in his soteriology. In the opening chapters, he dedicates most of his effort to denying Jewish particularism. While the Jews have the advantage of possessing the Old Testament law, the Gentiles are nevertheless quite capable of knowing sin. In any case, both transgress and require salvation through grace. Paul spends a number of verses describing the sinfulness of the group referred to as "Grecians" in the Geneva text and as "Gentiles" in the Tyndale text. As the summary at the beginning of the second chapter in the Geneva text of 1560 states, "he proueth all men to be sinners, The Gentiles by their conscience, The Jewes by the Law written." As Girard correctly notes, the universality of guilt furnishes an important theme of Paul's epistles, especially Romans. Moreover, as Kermode shows, the play insistently draws attention to the parallels between its Christian characters and "gentiles."[17] Kermode fails, however, to note that such parallels emphasize the characters' sin as much as their gentleness. The characters therefore contradict Pauline soteriology in their insistent distinction between gentile and Jew.

The Reformation directed renewed interest toward Paul's theme. A prologue to Romans constituted Luther's last addition to his translation of the New Testament.[18] Tyndale, in the bracingly shameless manner of the sixteenth century, plagiarized Luther, printing a prologue in his famous translation of the New Testament, which, David Daniell notes, "for the most translates Luther's prologue. The last five paragraphs are Tyndale's."[19] Tyndale's plagiarism pales, however, in comparison with the sheer perversity of Miles Coverdale, who furnished the second book of English translations of Erasmus's *Paraphrases* with a "stridently polemical tenor"[20] by adding Tyndale's, which is to say mostly Luther's, prologue. He thereby ascribed Luther's views, including a trenchant defense of predestination, to his polemical opponent. John Craig argues that "the *Paraphrases* was widely purchased and used, that it was instrumental in making the New Testament in English available and known to clergy and people, and that it was the chief means by which Erasmus was claimed for the English reformed church."[21] Luther's ideas would therefore have appeared ecumenical. Indeed, Augustine of Hippo had drawn on the same epistle in developing his own soteriology, also stressing the importance of grace. As Diarmaid MacCulloch has shown, a number of Luther's theological contemporaries arrived at conclusions similar to his, under the influence of Augustine,[22] though Alister E. McGrath argues that Luther seems to have achieved his theological breakthrough independently.[23] In any case, Luther's soteriology would have particular importance for English Protestant thought, especially given its wide circulation, albeit *incognito*.

Luther (or Tyndale, as the reader pleases) begins his preface by praising the epistle as "the principal and most excellent part of the new testament" and "a light and a way in unto the whole scripture" worthy to be memorized by "every Christian man" and to serve as "the daily bread of the soul."[24] The preface makes a striking use of the language of gift as well as that of debt, contrasting them in a manner oddly anticipatory of *The Merchant of Venice*. Lewalski notes parallels between the language of the play and that of the Lord's Prayer in the Geneva text: "Forgiue vs our dettes, as we also forgiue our detters."[25] This, she claims, makes "the debtor's trial in the court of Venice a precise analogue of the sinner's trial in the court of Heaven."[26] However, Luther draws upon the imagery of debt only to compare the receipt of grace to the violation of reciprocity: "Even as though thou were in debt to another man, and were not able to pay, two manner ways mightest thou be loosed. One way, if he would require nothing of thee, and break thine obligation. Another way, if some other good man would pay for thee, and give thee as much as thou mightest satisfy thine obligation withal. Of this wise hath Christ made us free from the law." The law still applies, Luther insists, but its demand has already been satisfied. As he says three paragraphs

earlier, "Yes there is sin remaining in us, but it is not reckoned."[27]
William Perkins echoes the language of Tyndale's translation:
"For even as a debt doth binde a man, either to make satisfaction,
or els to goe to prison, so our sinnes bindes us either to satis-
fie Gods justice, or else to suffer eternal damnation."[28] To Paul,
Luther, and Perkins, however, salvation consists in having such
debts forgiven. If Christ pays the sinners' debt to the law without
thought of recompense, the saved, in turn, obey the law without
desiring to earn salvation by their obedience.[29] Luther explains
Paul's most fundamental distinctions—of law and spirit, grace
and sin—in terms of the distinction between debt and gift. Paul's
language of gift ought to call into question the centrality of debt
and obligation on which the fictive society of Venice is built.

Paul, moreover, champions radical equality precisely at the
moment he declares the sinfulness of all and hence the need for
grace. Luther claims that Paul "mingleth both together, both the
Jews and the Gentiles, and saith that the one is as the other, both
sinners, and no difference between them, save in this only, that
the Jews had the word of God committed unto them."[30] Erasmus's
paraphrase of Romans follows Luther in making Jews and gentiles
equal first in sin and then in salvation: "Truely, touchyng the
free gyft of goddes grace offred by [the] ghospell, no poynte better is the Jewes state and condicion, than is the Gentiles." This
backhanded inclusion develops into the claim of Christian universalism that no special nation is particularly chosen because
"it hath pleased God, in the gospel of Christ to make all nacions
equal." The universality of God founds the universality of grace,
again understood as a gift: "sythe there is but one God ouer all,
good reason is it, that his gifte be likewyse commen to all."[31]
Contemporary readings of the Epistle to the Romans strongly
associate indifference to race with a doctrine of absolute generosity in the form of grace.

The other Epistles reemphasize racial equality and associate it
with the removal of the distinction between "bond" and "free."
The *Oxford English Dictionary* lists an early use of "bond" as

an adjective, "In a state of serfdom or slavery; not free; in bond-age" (n2 and a1) from the King James Version of the first letter to the Corinthians (12.13). However, the same usage can be found as early as Tyndale's translation, followed by the Bishop's Bible and the Geneva text. In all of these translations, the verse insists upon the equality under baptism of different groups. The Geneva text, for instance, claims, "For by one Spirit are we all baptized into one body, whether we be Iewes, or Grecians, whether we be bonde, or free, and haue bene all made to drinke into one Spirit." The Bishop's Bible follows Tyndale's language in contrasting Jews to gentiles, rather than Grecians. Colossians makes a simi-lar conflation, telling its readers to put on the new man, "Where is neither Grecian nor Iewe, circumcision nor vncircumcision, Barbarian, Scythian, bond, free."[32] Tyndale again uses "gentile" for "Grecian," though in this case is not followed by the Bishop's Bible. The translation of Erasmus's *Paraphrases* follows the lan-guage of the slightly later Great Bible, and also insists on equal-ity under baptism in its paraphrase of Galatians: "Throughe baptisme are we newe borne agayne, and sodenly altered, as it were into a newe creature. And as touching this gyft, it is layed to noman, nor passed upon, whether he were before baptisme, Jewe or Gentile, bonde man or free, manne or woman."[33] The epistles, in all sixteenth-century English Protestant translations, deny the relevance of the distinction between "bond" and "free," just as they conflate "Jew" and "Gentile," in maintaining that all are sinners, capable of salvation by baptism.

The characters in Shakespeare's play, on the other hand, insist upon the very distinctions that the gospels deny. Several char-acters pun on the proximity of "gentle" to "gentile." Lorenzo, Lancelot, and Graziano all call Jessica "gentle" or "gentile" (2.4.19–20; 2.4.33–34; 2.6.51), while she is escaping Shylock to convert to Christianity and become a gentile. Antonio, thinking Shylock's bond "kind," declares him a "gentle Jew" (1.3.174–75). The Christian characters identify their own religion with what the duke calls "human gentleness and love" (4.1.24) but in so doing they also identify themselves with the gentiles, the non-Jewish populace who, Paul assured his Roman readers, also lived under sin. Robert Zaslavsky draws a conclusion opposite to Kermode's: "The repeated puns throughout the play on 'gentle' and 'gentile,' whose Elizabethan pronunciation would have been virtually identical and which are etymologically the same word, underscore how far these gentiles are from being gentle."[34] The repeated pun would also draw attention to Paul's denial of the difference between gentiles and Jews. This difference structures the play's society; similarly, the distinction between bondage and freedom informs the central action of the play's plot, as Shylock makes clear in justifying himself by reference to Venice's practice of slavery (4.1.89–91) while insisting on his "bond" (3.3.12–13, for instance). The binaries that structure the play's world are those specifically denied by Paul but, more important, they are denied as part of his insistence upon the doctrine of salvation by grace. The terms in which Venice expresses its laws and culture place it in opposition to a Pauline soteriology of absolute generosity, which therefore appears countercultural, denying the basis not only of this fictive society but also, according to Mauss, of all societies.

One means of denying the equality of Jews and gentiles while maintaining the rest of Paul's claims is to gloss the word "Jew," taking it to mean two different things, as does Erasmus. In his "whole matier and argument" of the Epistle, he claims that Paul draws "sondrye allegories," such as when "he maketh two sortes of Jewishenes, two kyndes of circumcision, two degrees of Abrahās posteritie, two partes of Moyses lawe."[35] Similarly, the "argument" provided at the beginning of Romans by the Geneva translators holds out hope that members of both communities can be saved but by incorporating Jews into the true *ecclesia*. "The liberal mercie of God," they write, "at length wil stretch towarde the Iewes againe, and so father the whole Israel (which is his Church) of them bothe." Luther himself held out hope for the conversion of the Jews before his disillusionment soured into violent anti-Semitism.[36] Thomas H. Luxon bases his reading of *The Merchant of Venice* on the claim that the early modern world sharply distinguished the Jews of the Old Testament from their later co-religionists: "The 'Old Testament' Israelites, especially the patriarchs and heroes, were widely regarded as proto-Christian members of the true Church, elect from the beginning. But the post-advent Jews represented the worst form of stubborn and graceless apostasy." This leads Luxon to conclude that the Christian characters would have been recognized as closer to true Jews, analogous to the prophet Daniel invoked in court: "Grownup Jews are Christians like Daniel; Jews like Shylock are willfully stunted, pertinaciously puerile, literal-minded, and selfish."[37] In this sense, the Christian characters might follow Paul in conflating Jew and gentile but only to claim as their own the salvation promised to the Jews.

One might respond that the Christian characters never profess to be Jewish. Graziano does claim the name of Daniel for Portia but only in imitation of Shylock (4.1.336–37). More importantly, both groups might be conflated by their sinfulness, rather than their access to salvation. John Cunningham and Stephen Slimp quote Lawrence Danson to the effect that Antonio's malice "convicts him of being...himself spiritually a 'Jew'" and they draw attention to the liturgy for Good Friday, where the members of the congregation are addressed "in their crucifying sin as Jews."[38] Shylock, Thomas Fujimura notes, does not even include "man's rational soul"[39] in the otherwise wide-ranging list of human attributes that make up his famous speech beginning "Hath not a Jew eyes?" (3.1.55–69). The universality of what Luxon calls "carnal humanity"[40] seems, however, very close to Paul's universalizing of sin, identified throughout Romans with "flesh." Moreover, Shylock's famous speech ends in justifying his own desire for revenge: "And if you wrong us, shall we not revenge? If we are like you in the rest, we will resemble you in that" (3.1.62–64). The speech shows a very low common humanity, the commonness of sin, but this is precisely where it overlaps with the Epistle to the

Romans. Neither Paul nor Shakespeare present Jews and gentiles as equal in their everyday morality or even human rights but as radically equal in their sin and hence in their need for grace.

If all are equal in sin, conversely, baptism ought to unite all in salvation. To be sure, such Christian universalism bears little resemblance to cultural pluralism. Baptism effaces the differences between Judaism and Christianity, rather than recognizing or celebrating them. Cox expresses the argument against Christian universalism when she claims, "The ideal of a unified community pertains of course to a community unified in its acceptance not of categorical differences, of marginalized Others, but rather in its exclusive identity as Christian."[41] Baptism, however, fails to replace other identities in this play. Notoriously, Shylock continues to be referred to as "the Jew" after he has been condemned to baptism (5.1.292). The deferral of the sacrament means that he does not become a Christian in the course of the play, rendering the appellation technically correct, but no such excuse can be offered for Graziano's dogged reference to Jessica as "Lorenzo's infidel" (3.2.216). Though, as Jessica says, her husband has "made me a Christian" (3.5.17–18), Lancelot argues, using pagan logic, that she remains damned by "the sins of the father" (3.5.1). The characters do not recognize the assimilatory power of baptism to make all equal in God's mercy, because they do not recognize its role in overcoming sin and for that matter do not understand themselves as sinners in need of salvation. They reject, or remain oblivious to, the universality of the Christian faith and consequently the whole structure of salvation. Christian universalism does not crush Shylock; it is altogether ignored.

Portia's celebrated speech on "The quality of mercy" (4.1.181–202) shows clearly that she at least possesses a strong sense of the doctrine of grace. Portia argues with eloquence as well as orthodoxy:

> That in the course of justice none of us
> Should see salvation. We do pray for mercy,
> And that same prayer doth teach us all to render
> The deeds of mercy.   (4.1.196–99)

It is striking, however, that this doctrine is raised by Portia, an outsider in Venice. Moreover, the universal claim that "none of us should see salvation" is soon replaced by a specific law applicable only to "aliens." Marx notes, "discovering a statute that is selectively applied seems the opposite of Paul's endeavour to universalize the sectarian Jewish covenant between God and his chosen people."[42] As previously discussed, the injunction against murder seems to be Shakespeare's addition, not found in any of his sources. By his addition, Shakespeare illustrates the particularist nature of Venetian law and its distance from the Pauline universalism expressed in Portia's great speech.

Despite Portia's eloquence about mercy, it is anything but normative in Venetian society. The duke, in his appeal to Shylock, betrays a belief that the latter's mercy would be "more strange / Than is thy strange apparent cruelty" (4.1.19–20). Antonio abandons all hope of mercy, reducing Shylock to a pitiless racial identity: "You may as well do anything most hard / As seek to soften that — than which what's harder? — his Jewish heart" (4.1.77–79). Shylock's insistence on the law over mercy does not provide a contrast with the Christian characters, however, because they accept his argument. "If you deny me," he declares, "Fie upon your law! / There is no force in the decrees of Venice" (4.1.100–01). Portia gives voice to the obligation to forgive but also to the constitutional principle that "There is no power in Venice / Can alter a decree establishèd" (4.1.215–16). Shakespeare's play may reproduce a popular English view of the Venetian constitution, which took overt expression in 1615 when Lord Chancellor Ellesmere used the example of the Duke of Venice as a powerless ruler, bound by laws and without any prerogative power.[43] While Ellesmere dismissed such exaggerated legalism, the characters in the play seem largely to accept it. Reporting Antonio's misfortunes to Bassanio, Salerio uses Shylock's definition of justice: "[N]one can drive him from the envious plea / Of forfeiture, of justice and his bond" (3.2.280–81). Even Antonio accepts the need to uphold the law, explaining it in characteristically mercantile, if grammatically awkward, fashion:

> The Duke cannot deny the course of law,
> For the commodity that strangers have
> With us in Venice, if it be denied,
> Will much impeach the justice of the state,
> Since that the trade and profit of the city
> Consisteth of all nations.   (3.3.26–31)

A complex structure of laws buttressed the Venetian Republic, as any reader of Gasparo Contarini's *The Commonwealth and Government of Venice,* translated into English shortly after Shakespeare's play was written, would find in exhaustive detail. Portia's defeat of Shylock remains entirely within the structure of law. Much as they call on Shylock to show mercy, the characters of the play remain committed to the laws of their republic.

After referring to several critics who view the play's courtroom scene as a contest between common law and equity, William Chester Jordan concludes that, in the end, mercy does not triumph in this play, or even its analogues: "If it had, one of two things would have occurred. Either the lender would have been moved by sentimental arguments to withdraw his suit, or the court would have simply pardoned the debt."[44] Jordan notes that the story takes place in a far-off land, indeed "a strange universe in which strange devices uphold the moral order."[45] This strange order is, however, only an exaggeration of familiar societies, bound together by legal structures and social norms. The play poses in acute form the problem of reconciling absolute mercy with social order.

While none of the Christian characters wish to be responsible for enforcing the murderous contract, all shrink from violating the laws of Venice. The duke seems all too eager to delegate the case to "Bellario, a learned doctor / Whom I have sent for to determine this," welcoming Bellario's substitute "With all my heart" and urging "Some three or four of you" to "give him courteous conduct to this place" (4.1.104–05; 4.1.146–47). Bassanio similarly begs Portia to "Wrest once the law to your authority," desiring her to find some loophole in the law but not daring to simply violate it by, for instance, freeing Antonio by force (4.1.212). Where the duke defers to Bellario to find a solution to his jurisprudential quandary, Portia, in disguise, defers to Shylock to show mercy. Crocker even argues that the only expression of a superior Christian ethos occurs when the characters "conveniently and incongruously ask the archetypal Jew to act like a suppositious archetypal Christian."[46] Portia asks Shylock to have mercy and "Bid me tear the bond" (4.1.231), rather than herself denouncing the mercilessness of Venice's statutes. The appeals to Shylock transfer blame for the maintenance of Venice's laws and therefore Venetian society. Though horrified at its cost, the characters doggedly defend the Venetian legal and social order against the anarchic threat of pure forgiveness.

Just as everyone at the beginning of the trial defers to Shylock to show mercy to Antonio, after Shylock's defeat, Portia defers to Antonio to offer mercy to Shylock (4.1.374). Antonio's response offers Shylock the means of his own maintenance for the rest of his life (4.1.376–86). Hugh Short remarks upon "the generosity of such an act by a man who still thinks he has lost all of his ships and wealth." He proceeds to suggest that Shylock's line "I am content" should be read literally. Short refers to Antonio's action as "a miracle,"[47] but Antonio distinguishes his generosity from the miraculous by hedging it with conditions. Shylock purchases the remnant of his own wealth by conversion, subscribing to Antonio's provisions:

> that for this favour
> He presently become a Christian;
> The other, that he do record a gift
> Here in the court, of all he dies possessed
> Unto his son Lorenzo and his daughter.   (4.1.382–86)

The fine imposed on Shylock may make reference to an actual Venetian law recorded by Thomas Coryat, under which even willing converts from Judaism would be expected to forfeit "all their goodes."[48] Lewalski notes that such laws were common "throughout most of Europe and also in England during the Middle Ages and after."[49] The state's mercy therefore takes the form of a ruinous fine, which Shylock insists is tantamount to execution: "[Y]ou take my life / When you do take the means whereby I live" (4.1.372–73). The duke renders even this limited generosity conditional when he threatens to "recant / The pardon that I late pronouncèd here" (4.1.387–88). At such moments, his title of "Grace" (4.1.119 for instance) may seem ironic. For that matter, Portia's famous appeal to Shylock to "Be merciful" offers him "thrice thy money" to "tear the bond" (4.1.230–31).[50] While the Christian characters expect Shylock to show mercy—indeed, in the Duke's appeal, even to "Forgive a moiety of the principal" (4.1.25)—their forgiveness is not gracious, and they barely even expect Shylock to entertain the idea seriously. Rather than being freely given, like the mercy that "droppeth as the gentle rain from heaven" (4.1.182), that of the Christian characters toward Shylock is assimilated into a set of social obligations. While it is tempting to see this as an evasion of the high demands of radical mercy, one might also see this as an effort to accommodate the prayer that "doth teach us all to render / The deeds of mercy" (4.1.198–99) to the demands of a society in the world, governed by laws, and especially of a mercantile society, governed by exchange.

Certainly, Shylock's choice of terms in agreeing to Antonio's "mercy" need not represent anything more than the acceptance of a bargain, like Antonio's "content in faith" while agreeing to the bond (1.3.149). In an earlier play, Henry VI uses the same words in reluctant acceptance of a decision demanded by self-preservation and immediately denounced as cowardice,[51] whereas in a later play, Henry V uses an identical formula to accept a treaty with France.[52] Because reciprocal, indeed contractual, agreements serve as Shylock's habitual mode of human relations, he might indeed be content to find himself once more in a familiar world. In any case, he accepts the bargain. He could, Sigurd Burckhardt notes, kill Antonio anyway: "it is still in Shylock's power to turn the play into a tragedy, to enforce the letter of the bond and to take the consequences."[53] Portia anticipates Burckhardt, urging Shylock to "prepare thee to cut off the flesh" before reiterating the punishment if he does: "Thou diest, and all thy goods are confiscate" (4.1.320; 4.1.328). A true tragic hero would take his revenge and accept the mortal repercussions, Shell argues.[54] Instead, Shylock's self-preservation assumes the form of a series of efforts to renegotiate the bond, like Faustus offering to burn his books with his last line. Having learned that the bond permits "no jot of blood" (4.1.303), he maintains his threat against the life of Antonio while offering to forego revenge in favor of either three times the value of the bond (4.1.315–16) or, as he grows more desperate, "barely my principal" (4.1.338). Portia insists, however, that he "shalt have nothing but the forfeiture / To be so taken at thy peril" (4.1.339–40). Shylock's fate is the negotiation of a new exchange, of his life for Antonio's, a fact that he recognizes in his efforts to trade the threat against Antonio's life for a cash payment and that Portia recognizes in asking him "Art thou contented, Jew?" (4.1.389). As a bargain, the negotiation of Shylock's punishment echoes the bond that commences the whole plot and anticipates the later exchange of rings.

Lewalski notes that the conversion appears to be Shakespeare's "gratuitous addition" to his source, *Il Pecorone*,[55] but a more recently discovered analogue from fourteenth century France includes the conversion of the Jewish character. Miraculous intervention, however, inspires the conversion in the French text, with a visitation "by God and His angels."[56] Where the earlier religious drama makes conversion miraculous, Shakespeare's secular drama renders it the product of a process of negotiation and bargaining. Critics have noted the irony of a forced conversion as an act of mercy.[57] Of course, the conversion is not quite forced, though Shylock could only escape the baptismal font by fleeing into the grave. It is nevertheless striking that his choice seems entirely framed by secular concerns to preserve his life and property. Unless, with Short, one takes the most optimistic reading of Antonio's mercy, nobody tries to win Shylock by acts of charity. Certainly, nobody attempts to convert him with theological arguments. The question of how to view Shylock's conversion—whether as a generous offer or a savage, if symbolic, retribution—is not answered by the play, whose characters barely consider theology at all.

The first four acts concern Shylock's bond, while the last act concerns the bond of matrimony. An exchange of rings, backed by an oath, signifies Portia and Bassanio's union. Few critics seem to notice that the characters never solemnize their marriages. Indeed, Michael Radford boldly inserts the ceremony into his film. When told of Antonio's danger, Portia tells Bassanio "First go with me to church and call me wife, / And then away to Venice to your friend" (3.2.301–02). After hearing Antonio's letter, however, she tells him to "Dispatch all business, and be gone," presumably without hesitating for a formal service of matrimony (3.2.320). His return certainly occasions no marriage service, though Graziano seems eager to move to consummation as quickly as possible (5.1.300–05). Marriage constitutes an enormously powerful social institution but not a religious service.

Specifically, marriage is understood as a reciprocal exchange, which generosity would fatally undermine. Portia warns that because the fictitious doctor

> hath got the jewel that I loved,
> And that which you did swear to keep for me,
> I will become as liberal as you.
> I'll not deny him anything I have,
> No, not my body nor my husband's bed.   (5.1.224–28)

The consequence of simply donating the ring, and therefore giving away without exchange the marital commitment it signifies, would be sexual and therefore social chaos. In the absence of reciprocal bonds, only constant surveillance could maintain Portia's fidelity: "Lie not a night from home; watch me like Argus" (5.1.230). A new bond, to which Antonio serves as "surety" in a new exchange that co-opts Bassanio's love for Antonio, restores sexual order. Rather than a religious ceremony, the marriage of Portia and Bassanio is an immensely strong social bond. Social order is not reinforced by Christian doctrine; on the contrary, it is threatened by a doctrine of mercy.

Linda Boose and Anne Parten both ascribe the play's peculiar effect to the presence of a strong female character. Boose calls Portia "a wily artist";[58] Parten argues that she remains "a threat to the re-establishment of order."[59] Certainly, Portia asserts her power of ownership, talking once again of "my house" despite her earlier claims to give all to Bassanio (5.1.273). A few lines later, she gives Lorenzo "without a fee" the "deed of gift" by which he becomes Shylock's heir (5.1.290–92). He responds, "you drop manna in the way / Of starvèd people" (5.1.294–95). This clearly refers to the Old Testament, in which manna is produced as a "gift," as the act is described by the marginal notes to the Geneva text.[60] Thus, Lorenzo casts Portia as a god-like figure. Her gift, however, has been purchased in exchange for Shylock's life, and by Antonio, not herself. Shylock's wealth can be compared with the manna that falls "as the gentle rain from heaven," but only problematically.

Portia's appropriation of the miraculous exemplifies the effort required to reduce Christian grace to the network of reciprocal exchanges that constitute Venice's society. She forgives Bassanio's surrender of his ring only to bind him more dearly to herself by another bond. Similarly, the mercy offered to Shylock takes the form of a bargain and an exchange, expressed in a legal document. As Levinas suggests is true for the world as a whole, the play's world maintains social order by delimiting radical claims. While Levinas associates these with responsibility, a term he uses in a broad sense, we might equally associate them with mercy, forgiveness, or generosity. Specifically, sixteenth-century Pauline soteriology claims equality under sin and therefore denies the relevance of the play's central distinctions between Jew and gentile, bond and free. The characters, perhaps like their co-religionists in the audience, reconcile radical religious obligations with the exigent demands of an ordered society and thereby give them expression, at least allegorically, in the world. We need not, however, accept their effort as successful, any more than we need dismiss their society as profane or even hypocritical. The play illustrates the difficulty of reconciling a society, especially one understood as a network of Maussian gift exchanges, with a true gift, which would have to appear as not only gratuitous but also countercultural. Paul's theology of salvation by grace poses a contrast and a challenge to a society built on reciprocal exchange. The conflict that the play depicts between a Christian society and an anarchic doctrine of grace renders possible radically different readings of the play as a Christian allegory or a revelation of Christian hypocrisy.

THREE

"Nothing Will Come of Nothing"

Avoiding the Gift in *King Lear*

Mauss insists not only upon the ubiquity of exchange but also that a belief in pure generosity obfuscates it.[1] This assumption governs a number of readings of *King Lear*. William Flesch, for instance, cites both George Battaille and Pierre Bourdieu making much the same point, concluding, "Culture...is formed by the repression of the fact of equivalent exchange."[2] The characters of *King Lear*, however, like those of *The Merchant of Venice*, make the opposite repression, denying the possibility of a free gift under the pretense of exchange, self-interest, or social convention. Stanley Cavell famously argues that Lear "cannot bear to be loved when he has no reason to be loved, perhaps because of the helplessness, the passiveness which that implies."[3] One is reminded of Faustus, refusing the saving love of God in favor of maintaining his position as an agent, even if only an agent of his own damnation. Cavell notes that when Gloucester offers Lear love in act 4, the latter tries to label it as a solicitation.[4] Lear's response may serve as an example of how the characters reduce offers of

83

affection and kindness to reciprocal terms. S. L. Goldberg declares
that Goneril as "rampant ego can see personal relationships only as
power relationships." Most characters, however, share Goneril's
tendency to view human relationships in such impoverished
terms, because they share a need to, as Goldberg says, "keep the
world at bay,"[5] and render it comprehensible. Dollimore accuses
critics of obscuring "the awful truth" that "power and property"
exist "somehow prior to the laws of human kindness."[6] However,
both critics and characters make the opposite mystification,
ignoring the possibility of kindness by treating all relationships
as relationships of power and property. Exchange is normative to
the play's fictive society, as to that of *The Merchant of Venice*
and perhaps to every society, insofar as societies offer themselves
to a Maussian ethnology. If, in a Maussian analysis, "The cycling
gift system is the society,"[7] then generous acts can only appear as
antisocial and countercultural.

While some critics may, as Dollimore accuses, participate in a
"mystifying closure of the historical real,"[8] at least as many show
themselves to subscribe to a view of the world characterized by
the logic of exchange and therefore foreclose the possibility of
truly generous action. Leonard Tennenhouse writes as a new
historicist rather than as a cultural materialist like Dollimore,
but he nevertheless reads Shakespeare's plays as vehicles of
"Renaissance debates concerning the nature and origins of political power."[9] Some critics draw implicitly on Mauss's anthropology. In a fascinating feminist argument, Stephanie Chamberlain
describes how Cordelia functions as "a gift to the foreign power
that would receive her, creating future obligations to Lear and
England."[10] William O. Scott argues that Lear's "expectations of
reciprocity that go with his gifts resemble the social constraints
of the gift economy" and compares Lear's gift of the kingdom
with the contemporary practice of establishing a trust.[11] While
not all critics refer to Mauss's anthropology, most nevertheless
accept the ubiquity of exchange.

The importance of such a belief extends beyond literary criticism, and indeed *King Lear* evokes broad questions about whether the characters' understanding of their world is justified and whether their world represents a fair model of the world in general. In a retrospective of criticism published in 1980, G. R. Hibbard notes, "The very nature of the world we live in has much to do with the interest the play excites."[12] More recently, Lionel Basney remarks on "the philosophical and even theological reach" of *Lear* criticism, relating it to "our understanding of the world."[13] *Lear* evokes philosophical questions more reliably than any other play in Shakespeare's canon. Readings drawing on presuppositions similar to those of Mauss, therefore, reinforce a particular view of ourselves and other people.

Certainly the characters assume the ubiquity of exchange relationships, whether commercial or feudal. Lear premises his disastrous division of the kingdom on the assumption that every donation stakes a claim to reciprocation, thereby providing himself with a retirement plan and the play with its tragedy. *King Lear*, like *The Merchant of Venice*, illuminates the horrifying results of Mauss's *a priori* belief that all gifts elicit recompense. Moreover, this assumption handicaps the characters, leaving them unable to understand their own actions, including their own heroically charitable acts. The servant who attempts to defend Gloucester cannot account for his own behavior. Similarly, Kent fails to explain his loyalty to Lear by reference to the exchange of service for protection in feudalism. Only when deprived of all power and made liminal to the society they previously dominated can Lear and Gloucester abandon the assumption of exchange; only then can they express a generous concern for others and accept charity for themselves. Though the characters and their society do not understand generosity as anything other than a Maussian exchange, they nevertheless come to practice a very different generosity, in opposition to the assumptions of their society. In their fascination with interested exchanges and the Maussian social orders they support, characters as well as critics participate in a mystifying closure of the ethical real.

The characters champion a tradition of Western philosophy that, Levinas claims, is "fundamentally opposed to a God that reveals. Philosophy is atheism, or rather unreligion, negation of a God that reveals himself and puts truths into us."[14] I have argued elsewhere that the characters' habit of projecting their own needs and beliefs onto the Divine amounts to idolatry.[15] Their theological notions do not challenge their fidelity to exchange because they understand the gods as potentially fulfilling their requests and granting transcendent sanction to their beliefs. In this way, the characters resemble members of the cultures studied by Mauss, who explains that the "gods who give and return gifts are there to give a considerable thing in the place of a small one."[16] Such gods serve the needs of man, rather than vice versa. The characters show their paganism most forcefully in their insistence on exchange and indifference or even incredulity toward an absolute gift. Lear's repeated insistence that "nothing will come of nothing" (1.1.90) or that "nothing can be made out of nothing" (1.4.130) betrays his atheism not only because it denies creation but also because it, like Faustus's or Shylock's insistence on the letter of a bond, denies grace.[17]

Several characters treat people as the means of social advancement, placing them within an economy, though not one based on money. Regan offers Oswald "preferment" for the death of Gloucester (4.5.39–40). When they soon meet, Oswald regards the blind old man as preferment on the hoof: "That eyeless head of thine was first framed flesh / To raise my fortunes!" (4.6.223–24). He brushes aside Gloucester's status as a soul with a perfunctory order to "Briefly thyself remember" (4.6.225). The captain whom Edmund suborns to regicide also accepts murder as the means of self-advancement (5.3.39–40). Both Oswald and the captain attempt to exchange human lives for favors. Paula Blank argues, "Through arithmetic, Shakespeare reveals human identity as dependent on, and determined by, one's commensuration with others."[18] Human life becomes an item of exchange, imbricated within an economy like Antonio's pound of flesh. As Levinas writes, "The substitution of men for one another, the primal disrespect, makes possible exploitation itself."[19] The play invites us to recognize that people can be made interchangeable with one another, as Blank notes, but also to feel horrified at how easily they can be exchanged for land or advancement.

Exploitation forms a dense network in the final act. Edmund, faced with Albany as an obstacle, plans to convince Goneril to "devise / His speedy taking off" (5.1.65–66), thereby treating her as a weapon with which to eliminate her husband. Albany reciprocates his lack of fraternity: "I hold you but a subject of this war, / Not as a brother" (5.3.61–62). When they negotiate control over Lear and Cordelia, Edmund and Albany speak as enemies. Albany demands the prisoners as spoil, and Edmund plays for time, having already ordered their deaths. In fact, Edmund seems to view other people primarily as obstacles to or means of his own advancement, starting with his half-brother, Edgar. Goneril and Regan, in turn, treat him as a trophy over which to fight. Strikingly, neither sister considers the competition to be Edmund's to decide. Love can be won, like a battle, in Goneril's unfortunate but revealing comparison: "I had rather lose the battle than that sister / Should loosen him and me" (5.1.18–19). Goneril's poisoning of Regan merely carries the sisters' competition—by which the beloved becomes a thing contested—to its murderous conclusion.

At their worst, the characters assume that one person's gain always equals another's loss in a vicious and zero-sum game. Edmund seeks to have Edgar's rights transferred unto himself: "Legitimate Edgar, I must have your land" (1.2.16). This is still an exchange of sorts, in that it transfers one man's fortune to another. After his initial success, Edmund attaches an inevitability to his own rise at Gloucester's expense, expressing the principle in universal terms: "The younger rises when the old doth fall" (3.3.24). By his treachery, Edmund will gain "that which my father loses, no less than all" (3.3.23). Edmund views this process not only as inevitable but also as just — "a fair deserving" (3.3.22). Like Shylock, clinging to his bond, or Portia, applying an even more literal reading to the same bond, Edmund recognizes no justice beyond a process of exchange.

Edmund is self-consciously villainous but even generally sympathetic characters suffer from a sort of endemic category error, confusing what can be exchanged and what is excessive to exchange. The opening scene notoriously equates love and material reward. Lear bribes Cordelia, in whose "kind nursery" he hopes to live out his days, with the offer of "A third more opulent than your sisters" (1.1.124; 1.1.86). Similarly, Burgundy makes his love for Cordelia contingent upon her receiving a dowry from Lear. Lear anticipates this and mingles love and money when he demands to know:

> What in the least
> Will you require in present dower with her,
> Or cease your quest of love?　　　　　　　　　　(1.1.192–94)

Lear offers Cordelia within a dynastic exchange, as Chamberlain shows.[20] The love-test is an exchange not only between Lear and Cordelia but also between Lear and a future son-in-law.

The play's first lines introduce the tendency to treat persons as interchangeable and their values as expressed in material terms:

KENT:　　　　I thought the King had more affected the Duke of
　　　　　　Albany than Cornwall.
GLOUCESTER:　It did always seem so to us: but now, in the division
　　　　　　of the kingdom, it appears not which of the Dukes
　　　　　　he values most.　　　　　　　　　　　(1.1.1–5)

Both characters take it for granted that "affection" should assume material expression and that the division of the kingdom should measure Lear's feelings for his sons-in-law. Blank notes that the characters are concerned with "approximating human with material value, to make love or 'affection' proportionate with land and goods."[21] Having identified Edmund, Gloucester describes Edgar as "no dearer in my account" (1.1.18–19). Harry Berger argues that

Gloucester values his sons not as other people but as repositories of his investments in them, "the shares of pleasure, shame, trouble, sacrifice, and legal tenderness he has deposited in their characters."[22] Against such a reading of the play's first lines, Charles Spinosa argues that Gloucester is unnecessarily warm and emotive, pointing out that "whoresons, contrary to what Gloucester says, need not be acknowledged. They need not be introduced to royal counselors."[23] Gloucester, however, does not introduce Edmund, waiting for Kent to inquire awkwardly, "Is not this your son, my lord?" (1.1.7). Whatever Gloucester's feelings of paternal affection, the term "account" already had a longstanding financial meaning by the time Shakespeare wrote these lines.[24] Its use here illustrates Nicholas Visser's claim: "The language of commerce and law infiltrates itself into and debases the everyday discourse of the play." Visser lists multiple references to "dowries, portions, deeds, interest (in the sense of legal right), moiety, revenue, profit, property, inheritance, earnest (in the sense of money), hire, rent, monopoly, unpaid lawyers, cases in law, depositories (legalese for trustees), usurers, debts, and so on."[25] We need not understand the reduction of love to exchange as bluntly mercantile, however. Gloucester's love does not anticipate payment if Edmund will not inherit but it is nevertheless understood in delimited, measurable, and social terms. Spinosa exaggerates when he argues that "the claims of passion" to which Gloucester refers are "untempered by the stability of social forms,"[26] just as Berger exaggerates when he says that the metaphor of accountancy "measures the true limit of paternal affection."[27] Expression in monetary or at least reciprocal terms obscures the excess of affection. If Gloucester's affection is warmer than his turn of phrase would indicate, then its warmth must derive from something other than the networks of familial loyalties and reciprocal obligations that govern the society of the play—and which include the familial loyalties Edmund learns to manipulate with fiendish skill.

In such a network of reciprocal ties, donations stake claims. Incoherent with rage, Lear confuses giving with taking in banishing Cordelia: "So be my grave my peace, as here I give / Her father's heart from her" (1.1.125–26). Goneril and Regan compete for Edmund's love in a manner that serves as a variation on Lear's love-test, or perhaps a parody of Portia and Antonio's competition over Bassanio. Regan throws gifts at Edmund by way of claims. Before asking if he loves Goneril, Regan reminds him of "the goodness I intend upon you" (5.1.7). Two scenes later and with nearly her last breath, she marries him with the gift of

> my soldiers, prisoners, patrimony;
> Dispose of them, of me, the walls is thine.
> Witness the world, that I create thee here
> My lord and master. (5.3.76–79)

Like Portia's exaggerated marriage oath, this is an open-ended donation of self and property, but Regan's gift also stakes a claim.

Lear understands acts of generosity as claims to reciprocation in frankly contractual terms. Within the context of debt and repayment, we can understand the apparently irrational importance placed on the knights. His right to his martial entourage hinges upon his donation of "all," making his daughters "my guardians, my depositaries" (2.2.439–40). Goneril, in her practical way, imagines Lear being able to "hold our lives in mercy" (1.4.320). However, while directing the famous Soviet film version of *King Lear*, Grigori Kozintsev noted, "Not once are their swords unsheathed."[28] Despite their failure ever to deploy in his support, the knights reinforce Lear's power by serving as a possession he can claim by right, owed to him as a clause of the contract by which he divests himself of rule. Lear's entitlement to his knights is an assurance that he need not beg.

On the other hand, Lear asks nothing from the elements because he has given them nothing and therefore they owe him nothing:

> I tax not you, you elements, with unkindness.
> I never gave you kingdom, called you children;
> You owe me no subscription. Why then, let fall
> Your horrible pleasure. (3.2.16–19)

By extension, however, he taxes his children with unkindness, for failing to repay his generosity in love. The term "tax" implies sovereignty. Even the ability to make the accusation of unkindness provides a sort of recompense, almost a payment. The elements do not offer even this vicarious sense of righteousness, however. Scott compares Lear to Job, demanding justice from the heavens but also notes, "He has of course no contract with the gods" on the basis of which he could seek redress.[29] Lear alone refuses to complain about the weather. He will beg from the gods no more than he will beg for food and clothing from Goneril, or go to France and "squire-like pension beg, / To keep base life afoot" (2.2.403–04). His refusal differentiates him from King Leir, title character of an earlier anonymous play, who does journey to France to beg support and who accepts good fortune as a providential and unearned gift: "Come, let vs go, and see what God will send; / When all meanes faile, he is the surest friend."[30] Shakespeare's Lear at this point shows himself less Christian and more self-righteous, because he is incapable of the humility required to accept an absolute donation.

Within the context of a fictive world in which human relations are treated reflexively as power relations, Lear makes a concerted effort to draw all power to himself. Specifically, Lear intends to win forever the political struggle by making his gift so overwhelmingly large as to defy reciprocation. By giving his daughters "all," he can extract benefits indefinitely and provide himself with plenty of time to "Unburdened crawl towards death," in his grim image of retirement (1.1.40). Lear's position toward gifts is characterized by bad faith. He relies upon gifts to impose obligations but without assuming obligations of his own. Scott asks, rhetorically, how any assertions of love can "be commensurate, given Lear's own inflated estimate of the worth of kingship?"[31] In fact, the speeches do not provide even so asymmetrical an exchange. Berger draws attention to the form of the question that Lear poses to his daughters in the love test, pointing out that Lear does not ask "'which of you doth say you love us most,' but 'which of you *shall we say* doth love us most?'"[32] The daughters do not offer love in exchange for land, only speeches that Lear labels as love and assigns a value in land. The nonreciprocity of this all-important exchange may seem to violate Mauss's understanding of the gift. On the other hand, it follows logically from Mauss's insistence upon the ubiquity of exchanges. Lear's solipsistic love-test constitutes a reasonable strategy in a situation where donations threaten and human relations are understood as power relations. In such an agonistic context, power can only be retained by avoiding the receipt of any donation whatsoever.

The ungenerosity—indeed, unreality—of Lear's transfer of power illustrates his manipulation of exchange. Images such as parting the coronet pose difficulties; moreover, in banishing Kent, Lear issues a royal command after ceding power, as if deaf to his own resignation. "By Jupiter," he swears, "This shall not be revoked" (1.1.179–80). In principle, of course, Lear should be unable either to revoke or maintain his gift after he has already given it away, just as he should not be able to banish Kent after surrendering authority to Cornwall and Albany. Retention of a hundred knights, fifty knights, or even the clothes on his back belies Lear's claim to have given "all." Under the pretense of an absolute gift, Lear strives to impose an absolute obligation.

Cordelia's defiance goads Lear to an ever-greater insistence in his belief in the reciprocity of exchange. She claims a precisely divided love, one half each for her father and her future husband: "I love your majesty / According to my bond," she says, adding emphatically, "no more nor less" (1.1.96, 98). Basney argues that Cordelia's bond is not a contract that "is concluded on the basis of self-interest and can be withdrawn on the same basis. Cordelia means obligation as the unretractable offer of care—reciprocal according to pattern, but if not reciprocated then obligatory none the less."[33] Cordelia nevertheless states her obligation in reciprocal terms. Because Lear has "begot me, bred me, loved me" she will, in return, "Obey you, love you and most honour you" (1.1.95, 97). Dan Brayton calls this "a different economy of emotional exchange" but it is an economy nevertheless.[34] Peter

Holbrook rejects readings that align Cordelia's exchange with her sisters' when he says that they "distort the obvious dramatic contrast: it remains true that [Cordelia] is revolted by the love-auction while her sisters are not."[35] Cordelia may be revolted, but Lear obliges her participation. The love test, in which love takes the form of an exchange, constrains Cordelia's response. In her answer to Lear's curt order to "Speak again" (1.1.90), Cordelia merely acknowledges the explicit preconditions of Lear's test, by which land recompenses love, which therefore becomes an item in exchange. Lear calls her "untender" (1.1.107), but Cordelia's division of love only reflects the coldness of Lear's request. In turn, Lear extrapolates further the understanding of love as a series of exchanges: "Well, let it be so. Thy truth then be thy dower" (1.1.109). In response to Lear's network of exchanges, Cordelia measures her reply to what she owes him as an exchange for services rendered, such as begetting her in the first place. He, in turn, abjures any residual affection toward her, reducing her to "my sometime daughter" (1.1.121). Rather than revealing the ubiquity of exchange mechanisms, the disastrous and abortive exchange that opens *King Lear* shows the logic of exchange obscuring and even evacuating human affections. Because the characters will only acknowledge a gift that can be repaid in kind, the logic of love as a series of exchanges achieves its extreme and inhuman conclusion, whereby human relations disappear into increasingly mechanical, "untender," exchanges.

Perhaps, as Cavell argues, the love test is not a sign of naiveté in Lear so much as a bid for false love. Cordelia's nonanswer frightens Lear because he has a fundamental "terror of being loved, of needing love."[36] False love, on the other hand, would require only an exchange. True love confronts Lear with something of which he could not consider himself worthy, at least according to Cavell; moreover, true love represents a violation of the terms by which Lear understands his world and his own identity. One is reminded of Faustus, who is unable to accept grace. Berger argues that Lear's fundamental terror recurs when he encounters

Cordelia's troops near Dover. They offer him "anything." She will give all, generously, to which he can give nothing in return.[37] In response, he characterizes the situation as one of combat: "No seconds? All myself?" (4.6.190). The scene ends with the old king running away, fleeing a love he does not deserve and therefore cannot understand.

The evasion of gratuitous love extends to a refusal to even speak love's name. For Cordelia to confess her love for her father would place it within an economy, exchangeable for wealth and power. It would become the false love that Lear solicits and that Cavell suggests is all Lear can stand. The disjunction is not a Platonic one between ideal love and imperfect expression. Cordelia claims that "my love's / More ponderous than my tongue" (1.1.77–78).[38] Goneril also claims, "A love that makes breath poor and speech unable" (1.1.60), but makes this claim part of an act, involved in a network of exchanges, whereas Cordelia responds with silence. Both claim to be speechless but speak anyway. The distinction between the sisters' responses is not primarily a distinction between what is spoken and what is left silent, but between what is generous and what is exchanged within an economy. Cordelia is unable to offer false love not because she is any less eloquent than her sisters but because an expression of love coming from her would actually be true. "Nothing she could have done," Cavell argues, "would have *been* flattery."[39] Spinosa objects, "Common life, though, shows Cavell's position must be wrong. We can state many true things with inflections that are insincere."[40] Spinosa is, of course, correct but he misses the most important distinction. Goneril offers a false statement of love as an item of exchange; were Cordelia to make a false statement of true love, she would profane it. The form of the love-test, ostensibly that of an auction, evacuates its emotive content.

For the most part, Lear views his children in terms of what Levinas calls "the categories of power."[41] The king's rejection of Cordelia requires that he, like Gloucester, first assess his child in terms of his investments in her, of love or land, in order to be able to liquidate these investments and reduce her to a "little-seeming substance" (1.1.199). Leo Tolstoy objects, "Gloucester, like Lear, immediately believes the very grossest deception, and does not even try to ask the son who had been deceived, whether the accusation against him is true, but curses him and drives him away."[42] The gullibility of both characters, however, betrays their habitual anxiety, derived from an understanding of paternity as power. Berger explains the basis of Gloucester's actions: "The heir is a potential enemy and competitor, the eventual replacement whose appearance prophesies his father's death."[43] Montaigne makes a similar observation, claiming that parents cannot be friends to their children, citing filicidal cultures as well as patricidal practices to show that "naturally one dependeth from the ruine of another."[44] Certainly a number of the play's characters understand and indeed live paternity as political and mortal competition.

Berger's observation, though couched in broad terms, holds particularly well for the Gloucester family. Faced with the forged letter, Gloucester directs his anxiety toward Edgar, the legitimate heir destined to supplant him. The letter collapses love into "reverence" and paternity into "policy": "This policy and reverence of age makes the world bitter to the best of our times; keeps our fortunes from us till our oldness cannot relish them" (1.2.46–47). It voices Gloucester's own suspicions that his "legitimate" son will undo him, a suspicion that Berger finds Gloucester "almost too eager to entertain."[45] Gloucester's paternity is anxious because it is political. The career of Edmund illustrates the conception of fatherhood as a political position, beginning with his exploitation of Gloucester's fears to disown Edgar and appropriate his inheritance and continuing when, according to the quarto, Edmund wins "a dearer father" (3.5.24–25) by betraying Gloucester to Cornwall. As long as theirs are political roles, fathers can be changed like patrons or rulers. Edmund's assessment of the political system in which he operates proves horrifyingly accurate, with Cornwall, as an adoptive father, giving Edmund his natural father's title and territories. The seduction of Regan extends this pattern, as Edmund usurps the place of his second father in order to advance to plenary power.

Lear attempts to withdraw paternity by making charges of bastardy, or labeling himself a cuckold. The illegitimate child, as Edmund shows in his famous speech, stands to inherit nothing and therefore presents no threat. On hearing of Edgar's supposed treason, Gloucester responds with shocking brevity: "I never got him" (2.1.78).[46] Berger correctly interprets this as a gesture "disclaiming paternity," which "recreates [Edgar] as his wife's bastard."[47] Removing legitimate paternity exorcises the threat that the child imposes, but the child is only a threat if viewed as a competitor within a power relation. The Fool suggests in one of his apparently random catches both the threat and how to avoid it: "The hedge-sparrow fed the cuckoo so long / That it's had it head bit off by it young" (1.4.206–07). The child can rise to usurp or succeed the father, but by declaring the child a bastard and himself a cuckold, the father avoids this fate. "Degenerate bastard," Lear growls accordingly at Goneril, "I'll not trouble thee: / Yet have I left a daughter" (1.4.245–46). Later, he makes the legitimacy of Regan contingent upon her happy welcome:

> If thou shouldst not be glad,
> I would divorce me from thy mother's tomb,
> Sepulchring an adulteress.   (2.2.319–21)

If she is not glad to see him, then he can distance himself from her by declaring her a bastard and remove the threat of usurpation that only a legitimate child offers. Meeting Gloucester on the heath, Lear rejects the whole premise of legitimacy, summoning a universal orgy in its place:

> The wren goes to't, and the small gilded fly
> Does lecher in my sight. Let copulation thrive,
> For Gloucester's bastard son was kinder to his father
> Than were my daughters got 'tween the lawful sheets.
>   (4.6.111–14)

This passage evinces dramatic irony—Lear knows neither of Edgar's presence onstage as his father's guide nor that Edmund has been anything but kind—but has interest beyond that. Lear's readiness to believe ill of a legitimate heir echoes Gloucester's eager credulity. Because paternity is seen predominantly in this play in political terms, as patronage for instance, it often takes the form of competition. Motivating the anxiety toward children as threats and potential competitors is a prior anxiety toward an absolute gift that cannot be repaid—that is, in fact, not interchangeable with anything that might be offered as payment—and that therefore violates an entire worldview. The characters prefer to perceive their children as competitors within Maussian, agonistic exchanges, rather than to accept that familial love has no clear motivation.

If paternity is understood as a power relation then anyone with the means of offering patronage can become a father, as Cornwall does, and conversely, paternity can be revoked by withdrawing patronage. Lear first disowns Cordelia:

> Here I disclaim all my paternal care,
> Propinquity and property of blood,
> And as a stranger to my heart and me
> Hold thee from this for ever. (1.1.114–17)

He transforms Cordelia into his "sometime daughter," and reinforces her rejection with an image of "The barbarous Scythian, / Or he that makes his generation messes / To gorge his appetite" (1.1.117–19). "Against Lear's intention to liken Cordelia to the Scythian, the phrase likens the Scythian to Lear," as Berger points out.[48] A similar image occurs later, when Lear declares that Tom must have been impoverished by "pelican daughters" (3.4.74). Cherrell Guilfoyle notes a traditional image that compares Christ to a pelican, feeding his children with his own blood.[49] Lear's phrase, however, inverts the pelican image, transforming the daughters into potential victims. Even if one were to see the father as the "kind, life-rend'ring pelican," as Laertes

says in *Hamlet*,[50] Lear is still not giving generously but being can-
nibalistically consumed to nourish them. Lear's image expresses
his view of blood relationship as mortal competition; moreover,
it contradicts the usual Christian imagery of blood shed generously for sinners, as in Faustus's image of "Christ's blood…in
the firmament."[51] According to Guilfoyle, there is an element
of parody in this image, which shows that "Lear is not the true
Christ-figure."[52] Rather than loving his children unconditionally,
like Christ, Lear views his relationship with them as a matter of
exchange. Lear turns a depiction of generous giving, like the love
of God, into an icon of the hatred and murderous competition at
the heart of exchange mechanisms.

Such is the grip of models of society based on self-interest, that
even when characters do good, they seem unable to comprehend
their own actions. Ben Ross Schneider claims that Kent stands for
"feudal ties" that predate a movement where "the cash nexus"
takes the place of human relations and which Schneider identifies, following Karl Marx, with the rise of capitalism.[53] Kent certainly addresses Lear in feudal terms:

> Royal Lear,
> Whom I have ever honoured as my king,
> Loved as my father, as my master followed,
> As my great patron thought on in my prayers.   (1.1.140–43)

From his duty toward Lear, Kent gains a reason to be, if nothing else: "My life I never held but as a pawn / To wage against
thine enemies" (1.1.156–57). His loyalty outlasts that of those
who serve for immediate gain but so does that of Oswald, whom
no one would accuse of selflessness though his final request of
Edgar proves him loyal even in the face of death (4.6.242–46).
Kent insists, "No contraries hold more antipathy / Than I and
such a knave" (2.2.85–86), but contrasting feudalism with capitalism does not explicate their antipathy. On the contrary, if Kent's
expressions of duty were to take place only within the context
of reciprocal exchanges, then Kent's feudal service would be no

more generous than Oswald's mercenary service. Blank declares that, in his interview with Cordelia, "Kent's 'goodness' seeks its 'measure.' "[54] Kent himself, however, seems uninterested and even opposed to being rewarded for his services: "To be acknowledged," he tells Cordelia, "is o'erpayed" (4.7.4). In any case, Cordelia admits, "My life will be too short / And every measure fail me" (4.7.2–3). If Kent's service seeks its measure, it seeks in vain, because it extends service beyond that demanded by feudalism, indeed to "service / Improper for a slave" (5.3.219–20). At his best moments, Kent does not express nostalgia for feudal obligations but, on the contrary, exceeds them.

The anonymous servant who attempts to defend Gloucester against Cornwall also violates the limits of feudal service. Holbrook argues that "nothing, we imagine, could have been more unexpected to a Jacobean audience than this sight of a servant defying his master with force."[55] Richard Strier declares that the violence offered by Cornwall's servant against his master in a futile attempt to stop Gloucester's blinding constitutes "the most radical possible sociopolitical act."[56] Even Strier's description, however, fails to express its full radicality. If "service" is understood as an exchange, as in feudalism, then the servant's act is incomprehensible as the "better service" that he claims to be performing. Neither Regan, who calls him "you dog," nor Cornwall, who calls him "My villein," offer any reward for this service (3.7.74–77). Furthermore, no one, onstage or off, would expect them to. Gloucester's position negates his ability to offer a reward, and, in any case, the servant dies too soon to collect. Even extending the system of reciprocation to a metaphysical distribution of rewards and punishments fails to explain the servant's actions, because he dies without even seeking a reward from the gods in prayer. On the contrary, the servant's act exemplifies a generosity unconcerned with future reciprocation and therefore excessive to the exchanges that bind society. His defiance baffles Regan, for whom, as for her sister, the limits of power relations constitute the limits of the world: "A peasant stand up thus?"

(3.7.79).[57] In intervening for Gloucester, the servant performs a
heroically countercultural act.

Both Basney and Strier largely accept the servant's description
of his challenge to Cornwall as "better service." Basney, however, hints at an alternative explanation, arguing that the servant
"has served for so long in conventional ways that he hardly fathoms now what he is doing."[58] Dollimore considers pity in *King
Lear* to be a "residual expression of a scheme of values all but
obliterated by a catastrophic upheaval in the power structure of
this society."[59] However, the servant's courage violates the earlier "scheme of values" insofar as it also would express a "power
structure" built of reciprocal obligations. The servant's kindness
is not the legacy of a defunct belief system, though he explains his
action by reference to an ideal of service and to the loyalty that
has governed his life:

> Hold your hand, my lord.
> I have served you ever since I was a child,
> But better service have I never done you
> Than now to bid you hold. (3.7.71–74)

The ideal of service seems like an excuse, specifically one offered
to his master, rather than a convincing explanation. The servant
reflexively places his newly discovered duty of resistance within
conventional ideas of service, even while violating them, because
such ideas of service have always provided his motive and identity. His act defies even his own efforts to explain it within a
system of reciprocal exchanges.

The inadequacy, rather than the absence, of explanation in
terms of self-interest marks moments of generous kindness. Lear
tries to integrate Poor Tom into patterns of feudalism — "You, sir,
I entertain you for one of my hundred" (3.6.75–76) — but the next
few lines about replacing his wardrobe parody such efforts. While
the play depicts a large number of characters exchanging service
for love or money, often within patterns of social obligation, it
also allows the possibility of serving others for reasons that have

little to do with self-interest. Strier argues that the play may be read as "an extended meditation on the kinds of situation in which resistance to legally constituted authority becomes a moral necessity." He draws particular attention to how Gloucester aids Lear as his "old," in the sense of "former" master, to indicate that "Gloucester is insisting on a duty that does not depend on the immediate political situation."[60] The Old Man who guides Gloucester also explains his sense of duty on the basis of an obsolete feudal tie. The play as a whole, Basney argues, ascribes kindness to the most socially marginal, often anonymous, characters, "with a stage life of about ten lines."[61] Rather than serving as spokesmen for their society, these characters are the least imbricated in society and are sometimes cast out altogether as soon as they perform acts of kindness. In fact, as Frederick Turner points out in passing, the more important characters become "moral agents and creative beings" insofar as they become marginal to society, with Edgar transforming himself into Poor Tom and Lear and Gloucester reduced to wandering beggars.[62] Generously kind acts are performed by those least implicated in the social order because such acts are countercultural to a social order based on reciprocal, Maussian exchanges. The most substantial acts of kindness qualify as self-sacrificial, rather than self-interested.

Lear's famous recognition of the Fool inverts class sensibilities, and constitutes a sudden shift away from rantings about his own condition. Rather than understanding others by projecting his own condition unto them (as he does again when he encounters Edgar and immediately categorizes him as a disowned father), Lear recognizes his own condition by first recognizing that condition in the Fool, touchingly: "Come on, my boy. How dost my boy? Art cold? / I am cold myself" (3.2.68–69). After generously acknowledging the suffering of another, Lear moves away from the quid pro quo economic view of the world, in which he remained an active and powerful agent, and becomes able to accept gratuitous generosity: "Where is this straw, my fellow? / The art of our necessities is strange, / And can make vile things precious. Come;

your hovel" (3.2.69–71). The quiet words spoken to the Fool stand in contrast to the apocalyptic rhetoric of his earlier speeches in the storm scene, not one of which provides a certain example of Lear responding to anything said to him by someone else. Lear's acts of solicitude toward others in the storm represent a fundamental shift from concern with self to Other.

Rather than accepting the service of others as a feudal obligation, or attempting to bind them to him by Maussian gifts or promises, Lear accepts their generous aid and tries to help them, in turn. He insists that Kent "seek thine own ease" by entering the hovel, and that the Fool "go first" (3.4.23, 26). Lear's famous prayer extends concern for the Fool and Kent outward to all the wretches of the earth:

> Poor naked wretches, wheresoe'er you are,
> That bide the pelting of this pitiless storm,
> How shall your houseless heads and unfed sides,
> Your looped and windowed raggedness, defend you
> From seasons such as these? O, I have ta'en
> Too little care of this. Take physic, pomp,
> Expose thyself to feel what wretches feel,
> That thou mayst shake the superflux to them
> And show the heavens more just.   (3.4.28–36)

Dollimore argues that Lear cares about poverty only after experiencing it: "He has ignored it not through callous indifference but simply *because he has not experienced it.*"[63] The mere chronology of Lear's prayer, however, shows that Lear is driven to divest himself and expose himself to the elements "to feel what wretches feel" (3.4.34) only after he recognizes the suffering of the "poor naked wretches" (3.4.28)—not in order to recognize others but because he has already recognized them. The prayer, or at least its conclusion, might be dismissed as a supreme act of narcissism, presuming to be able to make the gods appear more just by his own actions, as if he were their agent. Such a dismissal would, however, be oblivious to the contrast that Lear's earlier prayers provide. He concludes one of his diatribes with the confident assertion, "I am a man / More sinned against than sinning" (3.2.59–60). Where he earlier presumes upon his own merits, calling on the gods to "Find out their enemies now" (3.2.51), his speech before entering the hovel concerns his own responsibility, his failure to take enough care of poverty, rather than his righteousness. Lear's prayer to the wretches shows a generous concern with others, whereas his prayer to the "the great gods / That keep this dreadful pudder o'er our heads" assumes his own worthiness (3.2.49–50). Lear's heightened awareness of the needs of others and of his own responsibility equips him to both give and receive with a new generosity.

In their final reconciliation, Lear and Cordelia place themselves below each other:

> O look upon me, sir,
> And hold your hand in benediction o'er me!
> No, sir, you must not kneel.   (4.7.57–59)

Lear's placement of himself below Cordelia is more than a simple inversion of the power relations with which the play started. Lear's blessing does not reinforce his position as patriarch, just as Cordelia's blessing does not humiliate her father, though he does take a place beneath her. Lear previously assumes the same posture when he illustrates to Regan the indignity of begging Goneril's forgiveness and support (2.2.342–45). The scene of Lear and Cordelia's mutual blessing does not, however, establish or confirm a hierarchy that places the giver of a blessing above its recipient: "When thou dost ask me blessing I'll kneel down / And ask of thee forgiveness" (5.3.10–11). They will be "poor rogues" together and in company with other "poor rogues":

> So we'll live
> And pray, and sing, and tell old tales, and laugh
> At gilded butterflies, and hear poor rogues[64]
> Talk of court news.   (5.3.11–14)

Humility does not become humiliation in either case because both characters defy the tendency, which their fictive world shares with our critical world, to understand human relations as power relations.

One might generalize the point that to give a blessing is not always to assume a position of power and note that several times in the play, a blessing appears as a genuine good wish to someone. Gloucester moves from a position of superiority to one of generous concern with another suddenly and with great pain. His first line after his blinding and before he learns of Edmund's treachery references his position as father and naturalizes the loyalty that his son owes him: "Edmund, enkindle all the sparks of nature / To quit this horrid act" (3.7.85–86). Having been robbed, or rather disabused, of this last remnant of command, however, he turns from concern with his exceedingly painful situation to his responsibility for another: "O my follies! Then Edgar was abused? / Kind gods, forgive me that and prosper him" (3.7.90–91). He wishes Edgar well again when he is about to commit suicide. In fact, he blesses Edgar, who may or may not live, then Poor Tom: "If Edgar live, O, bless him! / Now, fellow, fare thee well" (4.6.40–41). Gloucester's naming of Edgar at this point is not an assumption of a patriarchal role as lord over his household, because he has no household, no wealth, and, as far as he knows, no living family other than Edmund, who has already usurped Gloucester's social position. A blessing takes the form of a pure gift in these instances, not something to be exchanged for some other benefit or a ceremony recalling a hierarchy. In a sense, the blessing has no recipient, because Edgar cannot be expected to hear it (though ironically he does, disguised as Poor Tom) and may not even be alive to receive it. Nor, for that matter, does such a blessing have a clear donor. The person calling for blessing will not, in fact, provide any sort of tangible benefit, but will leave that task to the gods. He certainly would not expect to be repaid. At this point in the play, Gloucester has no ambitions for himself other than death, and his prayer before death does not request any sort of metaphysical reward. Gloucester does not, in this scene, make a gift in a Maussian sense, seeking a reciprocation and helping to create a network of obligations that would constitute his society while assuring his own place within it. On the contrary, he is an outcast from society and hopes soon to leave life altogether.[65] He does, however, make a generous gesture of concern toward an Other. In this more radical sense, Gloucester gives.

The characters of *King Lear*, like Faustus or the characters of *The Merchant of Venice*, strive to reduce all things to exchange. Many critics of the play join them and indeed, so do some of the theorists upon whose work those critics draw. Both critics and characters tend to view relations between people, if not in strictly contractual terms, at least in terms of reciprocal obligations between self-interested individuals or groups. They therefore partake in what Levinas calls "The sober coldness of Cain," who delimits his familial obligations, "conceiving responsibility as proceeding from freedom or in terms of a contract."[66] The characters' anxiety toward the gift is not merely about the prospect of owing a terrible debt. Instead, their anxiety concerns what would be unrepayable even in principle, and which therefore would frustrate efforts to understand the world as an arena of power. All of the characters agree, at least sometimes, with Goneril, that human relations are power relations and, accordingly, that gifts are aggressive acts. In the world of *King Lear*, relationships, culture, and laws are formed by the repression of gratuitous generosity. In moments of concern, however, the characters' actions fit poorly, if at all, with their own explanations. Generosity appears as countercultural and is most often expressed by socially liminal characters. In fact, social marginality appears almost as a precondition to generosity; Gloucester and Lear achieve a generous view of others only when robbed of their places in the social order. The a priori assumption that all gifts stake claims renders the characters mysterious even to themselves. Because the play raises philosophical issues about the nature of the world in which we live, criticism's participation in the repression of gratuitous generosity renders not only the play but indeed the world mysterious to us, as well.

FOUR

Speaking and Betraying Love

Despite a great deal of commentary, the nature of Antonio's love for Bassanio remains opaque. Antonio himself expresses bewilderment at his own emotions in the play's opening line: "In sooth, I know not why I am so sad" (1.1.1). After proposing that Antonio suffers a merchant's preoccupation with "his merchandise," Solanio goes on to suggest briefly "Why then, you are in love." Though Antonio brushes aside the notion with a couple of monosyllables—"Fie, fie" (1.1.40, 46)—many critics accept Solanio's second suggestion as correct. Graham Midgley, for instance, argues, "The cause of this sadness which Antonio has refused to acknowledge even to himself is revealed as soon as Antonio and Bassanio are alone together" when Antonio refers to Bassanio's suit to Portia.[1] Antonio's initial bewilderment and the nature of his affection toward Bassanio find simultaneous explanation by ascribing to Antonio a homoerotic desire for Bassanio.

In a thrice-anthologized article, Alan Sinfield makes a classic argument in favor of treating Antonio's affection as sexual. He quotes with approval Valerie Traub, who describes a whole group of plays that explore homoerotic pleasure until, as Sinfield says, they suffer "a failure of nerve" and revert to heteronormativity.

Sinfield's near certainty copes surprisingly well with the complete absence of overt eroticism in the play. "The fact," he argues, "that the text of *The Merchant* gives no plain indication that the love between Antonio and Bassanio is informed by erotic passion does not mean that such passion was inconceivable." On the contrary, the omission of such passion merely illustrates the manner in which "the Shakespearean text is reconfirming the marginalisation of an already marginalised group." Recognizing that "Whether Antonio's love is what we call sexual is a question which...is hard to frame, let alone answer," Sinfield thinks it sufficient to point out that "his feelings are intense."[2] Despite an absence of overt sexuality from the play, an unspoken and perhaps even unconscious sexual passion explains Antonio's sadness and commitment to Bassanio.

I will make here an alternative argument about why Antonio's affection remains unspoken. This is not to say that I wish to disprove, or even seriously contest, the argument that Antonio's love for Bassanio shows all the intensity of erotic passion, or more generally that, as Lewis has it, he is "ruled by irrational love."[3] Rather than joining the debate over the nature of Antonio's love, I want to draw attention to a shift over the course of the play in the expression and consequences of such a love. Antonio first gives his love the form of openhanded generosity, but he appears to seek a symbolic reciprocation by the trial scene. Initially, Antonio's love approximates the generous, excessive, and ultimately mysterious affection that Montaigne describes in his celebrated essay, "On Friendship." Whereas Montaigne thought his love to be exclusive, however, Shakespeare's play stages a competition between two loves. By finding expression, Antonio's initially nameless love becomes imbricated in the commercial exchanges of Venice and comes to compete with Portia's. Both of the claimants to Bassanio's affection begin with self-renunciation and generosity but end the play staking rival claims upon him. While a number of critics have blamed Antonio and Portia (mainly Portia) for the ungenerosity of their struggle over Bassanio, I rather draw attention to how their efforts at generosity fail by the very fact of finding expression. One is reminded of Derrida's claims regarding the impossibility of a gift. In Shakespeare's play, the gift is self-cancelling, because its generosity is undermined at the moment of its realization.

Antonio's initial generosity aligns his affection with the elevated friendship that Montaigne eulogizes. Sinfield finds intense friendship close to and even indistinguishable from erotic love: "While the entirely respectable concept of the friend was supposed to have nothing to do with the officially abhorred concept of the sodomite, in practice they tended to overlap."[4] Sinfield follows Alan Bray's seminal argument that early modern friendship shared many signs with the early modern construction of sodomical relationships. However, the friendship of which Bray writes largely consisted in political patronage and was therefore distinct from Montaigne's elevated sense of friendship, only possible between equals.[5] Everyday usage of the imagery of friendship, Bray claims, shows "something more immediately practical than the literary images at first glance reveal." Citing two letters that discuss politics, Bray asserts that sharing a bed might indicate such political friendship: "To be someone's 'bedfellow' suggested that one had influence and could be the making of a fortune." Similarly, "When two men kissed or embraced the gesture had the same meaning."[6] Bray argues that anxiety toward distinguishing between political friendship and sodomical love, whose signs could be identical, underlines much sixteenth-century literature and especially Marlowe's *Edward II*.

Montaigne describes friendship by contrast with political alliance and sexual desire, both of which are ultimately self-serving. In the classical example of the love of Tiberius Gracchus and Caius Blosius, Montaigne finds a relationship more important than loyalty to the state and its gods. Whereas common friendships remain governed by self-interest, Montaigne seeks and laments ideal friendship as "this noble commerce," in which "offices and benefits (nurses of other amities) deserve not so much as to bee accounted of." It is only in regard to other, "vulgar and customarie friendships" that Montaigne applies Aristotle's famous lament: "'Oh ye friends, there is no perfect friend.'"[7] The French is both more categorical and more plaintive than John Florio's translation would indicate: "O mes amis, il n'y a nul amy!"[8] In any case, Montaigne distinguishes the friendship of which he speaks from the sort of reciprocal exchange upon which Lear relies.

Derrida opens his essay, "The Politics of Friendship," a sort of prolegomenon to the book of the same title, by quoting Montaigne quoting Aristotle. Derrida recognizes the specificity of Montaigne's use of Aristotle, referring only to common friendships, "not 'the most perfect of their kind'; that is why 'there is no friend.'"[9] The example of an ideal and unusual, perhaps even unique, friendship allows Derrida to champion the necessity of friendship prior to political law: "before even having taken responsibility for any given affirmation, we are already caught up in a kind of asymmetrical and heteronomical curvature of the social space, more precisely, in the relation to the Other prior to any organized socius, to any determined 'government,' to any 'law.'" He finds Levinasian responsibility in an anarchic friendship, prior to political structures and the freedom of the self: "We are already caught, surprised in a certain responsibility, and the most ineluctable of responsibilities — as if it were possible to conceive of a responsibility without freedom." Though strangely he does not cite Levinas, he does cite Blanchot,[10] whose friendship with Levinas he would later describe in extravagant terms: "the absolute fidelity, the exemplary friendship of thought, the *friendship* between Maurice Blanchot and Emmanuel Levinas was a grace, a gift; it remains a benediction of our time, and, for more reasons than one, a good fortune that is also a blessing for those who have had the great privilege of being the friend of either of them."[11] Derrida describes this ideal friendship, as Montaigne describes his own, in terms of generosity. While claiming that it arises prior to social convention and law, Derrida nevertheless allows that it might find political expression. In fact, he argues in his wide-ranging way that "from Plato to Montaigne, from Aristotle to Kant, from Cicero to Hegel, the great philosophical and canonical discourses on friendship...will have linked friendship explicitly to virtue and to justice, to moral reason and to political reason."[12] Friendship, in Derrida's reading, combines a Levinasian responsibility with a political potential. Montaigne similarly places friendship outside or prior to political commitments but makes it exclusive and thereby seems to reject the possibility of it becoming generalized into politics.

The ideal friendship that Montaigne claims to have experienced with Étienne de la Boétie distinguishes itself not only from political alliance but also from sexual love, in both cases by its generosity. Montaigne contrasts friendship with both hetero- and homoerotic relations, including those which he finds in the literature of classical Greece, and declares all such relationships less generous than friendship. He describes marriage as a contract with commercial ramifications, "whereas in friendship there is no commerce or busines depending on the same but it selfe."[13] Montaigne dismisses heterosexual love between unmarried partners as primarily physical, with the lover seeking his own gratification: "enjoying doth lose it, as having a corporall end, and subject to satietie." One is reminded of Graziano's observation, that "All things that are / Are with more spirit chasèd than enjoyed" (2.6.12–13). Montaigne treats same-sex love as similarly corporeal, "simply grounded upon an external beauty." Such love may nevertheless take a relatively generous form: "If it fell into a more generous minde, the interpositions were likewise generous: Philosophicall instructions, documents to reverence religion, to obey the lawes, to die for the good of his countrie: examples of valor, wisdome and justice." Moreover, same-sex relationships have the redeeming characteristic of sometimes leading to friendship. Even this love, however, becomes at least metaphorically commercial, with the philosopher seeking to "establish a more firme and permanent bargaine." Friendship, on the other hand, "is enioyed according as it is desired, it is neither bred, nor nourished, nor increaseth but in jovissance, as being spirituall, and the minde being refined by use custome."[14] Florio translates the French *usage* with two words, "use" and "custome," both of which imply commerce; nevertheless, Montaigne argues that true friendship excludes even the exchange of gift-giving. In this relationship, the identity of the participants is so intense that "the union of such friends," causes them to expell from one another these words of division and difference: benefit, good deed, dutie, obligation, acknowledgement, prayer, thanks, and such their like."[15] Echoing such sentiments, Bassanio ties Antonio's virtues as "[t]he dearest friend" with his generosity, speaking of his "unwearied spirit / In doing courtesies" (3.2.290–92). Whereas marriage is a contract, lust extinguishes itself in consummation, and the pedagogical affection of the ancient philosophers devolves into an exchange, friendship is pure giving.

Rather than finding its explanation in mutual assistance, such friendship remains fundamentally mysterious. Montaigne admits his inability to explain it: "If a man urge me to tell wherfore I loved him, I feele it cannot be expressed, but by answering; Because it was he, because it was myself."[16] Both Alberto Manguel and Ricoeur place extraordinary importance on Montaigne's statement. Manguel traces its genesis in the copy of Montaigne's essays known as the *Exemplaire de Bordeaux*, annotated in his own hand. The words preceding the second comma in Florio's translation first appear in the edition of 1588, of which the *Exemplaire de Bordeaux* is a copy. In 1592, Montaigne added the words translated as "but by answering; Because it was he." Later, in a different ink and hurried hand, he inserted, "because it was myself." Manguel notes that in Montaigne's friendship "the separation between the 'I' and 'the other' is not denied"; rather, "the 'seam' that unites them, and which is consequently what divides one from the other 'cannot be found' in the eyes of the observer."[17] Friendship therefore does not resolve itself into fusion but maintains the distinction central to Levinasian ethics. More questionably, Manguel tries to render the relationship multilateral and a possible basis for society, though Montaigne clearly claims, "this amitie that possesseth the soule, and swaies it in all soveraigntie, it is impossible it should be double" never mind multiple or general.[18] Manguel may in his claim be following Ricoeur, who calls for "'a political friendship,' one that is essentially peaceful" and that would take the place of a Hobbesian competition of all against all as a basis for social solidarity.[19] Ricoeur concludes *The Course of Recognition* with Montaigne's extraordinary claim about his friendship with la Boétie and uses it as an instance of a reciprocal but peaceful generosity that maintains the independence of the participants: "We exchange gifts," he writes, "but not places."[20] Both Manguel and Ricoeur use the celebrated relationship between Montaigne and la Boétie as an instance of peaceful coexistence. In Ricoeur's use, it also instances a peaceful generosity, opposed to the competition of potlatch. Ricoeur and Manguel make different appropriations of Montaigne's concept, but they agree in characterizing it as generous.

Montaigne presumably reports on same-sex desire second-hand, and the pedophilic example of the ancients constrains his description.[21] In any case, the ruling distinction of his essay is not between homosexual and heterosexual love, but between generous love and love inspired by need, commerce and self-interest. "For generally," he writes, "all those amities nourished by voluptuousness or profit, publike or private need, are thereby so much the lesse faire and so much the lesse true amities, in that they intermeddle other causes, scope, and fruit with friendship, than it selfe alone."[22] We might paraphrase Montaigne's distinction by saying that all other relationships, in his estimation, combine generosity with self-interest. Levinas draws a distinction reminiscent of Montaigne's, when he compares "need" and "desire" in "The Trace of the Other." Here, he defines desire in opposition to need, arguing that whereas need seeks satisfaction, like a hunger, desire is infinite, increased by what it feeds on.[23] Levinas's depiction of need is close to Montaigne's description of heterosexual love "as having a corporall end, and subject to saciete."[24]

By the end of his essay, Levinas relates the infinity of desire to the infinity of responsibility. Earlier in the same essay, he describes works as directed toward the Other and not seeking a return, even in gratitude. Rather than promising the ultimately selfish satisfaction of receiving gratitude, works make goodness real, giving it concrete and historical form.[25] Levinas employs ideas surprisingly close to some of Montaigne's, though without citing or even alluding to his essay.

A gift within Montaigne's relationship would have the function that Levinas assigns to a work, as a means of expressing love. After arguing that true friends would not view their property as private in the first place and therefore could not make exchanges, Montaigne nevertheless claims that if a gift could be made in such a relationship, the giver and not the receiver would be most satisfied, and the receiver should be considered most generous: "For each seeking more than any other thing, to doe each other good, he who yeelds both matter and occasion, is the man sheweth himselfe liberall, giving his friend that contentment, to effect towards him what he desireth most." A gift given in such a relationship provides a means of expressing love. Montaigne notes parenthetically that la Boétie named him "with so kinde remembrance, heire and executor of his librarie and writings."[26] When Montaigne describes a gift that furnished the recipient with an occasion to express his love, he writes autobiography. In both Levinasian desire and Montaigne's friendship, generosity does not seek reciprocation. Instead, generosity provides an expression for love, thereby rendering it comprehensible.

Antonio essays such generosity. Certainly this is how some of the earliest readers of the play understood his actions. George Granville's adaptation of the play assigns Antonio additional lines echoing Montaigne: "My Friend can owe me nothing; we are one, / The Treasures I possess, are but in Trust, / For him I love."[27] A few critics still agree with Granville's assessment of Antonio's motivation. Murray J. Levith, for instance, contrasts Antonio with Faustus and notes that Antonio enters his bond for the sake of another, whereas "the magician signs over his soul for self-serving knowledge, worldly power, and fame."[28] In *Merchant*'s opening scene, the opportunity to express love obliges Antonio, as it would Montaigne's ideal friend. Bassanio's embarrassed apologies insult Antonio:

> You know me well, and herein spend but time
> To wind about my love with circumstance;
> And out of doubt you do me now more wrong
> In making question of my uttermost
> Than if you had made waste of all I have.   (1.1.153–57)

In the next lines he alludes to an obligation quite different from that implied by reciprocity, when he claims himself compelled by Bassanio's bare request:

> Then do but say to me what I should do
> That in your knowledge may by me be done,
> And I am pressed unto it.   (1.1.158–60)

Bassanio has already failed to repay earlier loans, so Antonio's obligation to help him is clearly not a reciprocal obligation. To be pressed can be a type of torture, as the term is used in *Measure for Measure*,[29] and one might be reminded of how Levinas uses persecution as a synonym of "responsibility for the Other."[30] In the context of Antonio's speech, however, "pressed" seems to stand in contrast to being bound, as by Shylock's contract. Antonio's generosity is neither self-interested nor compelled by the sort of obligation to repay that Mauss finds in every gift. Henry Smith draws a crisp distinction in his *Examination of Usury:* "Charitie rejoyceth to communicate her goods to other [men], and Vsurie reioyceth to gather other mens goods to her selfe."[31] By this definition, Antonio's loan to Bassanio would certainly qualify as charity, because it promises only to compound his losses. He rejoices in it nevertheless.

Both characters and critics reflexively suspect Antonio's generosity. Bassanio carefully describes his voyage to Belmont as a business transaction, promising "thrift" and the repayment of all his debts (1.1.175). Antonio's acceptance of Shylock's terms appalls Bassanio: "You will not enter such a bond for me. / I'd rather dwell in my necessity" (1.3.151–52). He understands that Antonio's generosity imposes obligations upon him and so he seeks to ameliorate them. Lewis notes that Antonio's "generosity has strings attached, as does Shylock's money." Certainly by the middle of the play, Antonio offers the forgiveness of debts as a sort of bribe for attendance at his execution, combining it with what Lewis calls "emotional blackmail":[32] "my bond to the Jew is forfeit; and since in paying it, it is impossible I should live, all debts are cleared between you and I, if I might but see you at my death. Notwithstanding, use your pleasure. If your love do not persuade you to come, let not my letter" (3.2.315–19). Lewis convicts Antonio of "often practicing some form of passive aggression."[33] Girard makes perhaps the most damning assessment of Antonio's generosity when he argues that it "may well be a corruption more extreme than the caricatural greed of Shylock" because "when Shylock lends money, he expects more money in return," whereas Antonio expects love. Of course, this reinforces Girard's wider argument that the Christian characters "do not live by the law of charity, but this law is enough of a presence in their language to drive the law of revenge underground."[34] For all Antonio's efforts to give to his friend, his expressions of love elicit damning suspicions.

Antonio's loan to Bassanio illustrates the inverse of Girard's point. Rather than greed being expressed in a language of charity which obfuscates it, generous love finds expression in financial terms that ultimately betray it. Antonio gives financial expression to his love for Bassanio simply because a loan provides him with an opportunity to express love. Girard acknowledges the possibility of true generosity later, in a particularly Roman Catholic way: "I would like first of all to make a distinction between sacrifice as murder and sacrifice as renunciation. The latter is a movement toward freedom from mimesis as potentially rivalrous acquisition and rivalry."[35] Without reference to Girard, Levinas agrees that communication with the Other requires "the gratuity of sacrifice."[36] Antonio attempts renunciation, even offering to become a literal sacrifice for his friend. His efforts, however, inevitably betray themselves because they take financial and therefore reciprocal form.

Expression complicates and undermines Antonio's love. He imposes claims by renouncing them. Parting from Bassanio, for instance, Antonio tells his friend:

> As for the Jew's bond which he hath of me,
> Let it not enter in your mind of love:
> Be merry, and employ your chiefest thoughts
> To courtship and such fair ostents of love
> As shall conveniently become you there.   (2.8.41–45)

Even in telling Bassanio to ignore the bond, Antonio draws attention to it. Moreover, in telling him to concentrate instead on "ostents of love," he stages his own ostent of love. According to Salerio, who reports the parting secondhand, Antonio's

>   eye being big with tears,
> Turning his face, he put his hand behind him,
> And, big with affection wondrous sensible
> He wrung Bassanio's hand; and so they parted.   (2.8.46–49)

Antonio carefully denies the claim he makes on Bassanio. This denial takes the form of silence—what he does not say as he turns his face away. Moreover, the gesture recalls the Biblical injunction from Matthew 6:2 (Geneva) to "let not thy left hand know, what thy right hand doth, that thine alms may be secret." Many critics read Antonio's denial of a claim on Bassanio as simply dishonest. His character remains equally consistent, however, if we imagine him attempting to be truly generous, to make no claims upon Bassanio with his generosity. The very fact of expression, however, destines Antonio's intent to fail; his generous act draws him into exchange. The bond with Shylock seems to be the first and only usurious transaction in which Antonio directly participates. "To supply the ripe wants of my friend" he reasons, "I'll break a custom" (1.3.60–61). By giving his love expression and therefore liberating it from its inarticulate state at the beginning of the play, Antonio imbricates it in the exchanges and transactions that structure Venetian society.

Antonio's near sacrifice of himself for Bassanio has been compared to that of Christ for sinful man. Girard sees Antonio only as the scapegoat, identified with Shylock by "their mutual hatred."[37] In taking on the role of Christ, Antonio participates in a whole dramaturgical and literary tradition. Crucifixions continued to be acted on stage after the Reformation; John Bale even composed a protestant Passion Play.[38] Earlier versions of the bond story identify the debtor with Christ as Jordan notes,[39] while in the *Processus Belial*, Christ is both accused and judge.[40] Lewis argues at length that all Shakespeare's characters named Antonio derive part of their imagery from Saint Anthony of the Desert, who "had collected about him an impressive number of parallels between himself and Christ—more, perhaps, than any other saint ever has." These characters, Lewis suggests, who would by their very name represent self-sacrifice to an early modern audience, all pose the question of "how can one love completely...when pure love is so easily subjected to selfish concerns, like pride, greed, and fear of rejection."[41] Lewalski draws a parallel with the Gospel of John (15:12–13, Geneva): "Greater love than this hath no man, when any man bestoweth his life for his friends."[42] An allegorical reading of the play identifies Antonio and Christ.

Such a reading accepts Antonio at his own estimate. He may not call himself the Lamb of God, but he does refer to himself as "a tainted wether of the flock, meetest for death" (4.1.113–14). Antonio echoes Christ responding to Pilate in the Synoptic Gospels when he merely acknowledges Shylock's accusation, responding to Portia's "You stand within his danger, do you not?" with "Ay, so he says" (4.1.177–78).[43] Like a martyr, he claims to:

> oppose
> My patience to his fury, and am armed
> To suffer with a quietness of spirit
> The very tyranny and rage of his. (4.1.9–12)

Facing death, Antonio describes himself in saintly and even Christ-like terms.

Such messianic imagery renders ironic Antonio's profane ambition in death. He makes no effort to pray, speaking to Bassanio instead. Antonio rejects the convention of urging survivors not to mourn:

> Repent but you that you shall lose your friend,
> And he repents not that he pays your debt;
> For if the Jew do cut but deep enough,
> I'll pay it instantly with all my heart.   (4.1.275–78)

Antonio secularizes the language of repentance. He does not repent for his sins; in fact, his only ambition seems to be to pay Bassanio's debt. In doing so, however, he imposes a new debt on Bassanio and can compel him to "Repent...that you shall lose your friend." Earlier he does pray, or at least uses the form of a prayer, when he exclaims, "Pray God Bassanio come / To see me pay his debt, and then I care not!" (3.3.35–36). This exclamation merely serves to emphasize that he directs his ambition in death toward Bassanio's mourning, rather than to any metaphysical afterlife. Antonio assumes a sacrificial and Christ-like role but only in order to impose an obligation on Bassanio.

R. Chris Hassel, in particular, notes the failure of Antonio's effort to assume a Christ-like role and describes it as inevitable in light of Protestant doctrine: "But every Renaissance Protestant would have insisted that Christ can be the only such perfect sacrifice. Only Christ could have fulfilled the Law of the Old Testament; only Christ, therefore, can have liberated mankind to his new commandment of love and forgiveness." Specifically, Antonio's "enactment of the 'sacrifice,' his act of 'greater love' cannot be offered selflessly."[44] To give with anything other than divine generosity stakes a claim to reciprocation. Engle argues that Antonio seeks self-sacrifice early in the play when he offers Bassanio "my purse, my person" and "seems to be imagining, even desiring, an 'occasion' for self-sacrifice."[45] In any case, he welcomes the chance to sacrifice himself, refusing to beg for life and

instead begging the court "to give the judgement" (4.1.240–41).
Unfortunately, giving his self-sacrifice expression in the world
frustrates it. Even if Antonio's affection for Bassanio consists in
"godlike amity," as Lorenzo assures Portia, his role as "a lover
of my lord your husband" (3.4.3, 7) places him in competition
with other lovers. His self-description as Bassanio's "love," in
fact, occurs in the speech where he asks Bassanio to tell Portia
the story of his death (4.1.273–74). Antonio's attempt to die for
his friend can furnish only a parody of Christ's sacrifice and one
eventually frustrated; moreover, it draws him into competition
with Portia. However generous its motive, the gift fails because
the expression it demands profanes it.

One way to understand the problem is to return to Montaigne's
insistence that a perfect friendship is unique. To prove his point,
he imagines different friends making competing claims: "If two at
one instant should require helpe, to which would you run? Should
they crave contrary offices of you, what order would you follow?
Should one commit a matter to your silence, which if the other
knew would greatly profit him, what course would you take? Or
how would you discharge yourselfe?" Neither can two friendships
conflict, nor can friendship conflict with erotic love. Montaigne
admits to enjoying both friendship and erotic love at the same
time, "but in comparison never: the first flying a high, and keeping a proud pitch, disdainfully beholding the other to passe her
points farre under it."[46] Montaigne imagines but dismisses competition between a friend and a lover, just as he imagines and dismisses competition between two friends. *The Merchant of Venice*
extends such competition into a drama. Where Antonio attempts
to sacrifice himself in Christ-like terms, Portia casts herself as
Hesione to Bassanio's Hercules:

> Now he goes,
> With no less presence but with much more love
> Than young Alcides, when he did redeem
> The virgin tribute paid by howling Troy
> To the sea-monster. I stand for sacrifice.   (3.2.53–57)

Of course, the imagery is no more than imagery. As Morocco com-plains, the strength of Hercules would prove impotent to choose the correct casket (2.1.31–38). Portia places herself rhetorically in the position of a sacrificial victim, but Antonio trumps this when he "courts risk" in offering his person for death.[47] As part of his insistence that friendship must be unique, Montaigne draws attention to the lavish generosity of a friend's donation, not only of things but of self: "For, this perfect amity I speake of, is indivis-ible: each man doth so wholly give himself unto his friend, that he hath nothing left him to divide else-where: moreover he is grieved that he is [not] double, triple, or quadruple, and hath not many soules or sundry wils, that he might conferre them all upon this subject."[48] Portia yearns for such self-multiplication:

> for you
> I would be trebled twenty times myself,
> A thousand times more fair, ten thousand times more rich,
> That only to stand high in your account
> I might in virtues, beauties, livings, friends
> Exceed account.   (3.2.152–57)

Portia converts herself into something to give; moreover, she does so in terms that echo Montaigne's desire to give beyond even the limits of the self. One is reminded of how Antonio, who identi-fies his purse and person, has recourse to credit in order to give to Bassanio: "That shall be racked," he says, "even to the uttermost, / To furnish thee to Belmont, to faire Portia" (1.1.181–82). Whereas Portia wishes to multiply herself, Antonio wishes to stretch his credit and possibly himself. By using the term "racked," a homonym for a form of torture, Antonio also describes a form of debasement.[49] Both Portia and Antonio offer excessively, but this is precisely how they enter into competition.

The struggle becomes most acute at the end of the play, when Bassanio finds himself indebted to both and therefore in the position Montaigne deems impossible. Bassanio's assump-tion that Portia would be satisfied "If you did know for whom I gave the ring" proves naive (5.1.194). Antonio defeats Portia's claim on Bassanio twice. First, as already mentioned, when facing death, Antonio demands that Bassanio describe his love to Portia (4.1.271–74). Bassanio accepts the terms of the comparison, expressing his love for Antonio as superior to that for his spouse:

> Antonio, I am married to a wife
> Which is as dear to me as life itself;
> But life itself, my wife, and all the world
> Are not with me esteemed above thy life.
> I would lose all, ay, sacrifice them all
> Here to this devil, to deliver you.   (4.1.279–84)

At this point, the idea of sacrifice shifts from renunciation—like that of Christ, or less successfully Portia or Antonio—to murder. Immediately after the trial, Antonio again trumps Bassanio's obligation to Portia: "My Lord Bassanio, let him have the ring. / Let his deservings and my love withal / Be valued 'gainst your wife's commandement" (4.1.445–47). Fujimura notes that Bassanio's gesture constitutes the sacrifice of something he very much values and therefore "shows the genuineness of his sentiments in the court scene."[50] By the beginning of the last scene, Antonio has reason to feel victorious. He has become, as Bassanio informs Portia, "the man to whom I am so infinitely bound," though Antonio is "well acquitted of" all bonds upon himself (5.1.135, 138). Antonio may not succeed in dying, but in giving his love expression he nevertheless manages to win Bassanio's love.

His victory, however, proves costly as well as short-lived. Lewis summarizes her critique of Antonio's efforts at self-sacrifice by writing, "In *The Merchant of Venice*, the claims of this world appear to bedevil the characters' every effort, however earnest and authentic, to practice idealism of any sort."[51] In setting the terms for Shylock's pardon from a capital crime, Antonio asks for half of Shylock's wealth "in use" (4.1.379). Shell notes that the phrase recalls "the Statutes of Uses of Henry VII and Henry VIII," and claims only the interest from Shylock's wealth. Shylock has obviously been defeated, but Antonio also suffers a loss, as he "has begun to think of himself as a kind of usurer."[52] Antonio extracts from Shylock "a gift / ... of all he dies possessed / Unto his son, Lorenzo, and his daughter" (4.1.384–86). The gift has become an object of exchange and indeed of extortion. Merely by giving his love expression, never mind making that expression a competition with Portia, Antonio robs it of its excessive character. His gift, when he generously offers "My purse, my person, my extremest means" (1.1.138) leads him to become "Engaged ... to his mere enemy" as Bassanio laments (3.2.260). Moreover, this generous donation binds Bassanio, who has "engaged myself to a dear friend" (3.2.259–60). This engagement to a friend threatens his engagement to Portia. Even if Antonio were ultimately victorious in the struggle for Bassanio's love, he would already have diminished it from the friendship that Montaigne praises, in which gifts are not even calculated.

Witnessing Antonio's loss of Bassanio to Portia, a number of critics have credited Portia with enormous and even wicked powers of manipulation. Szatek declares that Portia "like Machiavelli, will employ any means necessary to suit her end. The play evidences some of her tools to capitalize on her endeavors: manipulation, conspiracy, craftiness, humiliation, lies, fraud, disenfranchisement, and assuredly, that offshoot of capitalistic mercantilism, usury."[53] Though perhaps not as Machiavellian as Szatek proposes, Portia is nevertheless victorious, as Engle shows, noting "her absolute mastery of the systems of exchange in the play which have routed all blessings, economic, erotic, and theological, toward Belmont."[54] Most convincingly, she conscripts Antonio as "surety" to Bassanio's oath (5.1.254), making Antonio's earlier friendship subservient to her relationship, as Anne Barton notes.[55] Portia wins, but she triumphs by giving her love practical form and thus, like Antonio, simultaneously realizing and diminishing it.

The ring becomes a gift staking a claim to reciprocation. Initially, it merely represents Bassanio and Portia's relationship. Its loss would "presage the ruin of your love / And be my vantage to exclaim on you" Portia declares (3.2.173–74), but she does not indicate that the loss of the ring would actually precipitate the end of their relationship. It is only at the end of the play, after Bassanio has indeed parted with the ring, that Portia declares its retention the condition of her marital fidelity (5.1.223–28). She ignores Bassanio's reasoning in the previous lines: "Had you been there I think you would have begged / The ring of me to give the worthy doctor" (5.1.221–22). Ironically, she was there and did beg the ring in the person of the doctor. Instead of recognizing her own culpability in Bassanio's choice, or even recognizing Bassanio's argument, she simply stands upon her rights. The ring has become a claim upon Portia's body. The play ends with Graziano's obscene pun on "Nerissa's ring," conflating a piece of jewelery with a vaginal orifice (5.1.307). Over the course of the ring game, an object of donation becomes the means of asserting a claim. Portia's all-giving generosity transforms into a Maussian exchange.

Portia becomes most determined to reclaim Bassanio only after witnessing Antonio's victory over her in the court. Short points out the obvious counterfactual possibility: "She could at any point bring the issue to a close by simply opening those books and pointing to the pertinent law, as she does very late in the scene, giving the Duke grounds to arrest Shylock immediately, preventing him from carrying out the penalty for forfeit of the bond."[56] If she procrastinates Antonio's situation, she does so in order to determine the nature and intensity of her new husband's bond to his friend. She invites Antonio to make a final statement: "You, merchant, have you anything to say?" (4.1.260). When his scaffold speech elicits Bassanio's claim that he loves Antonio more than Portia, she comments "Your wife would give you little thanks for that, / If she were by to hear you make the offer" (4.1.285–86). Even Shylock sneers about "the Christian husbands" (4.1.292). Portia makes earlier efforts to defeat Antonio, or at least to obligate him, offering "To pay the petty debt twenty times over. / When it is paid, bring your true friend along" (3.2.305–06). Engle notes that when she hears Antonio's message, ending with the wheedling sentence, "If your love do not persuade you to come, let not my letter," Portia immediately echoes its claim upon Bassanio: "O love!" (3.2.318–20).[57] In both cases, Antonio's claim upon Bassanio inspires Portia's counterclaim.

Montaigne raises the possibility of divided loyalties only hypothetically, while Shakespeare's play dramatizes their struggle. In the face of such divided loyalties, the generosity that characterizes Montaigne's friendship dissolves into the sort of gift that stakes a claim. Montaigne's extraordinary friendship nevertheless serves, for Ricoeur, Derrida, and Manguel, as a model of a peaceful relationship of generosity. Ricoeur relates his own work overtly to Levinas's, in looking for an account of peaceful coexistence in "a philosophy of the originary asymmetry between the ego and the other."[58] He proceeds to note, "The philosopher of dissymmetry grants that 'there must be justice among incomparable ones.'"[59] Levinas also concedes that there would be no problem were we only confronted by a single Other: "If proximity ordered to me only the other alone, there would not have been any problem, in even the most general sense of the term....It is troubled and becomes a problem when a third party enters." The problem of how to adjudicate between them, Levinas argues, constitutes the rationale for pretty much all social thought: "The extraordinary commitment of the other to the third party calls for control, a search for justice, society and the State, comparison and possession, thought and science, commerce and philosophy, and outside of anarchy, the search for a principle."[60] Society, in the sense of social structures that can be studied by social science, rises from the fact that our obligations are never simple. In particular, radical generosity calls for political order: "A measure superimposes itself on the 'extravagant' generosity of the 'for the other,' or its infinity. Here, the right of the unique, the original right of man, calls for judgement and, hence, objectivity, objectification, thematization, synthesis. It takes institutions to arbitrate and a political authority to support all this." Our responsibility to the Other may initially be radical and absolute, but, Levinas argues, it also implies a responsibility for other Others, for third parties. In practice, of course, there are always third parties, unless, as Levinas pointed out in an interview, one lives on a desert island with only one other person.[61]

The commitment to the Other may not precisely resemble Montaigne's friendship but, like this friendship, it implies radical generosity. Excessive generosity initially characterizes relationships in Shakespeare's *Merchant,* as Antonio volunteers all his wealth and even his credit and Portia wishes to multiply herself in order to endow Bassanio with more than all she has and is. Unlike Montaigne's friendship, however, the relationships that Antonio and Portia share with Bassanio conflict with one another. They therefore lend themselves to adjudication, power struggles, and social norms. In Levinasian terms, "The state, institutions, and even the courts that they support, expose themselves essentially to an eventually inhuman but characteristic determinism—politics." Such determinism is not, however, without recourse, as Levinas states: "Hence, it is important to be able to control this determinism in going back to its motivation in justice and a foundational inter-humanity."[62] As Peperzak concedes, generosity might never be found in an absolutely pure state. In *The Merchant of Venice,* expression betrays the exorbitant demand of love but also grants it practical reality. The play dramatizes the movement from love to justice, to borrow Levinas's terms, or from absolute generosity to something that can have social status. In any case, the exorbitant demand of an excessive generosity precedes the social and political structures in which it finds expression.

FIVE

The "Dearest Friend" in *Edward II*

The theme of friendship commands attention in Marlowe's *Edward II*. The words "friend," "friends" or "friendly" occur a total of 55 times, compared to 37 times in the combined parts of *Tamburlaine* and only 11 times in the longer text of *Doctor Faustus*.[1] No other play by Marlowe comes close. In the play's second line, Edward describes himself as Gaveston's "dearest friend,"[2] and criticism of *Edward II* consists, in large measure, of an explication of that term. In particular, critics link friendship with same-sex desire. Lawrence Normand points out that "the signs of male friendship...were intense and physical,"[3] while Marie Rutkoski finds a parallel to Edward's "language of Renaissance male friendship" in Richard Edwards's 1564 *Damon and Pythias*. She nevertheless proceeds to show that the play's central love affair includes "corporal sexuality."[4] Like Sinfield writing about *The Merchant of Venice*, Rutkoski draws on Bray's seminal argument, expressed most famously in *Homosexuality in Renaissance England* but also in "Homosexuality and the Signs of Male Friendship in Elizabethan England," a 1990 article that uses Marlowe's play as an example. Bray argues that in the play, as in the culture of which it is a product, "The image we see is simultaneously both that of friendship and its caricature" in what the Renaissance labeled sodomy.[5] Following Bray, a number of critics argue that friendship and what the Renaissance understood as sodomy are indistinguishable in expression.

While Bray claims that the Renaissance distinguished friendship from sodomy by declaring the former generous and the latter self-seeking, I argue that same-sex love appears more generous than friendship in Marlowe's play. Edward's love of Gaveston expresses itself in excess and generosity. Other characters turn love, friendship, and the gifts through which both are expressed into the sorts of gift-exchanges that Mauss describes, constructing an entire society on gift exchange, like the characters in other plays. The love of Edward and Gaveston, however, proves recalcitrant to political relations because it violates the self-interest that is assumed to constitute the horizon of both friendship and eroticism. The king's relationship with his "dearest friend" is extraordinary, unique and, most importantly, exclusive.

Against the claim that friendship is a mere social convention, Levinas declares that the face of the Other founds sociality itself. A second but immediate movement founds political institutions: "If I am alone with the Other, I owe him everything; but there is someone else.... The interpersonal relationship I establish with the Other I must also establish with other men; there is thus a necessity to moderate this privilege of the Other; from whence comes justice. Justice, exercised through institutions, which are inevitable, must always be held in check by the initial interpersonal relation."[6] The self only becomes conscious "when the third party enters." In shared responsibility for a third party, the self and the Other are placed "on an equal footing as before a court of justice." Levinas generally describes this movement as automatic and necessary: "In the proximity of the other, all the others than the other obsess me, and already this obsession cries out for justice, demands measure and knowing, is consciousness." He links this automatic process to the movement by which "The saying is fixed in a said, is written, becomes a book, law and science."[7] While the face of the other commands, it also immediately opens to other faces. While ethics precedes politics, it also founds politics.

As a model for the face-to-face relationship, Levinas in some of his early works uses the erotic relationship, "where in the proximity of another the distance is wholly maintained."[8] He maps the difference of self and Other onto the difference between the sexes, to which he attaches ontological importance: "The difference between the sexes is a formal structure, but one that carves up reality in another sense and conditions the very possibility of reality as multiple, against the unity of being proclaimed by Parmenides." Against the Platonic notion that love seeks a lost unity, Levinas argues that its "pathos...consists in an insurmountable duality of beings." He compares this erotic relationship with the products of courtly love poetry, "the great themes of Goethe or Dante, to Beatrice and the *ewig Weibliches*, to the cult of the woman in chivalry and in modern society."[9] Feminist philosophy has responded either very positively or very negatively to this characterization of the feminine, leading Levinas later in life to try to avoid it altogether.[10] The same-sex love of Edward and Gaveston provides a test of how much this extraordinary eroticism—and the relationship with the Other with which it is associated—relies specifically on the gender dichotomy in which Levinas places it.

Levinas's treatment of the erotic relationship possesses further interest for the relationship of Edward and Gaveston. In *Totality and Infinity*, Levinas retreats from his identification of the erotic relationship with the face-to-face. He notes the equivocal nature of eros, which "does not transcend unequivocally—it is complacent, it is pleasure and dual egoism."[11] Edward seeks escape from the political world and its responsibilities into such dual egoism. The love of Gaveston and Edward precedes social conventions; as generations of critics have noted, it is bravely countercultural and, moreover, it is marked by excess. Its extraordinary claim does not immediately, however, extend to a third party, the "someone else" of Levinas's statement. Instead, it rests exclusively on the beloved, rather than evolving into wider political commitments to society, rules of justice, or the obligations of a constituted state. The exclusivity of Gaveston and Edward's affection renders it a paradoxically convincing instance of the radicality of love prior to cultural convention, reciprocal obligation, or even the language in which it takes expression.

Though Bray argues that early moderns contrasted their notion of the sodomite with that of the friend, he also declares this dichotomy fundamentally false. He presents the Maussian argument that the two sorts of relationship cannot be distinguished on the basis that only one is self-interested, because even the most idealized emotional bonds ultimately betray a self-interested motivation. Precisely because the sodomite and friend proved effectively indistinguishable, anxieties occasioned by their "uncompromising symmetry" haunted the early modern mind.[12] In the play, as in Bray's description of the early modern world, the word "friend" signifies a partner in a self-interested relationship. In the scene where the rebels muster their forces for invasion, Isabella, Kent, Young Mortimer, and John of Hainault all use the word "friend" to refer to allies. The first line, in which Isabella describes the failure of her embassy, establishes the pattern: "Our friends do fail us all in France" (15.1). Soon, however, a new group of friends gathers. Sir John of Hainault offers his services to the prince, asking "How say you, my lord, will you go with your friends?" (15.19). Young Mortimer uses "friends" as synonymous with members "of our party and faction" (15.51–54). A few lines later, speaking encouragingly of the military situation, he claims, "We will find comfort, money, men and friends" (15.65). The queen's coalition succeeds not only in invading England but also in importing its diction. Spencer signals defeat by informing Edward that Isabella's "friends do multiply, and yours do fail" (18.2). Friendship dominates the politics of the play's world.

Indeed, it drives the conflict. The barons consider themselves as the king's natural friends and therefore view Gaveston as a usurper of their own position. "My lord," Lancaster asks, apparently in genuine confusion, "why do you thus incense your peers, / That naturally would love and honour you, / But for that base and obscure Gaveston?" (1.98–100). As Claude J. Summers notes, "the political instability centered in the competition of king and peers is itself part and parcel of a larger social instability that mirrors a fundamental identity crisis."[13]

The nobles tie their identity closely to land, as Lancaster makes clear in inventorying his real estate while considering the feasibility of rebellion: "Four Earldomes have I besides Lancaster, / Darby, Salisbury, Lincoln, Leicester, / These will I sell to give my soldiers pay" (1.101–03). Gaveston mocks him as "the mighty Prince of Lancaster, / That hath more earldoms than an ass can bear" (3.1–2). Birth also, perhaps more fundamentally, founds nobility. The barons deploy their names as weapons when signing the order for Gaveston's exile. "The name of Mortimer shall fright the king," its bearer boasts (4.6). Conversely, the promotion of Gaveston is a particularly goading insult (2.9–15). Young Mortimer insists that Gaveston "hardly art a gentleman by birth" (4.29). Gaveston himself recognizes that the nobles "glory in your birth" (6.74).[14] The peers, as Gaveston recognizes, rely upon a model of nobility based on birth and control of land.

In opposition to this largely feudal conception of nobility, Edward and Gaveston propose an alternate model, based on education and cultivation. J. A. Nicklin suggests that Gaveston is a product of Marlowe's fascination with the Italian Renaissance and its renewal of interest in the arts: "The shows with which Gaveston proposes to entertain the pleasure-loving king would befit the court of an Italian despot better than a Plantagenet's palace at Westminster."[15] In Edward's mind, Gaveston's cultivation qualifies him as noble. "Ah, none but rude and savage-minded men" Edward exclaims, "would seek the ruin of my Gaveston;

/ You that be noble-born should pity him" (4.78–80). Gaveston declares himself superior to the nobles, that his "mounting thoughts did never creep so low / As to bestow a look on such as" them (6.77–78). Gaveston's self-conscious superiority insults the nobles. "Whiles other walk below," Young Mortimer complains, "the King and he / From out a window laugh at such as we" (4.417–18). Earlier, he declares, "We will not thus be fac'd and over-peer'd" (4.19). The pun on "overpeer'd," meaning not only surveyed from a position of superiority but also surmounted within the peerage, was noted as early as 1914.[16] Gaveston, who is low-born, reverses the social order when he literally looks down on the nobles. This act is sodomical in Bray's sense, reversing a hierarchy assumed to be natural. It also, however, implies a new model of nobility, by which Gaveston becomes a superior nobleman, closer to Edward and therefore more of a peer to him.[17] This new model of nobility explains Edward's preference for Baldock, who derives his status as a gentleman "from Oxford, not from heraldry" (6.241). Baldock may be "the first in a long line of displaced scholars who become the villains of Elizabethan and Jacobean tragedies,"[18] but he might also fulfill a new definition of nobility, qualified not by blood and soil but by achievement and learning.

The king's affection and proximity to the royal presence signify both this new construction of nobility and the traditional form of nobility that it attempts to displace. Forced to concede, Edward assigns the nobles positions within the royal administration:

> My lord, you shall be Chancellor of the realm;
> Thou, Lancaster, High Admiral of our fleet;
> Young Mortimer and his uncle shall be earls;
> And you, Lord Warwick, President of the North;
> And thou, of Wales.   (4.65–69)

Edward makes these appointments as an indifferent list, not even bothering to maintain the formal "you" throughout. Later in the same scene, however, when the nobles rescind the order for Gaveston's banishment, he makes similar appointments enthusiastically, as signs of reconciliation. Now restoring a political order in which the nobles find their natural place, Edward carefully and almost artfully relates sign and referent. "These silver hairs," he assures Warwick, "will more adorn my court / Than gaudy silks, or rich embroidery" (4.347–48). Similarly, Edward declares, "In solemn triumphs, and in public shows, / Pembroke shall bear the sword before the king," to which Pembroke replies, "And with this sword Pembroke will fight for you" (4.351–53). These relationships realize the socially sanctioned forms of love. "Now is the King of England rich and strong," Isabella declares, "Having the love of his renowned peers" (4.367–68). "Live thou with me," Edward invites Lancaster, "as my companion" (4.344). In finding positions of power in the kingdom, the nobles also obtain the king's affections.

Conversely, Gaveston's proximity to the king displaces the nobles from the position necessary to their own sense of self as noblemen. When Edward places Gaveston next to his throne, the Elder Mortimer demands, "What man of noble birth can brook this sight?" (4.13). When Lancaster and Young Mortimer attempt to kill the favorite, Edward punishes them with exile: "Dear shall you both aby this riotous deed. / Out of my presence! Come not near the court" (6.87–88). Banishment from court may seem a trivial punishment, especially compared to the mass executions later in the play, but Mortimer responds to it as a challenge to his identity: "I'll not be barr'd the court for Gaveston" (6.89). Mortimer simply ignores the royal command in favor of his own prerogative, as a peer, to enter the king's presence. Even in rebellion, the nobles are shocked to be refused entry by an anonymous guard (6.129–35). When they finally leave, they describe Edward as alone and unloved in their absence. "Who loves thee," Young Mortimer asks, "but a sort of flatterers?" A few lines later, he adds, "Thy court is naked, being bereft of those / That make a king seem glorious to the world; / I mean the peers, whom thou should'st dearly love" (6.168, 171–73). The king's love of Gaveston commands political importance because it violates an entire political structure based on conventional patterns of affection.

Edward gradually equips himself with an alternate set of loy-alties, also understood as friendship. The elder Spencer declares himself "Bound to your highness everlastingly, / For favours done" (11.41–42). As in the cultures studied by anthropologists, an affec-tive relationship is also a relationship of power, both ratified and realized in the exchange of gifts. Greeting Spencer Senior, Edward reverses the assumed relationship between love and nobility. Where the peers assume that he should love the nobles, Edward ennobles those whom he loves and who love him:

> Spencer, this love, this kindness to thy King
> Argues thy noble mind and disposition.
> Spencer, I here create thee Earl of Wiltshire.   (11.47–49)

Scene sixteen ends with Edward mustering his army—"Come, friends, to Bristol, there to make us strong"—and Isabella fol-lowing him onto the stage, welcoming "our loving friends and countrymen" of the invasion force (16.51, 17.1). Both belligerents in this civil war conflate friendship with alliance and do so within a few lines of each other.

Lancaster makes perhaps the most typical, though brief, use of the term, rejecting the recall of Gaveston. "I'll rather lose his friendship," he says of Mortimer, "than grant" (4.237). If friend-ship represents alliance, then it can be changed. Kent changes his alliance at least twice, serving alongside his brother until he real-izes that "your love to Gaveston / Will be the ruin of the realm and you" (6.205–06). In fact, Kent always stands on principle, against both self-interest and familial interest, as Sharon Tyler points out.[19] James Voss argues that Kent only changes sides because neither side is consistently honorable.[20] Rather than ren-dering him disloyal to everyone, this variability shows him to be uniquely consistent. At the end of the play, Kent shows a recog-nition of the political situation, telling himself to "Dissemble, or thou diest; for Mortimer / And Isabel do kiss, while they conspire" (18.21–22). His counsel of caution falls on his own deaf ears, however, and fails to stop him from boldly asking Isabella, "How will you deal with Edward in his fall?" (18.40). Within three scenes, he threatens to "haste to Killingworth Castle, / And rescue aged Edward from his foes, / To be reveng'd on Mortimer and thee" (21.118–20). This may even be an open threat, because the quarto stage directions place Isabella on stage to hear it. Edmund demonstrates political understanding but ignores it in self-sacrifice. He alone "seems never to relinquish" a "traditional world view" and dies maintaining it.[21] More to the point, Kent's changes of alliance render friendship a tactical relationship and subordinate it to the principles for which he fights and dies.

Sex, like friendship, finds political uses in the play. Gaveston actively exploits the king's sexuality for political gain, producing all-male plays on Ovidian erotic themes (1.56–70). The supposedly sodomical use of sex for power, however, fails to distinguish Gaveston from those around him. The play leaves "the erotic components" of several relationships "enigmatic," writes Curtis Perry, but shows that their "political impact is unquestionable."[22] Mortimer builds his power on sex with Isabella. "The Prince I rule," he claims, "the Queen do I command."[23] The partners in the play's dominant heterosexual couple leave each other and life itself with disquieting ease. After commenting upon the "empty rhetoric in Mortimer's acceptance of the turning wheel," Clifford Leech observes, "it would be difficult to find two other lovers in Elizabethan drama who parted with words so chill."[24] One might compare this unfavorably with Edward's pained parting from Gaveston before his exile, or Gaveston's desire to see Edward before his death, or even Spencer's invocation of chaos when Leicester takes Edward to Kenilsworth (4.106–40, 9.94–95, 19.99–103). The love of Isabella and Mortimer can be abandoned with such comparative indifference because it merely seals their alliance.

All affections, sexual or otherwise, prove contingent and political except for Edward's love of Gaveston. Whereas Mortimer takes Isabella as a lover in order to rule the kingdom, Lancaster changes his friendships for political benefit, and Kent has sufficient integrity to change his affections in favor of abstract principles, Edward alone among the characters does not waver in his affection. He favors the love of Gaveston over fraternity, ordering his brother, "Traitor, be gone; whine thou with Mortimer" (6.211). Kent remarks in a choric manner, "No marvel though thou scorn thy noble peers, / When I thy brother am rejected thus" (6.214–15). The love of Gaveston not only assumes a socially unacceptable form but also displaces the socially acceptable bonds of feudalism, marriage, and brotherhood. If the early modern world contrasted its construct of sodomical relationships, as self-interested and corrupt, to friendship, then Marlowe's play is even more subversive than Bray claims. *Edward II* depicts friendships and even love affairs as pragmatic alliances and offers Edward's love for Gaveston as a courageously generous and permanently fixed contrast. In Marlowe's play, same-sex desire is the only generous love.

The nobles prove inconsistent in their rejection of homosexuality. In his cry of "Diablo!" Lancaster labels the king's "passions" diabolical (4.320),[25] but Old Mortimer recites an impressive list of military, intellectual, and even moral heroes as precedents (4.392–98). In response to this "significant rhetorical defense of the king's sexual deviation,"[26] Young Mortimer denies that the king's "wanton humour" inspires his rebellion. Old Mortimer counsels public and political recognition on the assumption that the relationship will prove temporary. "Then let his grace, whose youth is flexible; /.../ Freely enjoy that vain, light-headed earl; / For riper years," he assures his nephew, "will wean him from such toys" (4.399–402). Lancaster anticipates young Mortimer's words earlier in the same scene when he comforts Isabella after Gaveston's exile: "Fear ye not, madam; now his minion's gone, /

His wanton humour will be quickly left." Isabella's response shows her recognition that her husband does not waver in adulterous love: "O never, Lancaster!" (4.198–200). With the word "wanton," the nobles accept Edward's love of Gaveston as sexual but think it therefore alterable, like their own relationships. Stephen Guy-Bray sums up the situation succinctly: "If Edward's love for Gaveston were truly nothing more than 'wanton humor,' both men might well have died of old age."[27] In fact, there seems a general critical consensus, shared by Purvis E. Boyette, Summers, David Thurn, and Ian McAdam, that erotic passion does not trigger the play's conflict.[28] Scott Giantvalley contrasts Marlowe's play with Drayton's treatment of the same subject matter where "the homosexual relationship itself…is seen as degrading."[29] Guy-Bray concludes that homophobic critics are most appalled that Edward treats Gaveston as his consort and not merely his minion. David Stymeist echoes him: "If Edward had maintained his male lover solely in a sexual capacity, then the nobles could simply categorize and dismiss Gaveston as catamite, whore, or ingle (male prostitute); what menaces them is Edward's demand that Gaveston be politically recognized and given official status as royal consort."[30] The barons seem considerably less perturbed by the sexual than by the political expression of same-sex love.

Before convicting the barons of being "only too eager to deny social and political legitimacy to homosexuals,"[31] however, it is worth asking whether any society, no matter how open-minded, would be capable of incorporating a relationship so extravagant. Edward's generosity violates the circulations that, according to anthropologists and the critics they inspire, are foundational to societies. Were Edward to treat his actual consort, Isabella, as he does Gaveston, he would be labeled insanely uxorious by critics and other characters. As Guy-Bray admits, Edward treats his homosexual relationship as not merely equivalent to marriage but superior to it.[32] The disjunction between what his society will accept and what Edward desires lies not between heteronormativity and homosexuality, nor between unconsummated love and overt sexuality, but between pragmatic relationships and an extravagant commitment. The nobles do not reject the relationship of Edward and his "dearest friend" because it seeks political expression, but because it is not political enough.

Edward indulges in the practice of giving away what he does not own and thereby promotes generosity above property. As Christopher Wessman argues, Edward gives away his public body, representing the kingdom's wealth and power, at the same time that he gives away his private body.[33] For that matter, he gives Gaveston the Bishop of Coventry's body, as Warwick specifies (2.1–2). He later presents Gaveston with a lucrative body in the form of a wealthy heiress:

> And, Gaveston, think that I love thee well,
> To wed thee to our niece, the only heir
> Unto the Earl of Gloucester late deceas'd.   (6.254–56)

As the new marriage of Edward and Isabella also indicates, the love of Edward and Gaveston is sexually inclusive. Their prior relationship, however, precedes and indeed motivates the exchange of women.

Gaveston appears not to merit Edward's love, a circumstance that marks the king's generosity as not only extreme and subversive but also gratuitous. As far as the title page of the first quarto is concerned, Gaveston is a complete nonentity, though the second and subsequent quartos add a reference to "the life and death of Piers Gaveston."[34] At least one early modern reader largely ignored Gaveston in his notes on the play.[35] Catherine Belsey observes that Gaveston "is arguably not worth what it costs to keep him" and finds the entire relationship "oddly unmotivated."[36] Unlike the elder Spencer, Gaveston brings Edward neither military nor political power. On the contrary, he draws all his power from the royal bounty, parasitically weakening his host. Lancaster notes that only Edward's immediate presence protects Gaveston (4.10–11). Finally capturing Gaveston, Lancaster tells him to "Look for no other fortune, wretch, than death! / King Edward is not here to buckler thee" (9.17–18). When he meets three masterless men at the beginning of the play, Gaveston can offer them nothing because "I have not viewed my lord the King" from whom all his wealth must derive (1.44). Soon, however, Mortimer has grounds to complain: "He wears a lord's revenue on his back, / And Midas-like, he jets it in the court" (4.408–09). Even Gaveston himself objects, albeit insincerely, to the four titles that Edward gives him as homecoming gifts: "My lord, these titles far exceed my worth" (1.156). He contributes nothing in reciprocation for Edward's bounty.

Nevertheless, Gaveston expresses his love for Edward in extreme terms. "Since I went from hence," he tells Edward, "no soul in hell / Hath felt more torment than poor Gaveston" (1.145–46). If Hell is the absence of God, as Mephistophilis assures Faustus with experiential certainty,[37] then Gaveston's statement amounts to a deification of Edward. Similarly, Gaveston compares Edward's presence to heaven. London will appear like "Elizium to a new come soul" but only because "it harbours him I hold so dear" (1.11–13). Where Gaveston's metaphor to Edward's presence as heaven recalls *Doctor Faustus*, his description of companionship with Edward recalls *Tamburlaine the Great*. He imagines himself "As Caesar riding in the Roman street, / With captive kings at his triumphant car" (1.172–73). This line shows not only the excess of Gaveston's affection but also its exclusion of third parties, reduced here to slaves. Gaveston's greed and manipulation should no more detract from the excess of his affection than from its self-destructive result. In his opening speech, he refers to "The king, upon whose bosom let me die" (1.14). Advancing a thesis on sexual roles, Jon Surgal sees this as a reference to orgasm,[38] but it also can be taken literally, expressing Gaveston's desire to die with Edward. Similarly, Gaveston's last words onstage express a desire to "see the king" (10.15). Self-interest marks and even characterizes Gaveston's love but does not measure its limit.

The two lovers ignore political imperatives, abusing political power and even fantasizing about escape from the state altogether.

Edward and Gaveston reinforce each other's most politically unsound actions. The first scene establishes the pattern in the attack on the Bishop of Coventry. Kent sees that this will lead only to problems, "For he'll complain unto the See of Rome." Edward ignores his brother's caution in favor of his lover's reckless advice: "Let him complain unto the See of Hell." Gaveston declares, "He shall to prison, and there die in bolts." Edward not only agrees but elaborates: "Ay, to the Tower, the Fleet or where thou wilt" (1.189–90, 196–97). Edward and Gaveston encourage each other's desires while ignoring other advice. They cut themselves off from third parties, the "someone else" in Levinas's statement, and even from God, in whose name Coventry curses them (1.198).

Gaveston's reputation and indeed self-description as an over-reacher would indicate political ambition frustrated by hubris (6.74–78), as at least three critics notice.[39] Perhaps because he is already king, on the other hand, Edward often seeks to escape social power and indeed society itself for a society of two, dreaming of "some nook or corner... / To frolic with my dearest Gaveston" (4.72–73). Being besieged appears to him like the realization of his desires: "Do what they can, we'll live in Tynemouth here, / And, so I walk with him about the walls, / What care I though the earls begirt us round?" (6.218–20). Edward seeks to escape the political world, which nevertheless demonstrates an insidious ability to reclaim him.

A number of critics note the indifference of most, if not all, characters to the public good. Joan Parks declares that Marlowe's play "recognizes the self-interest that lies behind all history and political action."[40] One might argue that she pays insufficient attention to Kent, but her point holds for most of the characters. Certainly, Edward's indifference to the state provides a contrast to his passionate interest in Gaveston. His claim that "Ere my sweet Gaveston shall part from me, / This isle shall fleet upon the ocean, / And wander to the unfrequented Inde" (4.48–50), establishes him as a tyrant indifferent to the country's good, but the image also promotes his love of Gaveston above the geological permanency of bedrock, rendered fluid in comparison. It is perhaps ironic, therefore, that Edward consents to Gaveston's exile, even if only after offering to "Make several kingdoms of this monarchy," and divide it between the barons (4.70). He assures his beloved that "long thou shalt not stay, or if thou dost, / I'll come to thee; my love shall ne'er decline" (4.114–15). Edward is as good as his word. Near death, he exclaims, "O Gaveston, it is for thee that I am wronged" (22.41). Though he adds loyalty to the Spencers among the causes for which he is prepared to die, he never repudiates his love of Gaveston. Edward's indifference to the state does not show self-interest but rather an excessive love.

Edward's escape from the political world and its responsibility takes aesthetic form in the "Italian masques by night, / Sweet speeches, comedies, and pleasing shows," which Gaveston promises to direct (1.54–55). Though Gaveston clearly ascribes to his dramaturgy an ability to "draw the pliant King which way I please" (1.52), James Voss argues that this and similar speeches "express a will to emotional and sensual fulfillment more than a will to power."[41] Jennifer Brady declares that Gaveston fantasizes "the emergence into visibility of a specifically gay culture."[42] However, rather than describing a new culture with a plurality of members, Gaveston imagines "pleasing shows" for an audience of two. Whatever he imagines revealing through dramaturgical productions, he imagines sharing it exclusively with Edward. His elaborate description of dramatizing the myth of Actaeon suggests an alternative reality (1.56–69) without consequences, where the boy-actor performing the role of Actaeon will only "seem to die" (1.69). Gaveston proposes a means of manipulation, which is also a retreat into an imaginary world. Such a movement is not only escapist, as McAdam correctly notes,[43] but also exclusive.

At times, the relationship of Edward and Gaveston threatens to collapse into identity. "Knowest thou not who I am?" Edward asks in greeting, "Thy friend, thy self, another Gaveston." Edward indulges in this self-description in order to deny the need for social deference—"Why shouldst thou kneel?" (1.141–42)—but it also indicates an exclusive relationship. Boyette and Summers both note that Edward's language borders, at least temporarily, on the neo-Platonic imagery of fusion,[44] which Levinas dismisses in his description of Eros.[45] Normand denies that this image of union can be applied to Edward and Gaveston, both because the image fails to account for the sexual element in their relationship and because they gradually abandon it as insufficient.[46] Of course the image must prove false: the lovers remain existentially separate, each dying alone. Nevertheless, each lover attempts a complete donation of self, while excluding third parties.

The king's most characteristic gifts identify himself with Gaveston by endowing the latter with his personal powers and authority:

> Fear'st thou thy person? Thou shalt have a guard.
> Wants thou gold? Go to my treasury.
> Wouldst thou be loved and feared? Receive my seal.   (1.165–67)

The gift of the seal allows Gaveston to make decisions literally in the name of the king. Edward gives his lover everything: power, titles, wealth, a woman and even, in the royal seal, his own name. Edward seeks to avoid any claim on Gaveston by asking for nothing in return. When Gaveston objects, Edward declares his gifts incommensurate with Gaveston's worth, which he rates "far above my gifts" (1.160). Edward's and Gaveston's gifts are both extraordinary, but they do not cancel each other out in reciprocation, simply because neither donor sees his gift as commensurate with the other's.

Edward recognizes that his donations are politically unwise but does not otherwise care about politics, "for but to honour thee / Is Edward pleased with kingly regiment" (1.163–64). He seems to understand power almost entirely as a means to express his love and, later, bloodily avenge his lover's death. Hearing of Gaveston's execution, Edward loses all reason to live:

"O, shall I speak," he asks, "or shall I sigh and die?" (11.122).
Spencer suggests that he convert his sorrow into rage, and Edward
continues the play motivated by vengefulness, a sort of inverse of
love. Revenge furnishes Edward with a renewed definition of kingship, as he promises the barons, "If I be England's king, in lakes
of gore / Your headless trunks, your bodies will I trail" (11.135–
36). This statement comes at Edward's only moment of military
effectiveness, echoing Tamburlaine's rhetoric.[47] Announcing the
executions, Edward giddily spouts a weak and morbid pun: "they
'barked apace a month ago; / Now, on my life, they'll neither bark
nor bite" (16.12–13). Edward's generosity to Gaveston, for all its
escapism, imbricates him in a political world of rivalry, property,
and violence. After his lover's death, revenge hurls him into a
career of war.

Though Edward's generosity draws him into political conflict,
he makes his donations before calculating their cost or political
importance; only when realized do they obtain political meaning. By depicting a commitment to an Other that resists social
forms and does not subjugate itself to the regulation of justice
or the state, Marlowe's play makes an extraordinary claim for
love. Politically aware criticism, drawing attention to the construction of homosexuality or to the heterosexism of the barons
or earlier generations of critics, contributes enormously to our
understanding of the play. That same criticism however, obscures
the most profoundly and doggedly antisocial aspect of Edward's
affection. Edward violates not only the heteronormativity of the
Elizabethan period and the power structures of feudalism but also
the assumptions of exchange that govern politics, social order,
and criticism.

Six

Listening to Lavinia

Emmanuel Levinas's Saying and Said in *Titus Andronicus*

King Lear and *Faustus* reveal exaggerated faith in the reciprocity of exchange as a tragic error. Even in the comedic world of *The Merchant of Venice*, the rejection of free gifts implies also the rejection of a doctrine of salvation. Edward's love of Gaveston, like Antonio's of Bassanio, essays generosity, but its own expression betrays it into politics. However, the possibility of a free donation is not always marked negatively. Pure gifts take positive form when characters such as the servant in *King Lear* recognize one another not for reasons of individual or collective self-interest but as part of an obligation to give that has very little to do with an expectation of repayment, self-interest, or social structure.

Titus Andronicus may seem the most counterintuitive choice of an early modern play in which to search for ethics. At least until recently, it rivalled *Pericles, Prince of Tyre* as the least admired work in Shakespeare's canon. As early as 1687, Edward Ravenscroft justified rewriting it by declaring, "It seems rather a heap of rubbish than a structure."[1] The success of Ravenscroft's new version,

143

which displaced Shakespeare's from the English stage until 1923, bespeaks the agreement of audiences. Eighteenth-century editors and critics were ashamed of the play, with Alexander Pope, Lewis Theobald, Edmond Malone, and George Steevens unanimously rejecting Shakespeare's authorship of the play on the basis of quality alone.[2] The Senecan orgy that Ravenscroft replaced features rape, murder, filicide, dismemberment, and even cannibalism, amounting to "an average of 5.2 atrocities per act, or one for every 97 lines."[3] Nevertheless, in the characters' responses to the brutality before them and especially to the suffering of Lavinia, Shakespeare produces a meditation on suffering, response, and language. The theater of blood illustrates how the suffering of others serves as an ethical imperative, one which, like Levinas's Saying, precedes signs and exchanges. Lavinia fails to offer signs and "shows how language itself is fragmented" as Gillian Murray Kendall argues, but she is not simply, as Kendall also argues, "a cipher in the sense of being a null."[4] On the contrary, the mutilated Lavinia makes a claim upon the attention of Lucius, Marcus, and especially Titus. This claim is not reducible to a function of exchange, since Lavinia's social value has been defaced, or to a product of her own power, because her mutilation robs her of the most basic forms of power. Neither can Lavinia's claim be reduced to a cultural norm, since Roman cultural assumptions collapse, nor, finally, to a product of language, since her claim to ethical concern precedes and summons language. If society is constituted by cycling gift systems, as Mauss holds, then Lavinia's appeal takes place outside society. The play's notorious violence renders Lavinia's appeal to her interlocutors a primordial claim, not a function of something else but basic and absolute.

The responses of the characters, rather than those of the audience, are my focus here. Shown his raped, mutilated, and tongueless daughter, Titus remarks, "Had I but seen thy picture in this plight, / It would have madded me; what shall I do / Now I behold thy lively body so?" (3.1.103–05). As audience, of course, we only encounter a representation of Lavinia, originally played by a boy actor. The experience of facing Lavinia remains Titus's trauma, not ours. The play therefore engages us in an ethical problem but does so in the realm of intellect, where ethics intersects with the question of language.

As early as *Totality and Infinity*, Levinas associates language as interruption with the face, the extraordinary summons of the Other: "Speech is not instituted in a homogeneous or abstract medium, but in a world where it is necessary to aid and to give."[5] Against the all-embracing circulation, which Mauss calls the gift-system and Derrida refers to as *oikonomia*, Levinas champions interruption and nonreciprocity. Bernasconi notes that what Levinas terms saying, most notably in *Otherwise than Being*, resembles the gift in making an interruption: "Saying always arises within a linguistic context. But it also interrupts that order, albeit it is readily reinscribed within it, just as is the case with the gift."[6] Whereas the Said includes both the amphibology of the verb and the signification of the noun, the Saying locates itself prior to both, in the concern that inspires language. Levinas defines it sweepingly: "Antecedent to the verbal signs it conjugates, to the linguistic systems and the semantic glimmerings, a foreword preceding languages, it is the proximity of one to the other, the commitment of one to the other, the commitment of an approach, the one for the other, the very signifyingness of signification."[7] Perhaps we could define Saying more briefly as a concern that elicits language. What Levinas terms the Said includes everything that we might consider content—the subject matter, choice of words, their arrangement, and so forth—and which might be misunderstood, intentionally or otherwise. Antecedent to this, however, is the radical fact of being addressed, the Saying, which Levinas compares to sincerity and even to silence: "Saying opens me to the other before saying what is said, before the said uttered in this sincerity forms a screen between me and the other. This saying without a said is thus like silence."[8] Marcus's and Titus's inability to communicate reciprocally with Lavinia threatens them with silence, but they remain concerned and indeed committed. When they actually do find means of communication, their concern finds expression, like Antonio's love for Bassanio or Edward's for Gaveston, but also betrays itself in the Said.

Bernice Harris best articulates the argument that Lavinia remains a signifier, "a means by which power is marked as masculine and is then transferred and circulated."[9] Clearly influenced by anthropology, Harris details Lavinia's role in the various exchanges in the opening scene that, to extend the argument, place her within a semiotic system and therefore what Levinas terms the Said. When she first enters, Titus treats her as the gift of a grateful state, addressing her only after thanking "Kind Rome, that hast thus lovingly reserved / The cordial of mine age to glad my heart!" (1.1.165–66). Even before she enters, Bassianus calls her "Rome's rich ornament" (1.1.52), establishing her value in material terms. However, whereas an ornament has value in itself, Lavinia soon becomes an item in exchange, "transferred and circulated," and therefore implicitly valued in relation to other goods and favors. Saturninus repays Titus "for thy favours done / To us in our election this day," by offering to marry Lavinia (1.1.234–35). Titus reciprocates by offering "My sword, my chariot, and my prisoners" (1.1.249). Powerful men exchange Lavinia to ratify their relations. When Bassianus later abducts her, Saturninus accuses him of "rape," though Bassianus objects that he did only "seize my own, / My true betroth'd love, and now my wife" (1.1.404–06). Where Saturninus reads the abduction as an illegal transfer of control, Bassianus understands it simply as the maintenance of his rights. Marcus helpfully explains, "*Suum cuique* is our Roman justice; / This prince in justice seizeth but his own" (1.1.280–81). Lucius goes further, offering to restore her "[d]ead, if you will," rather than to become Saturninus's bride, placing Bassianus's property rights above Lavinia's right to life (1.1.297). Amazingly, Lavinia objects to neither of her claimants, not that anyone pauses to inquire about her opinion. Passed from hand to hand, Lavinia circulates like the "changing piece" that Saturninus soon claims she is (1.1.309).

If she can be used to honor the Andronici, Lavinia functions equally well as an instrument to harm them. Her abduction by Bassianus furnishes Saturninus with all the excuse he needs to repudiate Titus (1.1.305–07). More gruesomely, Tamora, giving Lavinia to her sons to rape and dismember, declares that she wishes to inflict revenge against Titus and at least in part considers the rape of Lavinia a means to this end:

> Remember, boys, I poured forth tears in vain
> To save your brother from the sacrifice,
> But fierce Andronicus would not relent.   (2.3.163–65)

At least three critics have noted the difference between the definition of rape applicable to Bassianus's abduction of Lavinia and that active in Tamora's revenge. Emily Detmer-Goebel and Carolyn D. Williams both cite Nazife Bashar on the growing recognition of rape as an independent crime, separate from abduction, over the course of the sixteenth century, whereas in medieval law, rape was an offense against the property rights of the victim's father.[10] Harris summarizes the distinction: "In the exchange of women, it is as if, on the one hand, when ownership presumptions are violated, rape is the resulting charge and it is the original owner who is the victim. On the other hand, if an exchange is mutually agreed upon between men, no matter how politically invested the exchange is, it is as if there were no victims."[11] Bassianus's abduction of Lavinia victimizes Saturninus, whereas in Chiron and Demetrius's assault, Lavinia serves as an instrument whereby her father might be injured. The argument that Lavinia signifies power relations seems irrefutable, at least for the opening scenes.

However, her function as a token of exchange in the opening scenes makes her continued importance later in the play all the more striking. A second authorial hand may partially explain the difference. Brian Vickers concludes a detailed chapter in his *Shakespeare, Co-Author* by declaring, "Over the last eighty years scholars have applied, by my count, twenty-one separate tests to the play, each of which has confirmed the presence of a co-author....Surely this quantity of independent tests, mutually confirming each other, will now be enough to gain [George] Peele recognition as co-author of 'The Most Lamentable Romaine Tragedy of *Titus Andronicus*.'"[12] While Vickers assigns four scenes to Peele, all but one of them precede Lavinia's rape and dismemberment. These include almost all occasions on which Lavinia is assigned a monetary value or deployed as a mute token of exchange. Perhaps it is appropriate that "the son of James Peele, author of the first native double-entry manual"[13] would track exchanges of Lavinia with a bookkeeper's precision. On the other hand, other than the scene in which Lavinia finally succeeds in identifying her rapists, all of the scenes in which the Andronici respond to her or attempt to comfort her are nearly unanimously assigned to Shakespeare. "In this world," Sara Eaton writes, conflating the works of both collaborators, "Lavinia is a 'changing piece' (1.1.309), her humanist education but an ornament, her only 'real' value the possession of her chaste femininity."[14] In his own contribution, however, Shakespeare examines how Lavinia continues to command attention after her loss of value. That anyone is concerned with her at all in the later parts of the play would indicate that Lavinia's role as a "changing piece" does not exhaust her importance.

Raped, silenced and dismembered, Lavinia's value certainly declines. Marcus's apparently impertinent speech upon discovering her takes the form of a blazon, a list of her charms, inventorying what has been lost. He calls her hands "sweet ornaments," "lily hands," and "pretty fingers" (2.4.18, 2.4.42–45). Similarly, in describing "the heavenly harmony / Which that sweet tongue hath made" (2.4.48–49), Marcus only emphasizes how it, too, is gone. Alexander Leggatt argues that Marcus's language echoes that of the rapists: "Desperate to understand and deal with what has happened to Lavinia, Marcus unwittingly re-enacts the offense, eroticizing her body and making her bleed."[15] This is a significant charge, because, as Karen Cunningham has noted, "the brutal tongue-lashings of the rapists" succeed in "bringing words dangerously close to instruments of torture."[16] In a fascinating essay, she compares the interrogation of Lavinia to trial by ordeal, in which the body is forced to reveal its secrets. Marcus's solicitude toward Lavinia—what Levinas would call his facing her—seems quite distinct from the rapists' sadism, however. While Chiron and Demetrius note Lavinia's charms before erasing them, her uncle mourns their loss. However, both Lavinia's rapists and her uncle agree that, raped and mutilated, Lavinia loses sexual and social value. The judgment seems unanimous in the play. No one tries to marry her again.

Lavinia loses agency as well as value. With her tongue, she loses voice. Whereas in Ovid, as Marcus recalls, Philomela loses only her tongue and nevertheless reveals the identity of her assailant using her hands, a "craftier Tereus" (2.4.41) has the foresight to compound Lavinia's mutilation. Eaton follows Jonathan Goldberg in claiming that "the writing/written self in humanist ideology is a supplementary—or self-conscious—one."[17] The "written/ writing self" rises in importance once the voice has been lost, so that the double amputation completes Lavinia's locked-in condition by removing not only her voice but also its supplement. Hands not only serve as objects of humanist ideology and pedagogical discipline but also, in phenomenology, the primary means of agency. "Knowledge as perception, concept, comprehension," Levinas summarizes Edmund Husserl, "refers back to an act of grasping. The metaphor should be taken literally."[18] Lavinia does not merely lose a supplementary means of communication but the primary means of relating to and obtaining power over the world. The obligation that Lavinia imposes on the Andronici is not of her own power or even intention. In fact, her appeal occurs against her desire, because, as Marcus notes, she tries to hide herself in her shame (2.4.11, 2.4.56, 3.1.88–90). Lavinia's claim on the Andronici is not a triumph of will over a handicap.

Although stripped of the means of agency, Lavinia nevertheless elicits a response from others, expressed in frustrated efforts to acknowledge and understand. Marcus's speech when encountering her is replete with Ovidian imagery and aestheticization, but it also represents, Brian Gibbons argues, "an effort of love, to overcome repulsion and fear, to recognise and identify sympathetically with the sufferer." By inventorying Lavinia's defunct charms, Gibbons continues, Marcus returns to the horror of her wounds and her suffering: "The speech transmits shock, but it also insists that Lavinia still has emotional meaning as Lavinia, for her former self is in mortal peril of obliteration."[19] Titus insists on her continued importance, in spite of the loss of her value and agency. When Marcus introduces her with the words "This was thy daughter," Titus responds with touching immediacy and a more than categorical certainty: "Why, Marcus, so she is" (3.1.63). "He changes the tense from past to present," observes Gibbons. "It is a moment of great simplicity and power."[20] Two definitions of "daughter" seem to be offered. Lavinia "was" Titus's daughter, in Marcus's phrase, when she served as a token of exchange, the usual role of a daughter in the power relations of Titus's fictive Rome. She "is" his daughter in his response, because she appeals for his paternal care. When Lavinia has lost her social value and even existential agency, she elicits an ethical response.

Marcus, still waxing metaphorical, describes Lavinia "seeking to hide herself, as doth the deer" (3.1.89). Titus seizes on the simile as an occasion for a dreadful pun: "It was my dear, and he that wounded her / Hath hurt me more than had he killed me dead" (3.1.91–92). Both folio and quarto texts aid the pun by spelling both words as "Deare" (through line numbers 1229–31 in the folio). The play on words displays bad taste, in part because it conflates endearment with an accouterment of noble rank. In adopting the metaphor, Titus echoes Aaron, who deploys a similar comparison in suggesting the rape: "What, hast thou not full often struck a doe, / And borne her cleanly by the keeper's nose?" (2.1.94–95). Greenblatt uses this quotation to illustrate how deer poaching served in Shakespeare's time as "a skillful assault upon property, a symbolic violation of the social order, a coded challenge to authority."[21] In Titus's use, however, the metaphor is overwhelmed when Lavinia's fate inflicts on Titus a pain greater than death, never mind loss of property or prestige. Only ten lines later, he places his concern for Lavinia above concern for salvation, referring to "dear Lavinia, dearer than my soul" (3.1.102). The language of possession survives, briefly, in the form of a metaphor for value, until concern for the Other overwhelms the metaphor in which it is expressed.

Not only is Lavinia unable to speak, but also she frustrates efforts to describe her, as though her physical silencing symbolizes her recalcitrance to language. Nevertheless, precisely because Lavinia cannot be reduced to a sign and a meaning, she commands concern from the men in her family. On first realizing her mutilation, Marcus wishes to "rail" at the rapist "to ease my mind" but then offers a general observation: "Sorrow conceal'd, like an oven stopped, / Doth burn the heart to cinders where it is" (2.4.35–37). If expression eases suffering, then listening already offers comfort. "Repeatedly," Pascal Aebischer observes, "the playtext insists on the fact that even inadequate expression gives more relief than silence."[22] Marcus's first words, on encountering the mutilated Lavinia, ask her for a response (2.4.12). Titus and Lucius echo him in asking her to name her assailant (3.1.66; 3.1.81). Leggatt argues that in this situation "[j]ust to ask her a question...is an act of cruelty" that emphasizes Lavinia's powerlessness.[23] The cruelty seems an unintended consequence, however, of the male characters' desperate efforts to elicit her voice. They seek it, searching for some means of communication, because they assume that expression would bring her comfort. Ironically, everyone is prepared to listen to Lavinia only after mutilation has reduced her to silence.

The problem of language assumes centrality after the loss of Lavinia's tongue. She is, Cunningham observes, "the interpretive problem made flesh," both eliciting and resisting interpretation.[24] The play, however, is more than a "whodunit" as Cunningham claims, because Lavinia also poses an ethical problem of how to respond. Unable to exchange words with her, Titus proposes mimetic expressions of sympathy:

> Or shall we cut away our hands like thine?
> Or shall we bite our tongues, and in dumb shows
> Pass the remainder of our hateful days?
> What shall we do?   (3.1.130–33)

When Aaron suggests that either "Marcus, Lucius, or thyself, old Titus" (3.1.152) should amputate his hand to ransom Quintus and Martius, each of the Andronici eagerly claims the right to offer his own. Lucius reasons, "My youth can better spare my blood than you" (3.1.165), while Marcus argues that as a noncombatant, "My hand hath been but idle" (3.1.171). Finally, Titus tricks them into leaving to find an axe, in order to give himself the opportunity to cut off his own hand and to create another of the dreadful puns to which he is evidently addicted, when he elicits Aaron's aid: "Lend me thy hand, and I will give thee mine" (3.1.186). Leggatt argues that Titus attempts to identify with Lavinia's pain, to make her pain his, "yet by a crudely literal measurement he is less than half-way there."[25] Titus aims, however, not to become Lavinia but to comfort her and therefore to offer signs. Insofar as he fails to make her pain his own, this merely reproduces the insurmountable distinction of self and Other. Were he, impossibly, to succeed in feeling her pain bodily, he would still be left with what Cavell, in a thought experiment that precedes his famous essay on *King Lear*, refers to as the "phenomenological pang in having to say that knowing another mind is a matter of inference."[26] In any case, neither such sympathy nor its inevitable failure seriously interferes with a claim for ethics, which Levinas locates precisely in the distinction between self and Other. Aaron's treacherous offer not only provides the characters with a glimmer of hope but also seems to answer their achingly open question, "What shall we do?"

   Titus is extraordinarily bookish and overt in its use of intertexts. Even the Goths and Aaron the Moor share a classical education, with Chiron confidently identifying lines from Horace which he read "in the grammar long ago," Aaron grasping their import, and Demetrius adapting lines from Seneca to express his rapine lust (4.2.22–28; 2.1.136). Several characters independently offer comparisons between Lavinia and Philomela, raped and muted by Tereus in Ovid's *Metamorphoses*, a copy of which appears as a stage property. Noticing that his niece's hands as well as tongue have been cut away, Marcus ascribes begrudging admiration to a "craftier Tereus" (2.4.41).[27] Titus's revenge, cooking the rapists' brains in a pie and serving it to their mother, shares the same literary precedent: "Worse than Philomel you used my daughter," he declares, "And worse than Procne I will be revenged" (5.2.194–95). All the characters appear to share a familiarity with Shakespeare's source. Aaron adopts it as his own inspiration (2.3.43), but all it teaches him is how to commit rape while escaping punishment. Titus even describes the scene of the rape as "Patterned by that the poet here describes, / By nature made for murders and for rapes" (4.1.57). In Titus's expression, nature appears to imitate art. Marcus asks if the place was created because "the gods delight in tragedies" (4.1.59). Ovid provides a precedent for crime, perhaps even to the natural world or the pagan gods. In any case, the characters reach instinctively for literary antecedents to guide and give meaning to their actions.

Unfortunately, language not only offers comfort but also inflicts pain. According to Kendall, "The world of *Titus* is not simply one of meaningless acts of random violence but rather one in which language engenders violence and violence is done to language."[28] Aaron employs language to frame Lavinia's brothers for the death of her husband, to "Accuse some innocent, and forswear myself; / Set deadly enmity between two friends" (5.2.130–31) and most of all, to taunt:

> If there be devils, would I were a devil,
> To live and burn in everlasting fire,
> So I might have your company in hell,
> But to torment you with my bitter tongue.   (5.2.147–50)

If "sorrow flouted at is double death" (3.1.244), as Marcus declares, then Aaron seems determined to murder everyone twice. Mary Laughlin Fawcett argues that Aaron indulges in a "freer, more self-expressive form of speech, based on a love of the tongue as opposed to the pen."[29] He shares, however, the reliance on literary antecedents of other characters and is happy to write, as long as his texts cause misery. He boasts to Lucius that he "wrote the letter that thy father found," which served to convict Quintus and Martius, and claims to have "carved in Roman letters" messages on the skins of the dead to taunt the bereaved (5.1.106, 139). As Grace Starry West has shown, Aaron converts written language into just another instrument of torture, and Shakespeare's play therefore damningly refutes the humanist claim that literary education leads to moral improvement.[30] One cannot ascribe the efforts of the Andronici at comfort to their education or to a function of their language because, in this play, literature teaches crime and cruelty as often as concern. Marcus's and Titus's condolences cannot be distinguished from Aaron's and the rapists' taunts by their use of language.

Even as a means of conveying information, the written text proves almost completely useless. When Lavinia tries to explain her situation by indicating the Ovidian intertext, her nephew runs from her in horror, though he retains enough presence of mind to propose a literary precedent for his fears: "I have read that Hecuba of Troy ran mad for sorrow" (4.1.20–21). The literary precedent blocks communication, rather than serving as its instrument. More generally, multiple intertexts frustrate narrative clarity. Titus, Marcus, Lucius, and even Aaron refer to the rape of Lucrece (4.1.63; 4.1.90; 3.1.297; 2.1.109), but the reference misleads, suggesting Saturninus as the rapist, at least to Titus. Even those equipped with the correct intertextual key find Lavinia maddeningly opaque. The Ovidian parallel presents itself spontaneously to Marcus, but Lavinia nevertheless must painstakingly write the word "*Stuprum*" (4.1.77). When she indicates a copy of the *Metamorphoses*, Titus assumes that she seeks literary escapism: "Come and take choice of all my library, / And so beguile thy sorrow," he urges her, "till the heavens / Reveal the damned contriver of this deed" (4.1.35–36). Her father and uncle remain baffled by her signs. Raising her two stumps might indicate "that there were more than one / Confederate in the fact" or merely that "to heaven she heaves them for revenge" (4.1.38–40). Fawcett argues that the Andronici are text-bound, while West points to a general obsession throughout the play "with writing things down."[31] The instinctive reference to text, however, serves as often to frustrate as to facilitate communication. Texts do not inspire ethical concern in this play; on the contrary, ethical concern draws forth texts.

Kendall notes that throughout the play, metaphorical language reveals its own failure: "In *Titus* the seams keep coming apart with the discovery of very real disjunctions between metaphor and reality, between figurative and literal usage."[32] Despite its failure to carry content, language is nevertheless offered as a form of recognition or acknowledgement, as in Marcus's desire to mourn with Lavinia. The Saying precedes the Said in the play as in Levinas's philosophy; moreover, the Saying must seek realization in the Said: "The subordination of the saying to the said, to the linguistic system and to ontology" Levinas declares, "is the price that manifestation demands."[33] Shakespeare's play extends the helplessness of Lavinia from an anonymous chapbook that probably served as a source, and his folio text adds an additional scene, extending her helplessness even further from the presumably earlier quarto text.[34] Lavinia's suffering body, simultaneously eliciting and frustrating response, delays and therefore dramatizes the process by which the Saying surrenders itself to the Said.

Lavinia's loss of meaning as a signifier of power relations exemplifies the rapid collapse of the whole Roman political and social structure, the language that expresses it, and the system of exchanges on which it is based. A struggle for sexual control of a woman named Lavinia founds Rome in the *Aeneid*, and in Shakespeare's play, Titus's daughter, "Rome's rich ornament," seems to represent the state. Conversely, her loss of meaning symbolizes the collapse of the social order that establishes her value. The wars with "the barbarous Goths" (1.1.28) from which Titus returns imply a binary distinction between Rome and its enemies. Marcus gives this distinction aphoristic form, scolding his brother's refusal to inter Mutius: "Thou art a Roman; be not barbarous" (1.1.378). Titus's sacrifice of Tamora's son in the first scene of the play already elicits comparisons with the barbarism of Scythia and therefore casts doubt upon the distinction of Rome and its enemies (1.1.131). The Goths, for their part, remember a time past "When Goths were Goths, and Tamora was queen" (1.1.140). Rather than reclaiming their Gothic identities, they soon find themselves "incorporate in Rome" (1.1.462), as Tamora says after being chosen as empress. Conversely, the Goths whom Lucius leads against Rome in act 5 seem to have disowned those brought as captives in act 1, vowing to "be advengèd on cursèd Tamora" (5.1.16). Barbarity and Rome cease to be opposites when the Goths become Romans and a Roman leads the Goths.

Titus finds himself suddenly excluded from the center of Roman political life. At the beginning of the first scene, everybody defers to Titus's greatness. Both Marcus and a captain who serves as herald announce Titus in fulsome terms (1.1.20–38, 64–69). Even Tamora, pleading for her son, calls him "Thrice-noble" (1.1.120). His rage at Mutius's insubordination measures his wounded sense of importance: "What, villain boy, / Barr'st me my way in Rome?" (1.1.290–91). Titus's choice of terms locates the respect he feels he deserves not within the family but within the state. He finds it particularly galling to be stopped in Rome, where he enjoys all the prestige of a conquering hero. In this context, the word "villain" probably retains its meaning of "Low or mean in respect of birth or position."[35] Though Titus and Mutius obviously share the same class, Titus treats his son as far beneath him. A few lines later, Titus finds to his surprise that "I am not bid to wait upon this bride" (1.1.338) and left alone, reduced from public declamation to private self-address: "Titus, when wert thou wont to walk alone, / Dishonoured thus and challengèd of wrongs?" (1.1.339–40). When Tamora rises to imperial power, Titus suffers a corresponding marginalization. Internecine violence replaces the struggle against an external threat in Titus's duel with Mutius. Within a few scenes, he declares, "Rome is but a wilderness of tigers" (3.1.54), after the tribunes refuse to so much as hear him plead. The symbolic silencing of Titus not only counterpoints the physical silencing of Lavinia, but also shows that the value system that prized Titus and his worth, like the one that prized Lavinia as "Rome's rich ornament," has broken down.

In keeping with Mauss's description of gift-giving as "total services" in which everything is exchanged, the principal figures of the Roman state exchange women, prisoners, and honors. These relationships soon collapse in mutual recrimination, however. Though Tamora early in the play warns Saturninus against "ingratitude / Which Rome reputes to be a heinous sin" (1.1.447–48), he nevertheless returns Titus's hand, inciting the messenger to observe, "Ill art thou repaid" (3.1.233). This most callous gesture marks the collapse of the system of exchanges within which Lavinia serves as a marker of value and Titus acts as an important agent. Marcus describes Roman values as the opposite of barbarian and Tamora identifies gratitude as a central value. Once Rome becomes barbarian, however, "a wilderness of tigers," the exchange system ceases to apply. Lavinia's loss of value symbolizes the collapse of the whole system of exchanges that assigns her value.

The deterioration of Rome's religion provides a measure of the breakdown of Roman values. Eugene Waith comments on the highly ritualistic character of the play's dramaturgy, beginning with an "almost uninterrupted series of spectacles in the first act,"[36] but this only serves to emphasize the failure of ritual. A Girardian might note that the sacred violence of scapegoating fails to unify the community. Instead, as often in the myths that Girard discusses, "violence that should be present in but contained by the religious ritual is released into the community."[37] Stephen X. Mead argues that the play's world suffers from "the failure of sacrifice to protect a community from its own violence by channelling that violence into a meaningful experience."[38] On the contrary, the most spectacular ceremony, the sacrifice of Alarbus to the ghosts of Titus's dead sons, begins the whole sanguinary spiral. The sacrifice of her son drives Tamora to oxymoron: "O cruel, irreligious piety" (1.1.130). The Romans, however, accept this piety as an expression of religion and concern for the dead: "Religiously," Titus says of his sons, "they ask a sacrifice" (1.1.124). Titus himself, "surnamèd Pius" (1.1.23) serves as a pillar of this Roman value system. Although sacred traditions may be artificial—Titus proudly declares that he has "sumptuously re-edified" the family tomb (1.1.351)—they structure responses to the suffering of others and thereby contain grief. Mutius becomes the first occupant of the family monument to be, as Titus declares with striking indifference to his own culpability, "basely slain in brawls" (1.1.353). His kinsmen nevertheless repeat a customary formula: "No man shed tears for noble Mutius; / He lives in fame, that died in virtue's cause" (1.1.389–90). Apparently these words furnish an actual imperative, not merely an obsequious prayer. Titus entombs his grief along with his sons in the family monument. The ethical response finds expression, in words and rituals, in what Levinas would call a Said, where it is entombed like Titus's sons.

When their religion fails, the characters must face the suffering of others without a customary form of mourning. This shift from pagan religion to human comfort manifests after Titus, having chopped off one of his hands to ransom his sons, implores the gods for revenge (3.1.207–8). Mockery answers his prayers. A messenger arrives bearing the heads of Titus's sons, along with "thy hand in scorn to thee sent back" (3.1.236). Later in the play, when Titus again calls on the gods, a clown enters instead. "Shall I have justice? What says Jupiter?" (4.3.79) Titus demands of the uncomprehending bumpkin. The hollowness of the ceremonies of Roman duty renders Lavinia's demonstration of sympathy, joining her father in prayer, all the more remarkable: "What, wouldst thou kneel with me?" (3.1.208). Even the messenger who brings the heads of Titus's sons finds an empathy beyond the demands of Roman piety: "woe is me to think upon thy woes, / More than remembrance of my father's death" (3.1.238–39). The call for an ethical response in concern for the Other, which Levinas terms Saying, does not evaporate with the pagan religions in which it found expression. On the contrary, it assumes renewed importance.

Hence, the difficulty of understanding Lavinia in no way discourages Titus from laboring doggedly at the task. When she frightens Young Lucius, Titus assures him, "She loves thee, boy, too well to do thee harm" (4.1.6). Titus bases his trust of Lavinia on neither literary precedent nor hermeneutical meaning; on the contrary, he strives to understand her meaning because he first trusts and loves her. "Fear her not, Lucius," he assures her terrified nephew, "somewhat doth she mean" (4.1.9). When the sight of Lavinia knocks her sole surviving brother to his knees, Titus insists that he summon the courage to "arise, and look upon her" (3.1.65). A primordial ethical appeal inspires an effort to face Lavinia. Titus's response seeks semiotic form when he asks his daughter to "make some sign how I may do thee ease" (3.1.121). In the next scene, he offers to study her gestures, in order to develop a common language:

> In thy dumb action will I be as perfect
> As begging hermits in their holy prayers.
> Thou shalt not sigh, nor hold thy stumps to heaven,
> Nor wink, nor nod, nor kneel, nor make a sign,
> But I of these will wrest an alphabet,
> And by still practice learn to know thy meaning.   (3.2.40–45)

Kendall notes that Titus "realizes the need to build language anew."[39] Titus anachronistically compares his effort to the rigorous discipline of monastic prayer, attentive to the silent voice of the absolutely Other. Lavinia's condition both frustrates and elicits language, driving the men around her to construct semiotic systems in search of a means of communication.

Having patiently learned the names of Lavinia's assailants, the Andronici do not call on her again. Detmer-Goebel concludes that identifying the guilty exhausts their interest in Lavinia's voice: "As soon as Lavinia dutifully writes in the sand the names of her attackers, she is not addressed or consoled, but told to kneel down with the others present and swear revenge."[40] Both Marcus and Titus nevertheless treat her words with extraordinary importance and attempt to fix Lavinia's message permanently. Marcus proposes an oath, on the precedent of that taken by Junius Brutus to revenge Lucrece (4.1.88–93), while Titus quotes Seneca in Latin (4.1.80–81), before devising an elaborate allegory, practically a fable, in which the rapists, their mother, and her husband take symbolic form as animals (4.1.95–99). After proposing literary precedents and narrative expressions, Titus resorts to giving the words physical form: "I will go get a leaf of brass, / And with a gad of steel will write these words" (4.1.101–02). His choice of materials might be suggested by the description of the books of fate at the end of the *Metamorphoses*.[41] In any case, both literary form and precedent, like inscription in brass, fix Lavinia's words within the Said; there, they become separable from the person who offers them. Marcus and Titus do not address Lavinia again because the content of what she says eclipses the fact of her address in which she faces them and commands their attention. Paradoxically, the Andronici silence Lavinia by assigning her words extraordinary importance. In the Said, Levinas argues, the Saying finds both expression and betrayal.

The Andronici take revenge, at first symbolically, on paper, but then physically, on the bodies of their enemies. After learning the rapists' identities, Titus sends them a gift, as Aaron says, "wrapped about with lines, / That wound beyond their feeling to the quick" (4.2.27–28). Other than Titus, no one understands this as an effective revenge: Aaron seems amused, Chiron and Demetrius remain oblivious, and Marcus confuses Titus's revenge with forgiveness (4.1.127). Titus sends a similar message to Saturninus, but this only angers the emperor, who orders the messenger to be executed (4.4.44), then plots Titus's death: "For this proud mock I'll be thy slaughterman" (4.4.57). Saturninus would probably carry out his threat if the news of Lucius's Gothic army did not impose an imperative distraction. Later, Titus writes "sad decrees" in blood, which seem only a desperate effort to assure himself that "what is written shall be executed" (5.2.11, 15). Titus's efforts to give his revenge textual form prove futile even when they are not self-defeating.

Only when Tamora, crazed with confidence in her own rhetorical power and cunning (4.4.94–98), brings Chiron and Demetrius to Titus can Titus follow his Ovidian precedent to its cannibalistic climax. He does not write another word in the play, even sending Marcus to summon Lucius by word of mouth (5.2.122–30). Henceforth, literature becomes for Titus an applied art. He dispatches Lavinia on the strength of the "pattern, precedent, and lively warrant" of "rash Virginius," who similarly killed a ravished daughter (5.3.43, 36). One might argue with Deborah Willis that Titus merely avenges his honor,[42] but he speaks only of his pain. Moreover, Lavinia begged for death with some of her last words (2.3.173), and Chiron and Demetrius boast sadistically of robbing her even of the means to hang herself (2.4.10). One is reminded of Gloucester in *King Lear*, frustrated by the failure of his suicide attempts. The chapbook prose history declares that "at his daughter's request, he killed her," though it fails to offer any sense of how Lavinia might convey her request.[43] Kendall objects that Lavinia ought to have been capable of at least requesting death, if not suicide.[44] The question of whether the death of Lavinia should be considered an honor-killing or a mercy-killing remains open. In either case, Titus locates a literary precedent to provide him with a response to Lavinia's suffering. He answers the question "What shall we do?" (3.1.133) in a most macabre way. We ought not to forget, however, that the question itself expresses the extraordinary ethical demand made on the Andronici by Lavinia.

Manifestation, Levinas insists, demands betrayal. The last scene of the play shows how language as an exorbitant concern yields to a Said. Marcus's speech to the Roman people constitutes a *tour de force* of spontaneous rhetoric, mixing claims on pity with humility before the popular judgment. Instead of introducing his nephew as *candidatus*, Marcus compares him with Aeneas, "our ancestor" and founder of the state (5.3.79), then conflates "our Troy, our Rome" in case the parallel has somehow escaped his auditors (5.3.86). In a flurry of metaphors, Marcus likens the state to "a flight of fowl," "scattered corn" and finally a severed body, with "broken limbs" (5.3.67–71). Kendall argues that in this final scene, "the rhetoric seems more artificial than ever (because of what has gone before),"[45] but the rhetoric actually draws authority from what has gone before. Whereas earlier, Lavinia's body loses meaning, other bodies now serves as a means of expression and even as evidence. Marcus appeals to his "frosty signs and chaps of age" as "Grave witnesses of true experience" (5.3.76–77). Lucius proclaims, "My scars can witness, dumb although they are, / That my report is just and full of truth" (5.3.113–14). Finally, the very color of Aaron's child witnesses to Tamora's infidelity (5.3.118–20). While Lavinia's body calls, mutely, for response and offers no statement or meaning beyond her suffering, the bodies of Marcus and Lucius signify truths and ratify their words. In a Rome where the moral and political system is in collapse, Titus's tears and scars can command no more pity than the presentation of his hand to Saturninus. In the final scene of the play, however, scars are restored to their role as signs of truth. Indeed, Marcus deploys silence as a trope, claiming to be unable to speak for tears:

> floods of tears will drown my oratory
> And break my utt'rance, even in the time
> When it should move ye to attend me most,
> And force you to commiseration.   (5.3.89–92)

The silence that represents an absence of signification and an appeal prior to meaning in Lavinia becomes just another sign in Marcus's final speech. The Said (the word as text and meaning) both expresses and betrays the Saying (an extraordinary proximity to the Other and imposition of responsibility).

Moreover, the body's various significations serve as arguments in a political arena. Without even overtly requesting it, Marcus secures the empire for his nephew. It would be churlish to insist that Marcus merely feigns distress on the grounds that he exploits the claim of silence rhetorically and for political gain. The option of suspecting Marcus of bad faith, however, shows that his suffering has become a Said. Umberto Eco famously defines the domain of semiotics as "everything which can be used in order to lie." Of course, as Eco continues, "If something cannot be used to tell a lie, conversely it cannot be used to tell the truth: it cannot in fact be used 'to tell' at all."[46] What allows Marcus to express his suffering also introduces the possibility of its falsehood. "In language qua said," writes Levinas, "everything is conveyed before us, albeit at the price of a betrayal."[47] As with other references to the body, Marcus's tears signify and even guarantee the truth of his claims, as does his offer, on behalf of his nephew and Young Lucius to "hand in hand all headlong hurl ourselves, / And on the ragged stones beat forth our souls, / And make a mutual closure of our house" (5.3.131–33). The traumas that these "poor remainder of Andronici" (5.3.130) have survived render the offer credible. As when the Andronici perform their obsequies in the play's first scene, however, rhetorical form gives feeling expression and therefore allows it to be suspected of falsehood.

One is left with the sense that Roman government and society has undergone permanent change. Titus will join his sons in "our household's monument" (5.3.193), and even Saturninus receives the dignity of burial "in his father's grave" (5.3.191). Whereas Titus demanded stoicism, however, Lucius invites his son to "learn of us / To melt in showers" (5.3.159–60). Lucius ratifies his own and his son's public mourning but forbids pity toward Aaron: "If anyone relieves or pities him / For the offence he dies" (5.3.180–81). The coldly traditional sacrifice of Alarbus appears merciful by comparison with Aaron's slow starvation. Similarly, Lucius denies Tamora burial, commanding that her body be thrown "forth to beasts and birds of prey" (5.3.197) outside the city walls. After the semiotic crisis of the play, Lucius establishes a new order, reiterating the distinction between Roman and barbarian. New burial rites replace old obsequies. Suffering reclaims expression and social discourse assimilates its signs.

In the course of the play, a society based on exchange loses its values. The distinction between Rome and its other disappears; the expectation of repayment for gifts in gratitude also disappears. This change is both symbolized and realized in the devaluing of Lavinia, whose initial status as "Rome's rich ornament" marks her as both a token of exchange and symbol of her society. Moreover, her loss of language both symbolizes and realizes a semiotic crisis. Her silence seems contagious, affecting those who would respond to her suffering. Despite the failure of systems of gratitude, the society that they constitute, and even the language in which they are spoken, ethical concern persists and moreover renews itself, in radical independence from such structures. Concern with Lavinia furnishes an example of a pure gift, for which no recompense could be expected. Of course, to be meaningful and effective, such a gift must take form in a society, in signs and actions. The Saying must betray itself to the Said. Its inevitable betrayal, however, should not delude us into believing that such generosity is a mere social product, derived from the cycling gift system itself, or commanded by the need to reciprocate. Like Antonio's love of Bassanio, or Edward's for Gaveston, Titus's concern with Lavinia precedes its own expression, and therefore shows itself anterior to the exchanges, negotiations, and circulations that we all too often regard as the limits of the early modern world and even of our own.

SEVEN

Returning to the World

PROSPERO'S GENEROSITY AND POWER

"'The true life is absent,'" Levinas writes, quoting Arthur Rimbaud, in the opening words of *Totality and Infinity*. "But," Levinas continues in his own voice, "we must live in the world. Metaphysics arises and is maintained in this alibi."[1] In *The Tempest*, Prospero, magician and protagonist, does not merely come to the realization with which Levinas begins one of his most important works but also dramatizes the movement into the world from the "true life" of metaphysics, found on the island or in his study. By returning to Milan, to ducal power and to mortality, Prospero returns to human society, political responsibility, and existential temporality. Milan is a historical location, unlike the island, which is fictive, geographically unspecific, and magical. Prospero returns to the world—to history, politics, and economics—but generosity motivates his return.

Attempts to explain Prospero's motives by way of ambition proceed from a general view of the world itself that privileges self-interest as fundamentally real and discounts generosity as bad faith. On the contrary, Prospero divests himself of wide-ranging

165

magical power by leaving the island; moreover, he does so in the interests of another, clouding his actions in secrecy so as to avoid repayment even with thanks. In a sense, his goal is not even his own, because he anticipates nothing in Milan but a prologue to death. Miranda, not Prospero, will enjoy life in the world he once left for exile. He sacrifices his own life along with his enormous power on the island so that Miranda may reach maturity and enjoy marriage. Unlike Gloucester in *King Lear*, possessed by fear of the sons destined to replace him, Prospero sacrifices himself for his child.

Prospero recalls only one sex partner, notoriously dismisses her in two lines, and only mentions her for Miranda's sake, endorsing the legitimacy of her birth.[2] He expresses no nostalgia toward his defunct sex life and, for a man escaping both imprisonment and a desert island, greets the possibility of its renewal with frigid indifference. In contrast, Prospero's seemingly obsessive return to Miranda's sexuality, demonstrated by his warning to Ferdinand, might indicate some sort of sexual magic at work,[3] or a strange and incestuous fascination.[4] Yet it might just as easily dramatize the difficulty of letting go, of accepting that the maturity of one's own children implies one's own death and of making the self-sacrifice of embracing it. In what James Black describes as Prospero's elaborately legalistic donation of Miranda to Ferdinand,[5] he refers to his daughter as "a third of mine own life, or that for which I live" (4.1.3–4). This echoes his later anticipation of a grim life in Milan, "where / Every third thought shall be my grave" (5.1.310–11). Critical speculation over the other two thirds in each case[6] emphasizes the verbal parallel, which aligns the child's marriage and maturation with the father's mortality and displacement. In fact, Prospero's resolution toward death immediately follows reference to "the nuptial / Of these our dear-belov'd" (5.1.308–09). By inviting his own death as the price of his child's maturation, Prospero becomes the very opposite of Gloucester.

Prospero's acceptance of his inability to transform those around him accompanies his return to the world. He commands neither penitence nor mercy, as David Evett shows.[7] In any case, it seems unlikely that anything could ever change Antonio. William M. Hamlin suggests that he and Sebastian could be as easily described as "born devils" as Caliban.[8] Lewis notes that Antonio remains opaque at the end of the play,[9] while Harry Berger claims that Caliban troubles Prospero with his opacity.[10] To live in the social world, however, is to be surrounded by others whose opacity measures their alterity. Though Prospero famously declares, "This thing of darkness, / I acknowledge mine" (5.1.275–76), Caliban remains dark. If anything, he becomes darker still when Prospero abandons his magical powers of surveillance. Like the rest of us, Prospero must live among persons he cannot control or even fully comprehend.

The opening scene of the play distinguishes political power from control over the natural world. "What cares these roarers for the name of king?" (1.1.16–17), the boatswain asks rhetorically. John S. Hunt argues that the play's opening scene "emphasizes the limitations of political authority itself,"[11] beyond which counselors and princes cannot hope to command. In contrast to an impotent politics, the storm seems endowed with the power of mortality itself. The boatswain advises Gonzalo, a landlubberly statesman, to "give thanks you have lived so long and make yourself ready in your cabin for the mischance of the hour, if it so hap" (1.1.23–25). He claims that noblemen and courtiers are powerless in the face of the storm but soon finds himself equally impotent, able to command men but only to defy the elements. "Tend to th' Master's whistle!" he orders the sailors before turning to address the winds that mock the master's ineffectual breath: "Blow till thou burst thy wind, if room enough" (1.1.6–7). The first scene appears to establish firm limits on human power.

The next scene, however, violates these limits, revealing that the storm is indeed under human control, specifically Prospero's. He may have reached the island by "providence divine" (1.2.159), but he arrogates the attributes of providence by controlling nature. The source and nature of Prospero's control over the natural world has, like much about this play, attracted a great deal of critical commentary.[12] Caliban curses with reference to natural forces and associates his mother's magic with the night (1.2.321–24; 1.2.339–40), and the gods she teaches him to adore include the man in the moon (2.2.132–35), but Prospero also controls the natural elements, as Miranda recognizes in her first lines: "If by your art, my dearest father, you have / Put the wild waters in this roar, allay them" (1.2.1–2). Karol Berger notes that Prospero controls the four elements: "he can produce winds in the air, raise waters of the sea in storm, flash fiery lightnings, and make the earth shake."[13] While critics have debated what type of Renaissance magic Prospero should be understood as employing, they all agree that he controls nature. Rather than forming the horizon of Prospero's power, the natural world serves as its arena.

Prospero boasts expansively of his power, specifically claiming power to raise the dead and appropriate the thunderbolt: "to the dread rattling thunder / Have I given fire, and rifted Jove's stout oak / With his own bolt" (5.1.44–46). In the course of the play, we see him do neither of these things, and he only once claims to raise the dead.[14] Hunt notes, "Prospero thinks of himself as a kind of god."[15] Prospero's claims soar blasphemously. In the voice of Ariel he self-righteously conflates his own revenge with that of "[t]he powers" (3.3.73). Earlier, Ariel claims that the magic of which he is the agent imitates and even threatens the gods of ancient myth:

> Jove's lightning, the precursors
> O'th' dreadful thunder-claps, more momentary
> And sight-outrunning were not; the fire and cracks
> Of sulphurous roaring the most mighty Neptune
> Seem to besiege, and make his bold waves tremble,
> Yea, his dread trident shake.   (1.2.202–06)

According to Walter Clyde Curry, the theurgist eventually rises to be "completely assimilated to the gods," and thereby "becomes impassive like them and is able to exercise all the powers of the gods themselves."[16] If so, then Prospero cannot be understood as a theurgist, not only because he never achieves impassivity, but also because he claims to have risen higher yet, bullying the gods. Caliban, evidently impressed, declares that Prospero's art "would control my dam's god Setebos, / And make a vassal of him" (1.2.372–73). Insofar as Prospero gives up his magic to return to his dukedom, he surrenders the power of a god for the weakness of a man.

Prospero claims a need for Caliban's services, but this claim strains credulity. In his reminiscence of their earlier relationship, Caliban relates an exchange in which he presented indigenous knowledge in exchange for Prospero's patronage:

> I loved thee,
> And showed thee all the qualities o'th' isle,
> The fresh springs, brine pits, barren place and fertile —
> Cursed be I that did so!   (1.2.336–39)

Dogged in his search for a deity, Caliban offers the same services to Stephano (2.2.154–58). Prospero tells Miranda, "We cannot miss [Caliban]. He does make our fire, / Fetch in our wood, and serves in offices that profit us" (1.2.311–13). However, it is difficult to imagine why someone who commands the thunderbolt needs the services of a fire-kindler, or why spirits that can "fetch dew / From the still-vex'd Bermudas" (1.2.228–29) suffer from a strange incapacity to transfer wood. It is not clear why Prospero keeps Caliban around, except perhaps to demonstrate his own power.

This is, of course, to imagine counterfactuals. Nevertheless, it illustrates that the problem of the distribution of scarce goods in a human community barely marks Prospero's life on the island; insofar as it does, he wins any struggle by overwhelming force. His relations with Caliban do not rise to the level of negotiation. Prospero may have exchanged his own erudition for Caliban's local knowledge when he first arrived, but he has long since ceased to trade when he can command: "Fetch us in fuel, and be quick, thou'rt best, / To answer other business—shrug'st thou, malice?" (1.2.365–66). Prospero and Caliban no more engage in the exchange of gifts characteristic of primitive economies than they participate in monetary exchange. At least in economic terms, Caliban is justified in calling Prospero "the tyrant that I serve" (2.2.156). Prospero does not even offer anything for his magic, as Faustus must in his formal "deed of gift."[17] Moreover, insofar as Prospero has material needs, they are already met. If politics and economics consist in negotiations with others, his life on the island is neither economic nor political.

This certainly does not handicap his enjoyment of it, however. He boasts about "mine art" to Ariel (1.2.291), partly in order to awe him into submission but mainly, one suspects, because he enjoys boasting. His first order to the newly humbled sprite is a gratuitous bit of theatrical business: "Go, make thyself like to a nymph o'th' sea. / Be subject to no sight but thine and mine, invisible / To every eyeball else" (1.2.301–03). Prospero's call for an invisible display borders on contradiction. He feels no need for any further audience, however, to enjoy his own power. His magic is fundamentally solipsistic, cutting him off from human relations. In fact, he often uses it against other people. David Lucking compares him to Marlowe's magician and points out that, like Faustus, Prospero punishes his enemies,[18] attacking them with dogs whose very names—"Fury" and "Tyrant" (4.1.258)—seem to designate them as aspects of his own personality. Indeed, Peter Lindenbaum notes that Prospero spends a great deal of the play either alone or acting the role of furious tyrant, only shifting the objects of his rage from Ariel, to Caliban, to Ferdinand, to Miranda, and to Ferdinand again.[19] By the end of the second scene, Hunt argues, "our introduction to an emotionally unbalanced policeman is complete."[20] Moreover, Prospero shows off his power, waxing metatheatrical in his self-aggrandizement. "He is obviously more at home in roles allowing him to cleave the ear with horrid speech, make mad the guilty and appall the free," Harry Berger observes.[21] Like Bottom in *A Midsummer Night's*

Dream,[22] he enjoys the role of tyrant, though unlike Bottom, he expresses no desire to play a lover, never mind every other role in the cast list. Perhaps this is part of the reason why he maintains Caliban, an otherwise redundant slave, whom one suspects that he taught to curse by example.

Prospero's obvious and distasteful tendency to take pleasure in the exercise of power makes his renunciation of it all the more remarkable, however. His most grandiloquent claims, in fact, come precisely as he promises to abandon them. He threatens Ariel with imprisonment in an oak "till / Thou hast howled away twelve winters," as a prelude to promising him liberty "after two days" (1.2.295–98). His extraordinary claim to raise the dead ends at the beginning of the line in which he declares that "this rough magic / I here abjure" (5.1.50–51). One is reminded of Edward II clinging to the crown even as he gives it up. "The king rageth" reads the stage direction in the quarto of Marlowe's play.[23] Prospero also rages as he gives up power; unlike Edward, however, he does so at his own initiative. Prospero indulges his enjoyment of power, in the knowledge that he will soon lose it.

Insofar as politics involves life in community with others, Prospero abandons it for the island; insofar as it involves the exercise of power, however, he consummates it on the island. John D. Cox claims, "he literally embodies the fantastic vision of kingly power that was repeatedly presented as a flattering image to King James in court masques," though, as Cox notes, Prospero's power rises above mere dramaturgy. Prospero incapacitates Ferdinand effortlessly, for instance, and commands "an absolutely reliable and accurate espionage system."[24] On the other hand, Prospero barely even engages with the problems of negotiating power relations and certainly is not confined by a constituted state. He wields enormous magical power, but it barely even qualifies as secular, let alone political or economic. The assumption that everything is political has become a convention or even cliché of Shakespeare criticism, especially the criticism of *The Tempest*. Meredith Skura argues that "revisionist" readings of *The Tempest*

emphasize the play's status as "a political act." The critics Skura
describes repeat older critics, but with particular attention to
"power relations and to the ideology in which power relations are
encoded."[25] Hunt claims that New Historicists regard Prospero
not as the play's "hero" but "instead as a kind of mask for economic and political power, amoral, impersonal, and ruthless."[26]
Stephen Orgel's subtle and original reading exemplifies such
criticism. He argues that Prospero's apparent generosity in giving away Miranda allows him to exclude Antonio permanently
from the Milanese succession in favour of his grandchildren.[27] To
a critic armed with the right presuppositions, even acts of paternal generosity can be read as political gambits in *The Tempest*, as
they clearly are in *King Lear*. For the time being, it suffices to note
that critics who assign everything to the political implicitly agree
with the play's antagonists. While suborning Sebastian to fratri-
cide, Antonio equates abandoning hope of Ferdinand's survival
with "Another way so high a hope that even / Ambition cannot
pierce a wink beyond, / But doubt discovery there." As Orgel notes
in his Oxford edition, "the syntax is confused" but the sense is
clearly that "ambition cannot conceive of anything higher than
the hope of a crown" (2.1.239–241 and note). A few lines later,
Antonio compares Sebastian's anticipated rise in power to awak-
ening and therefore ambition to consciousness itself: "How shall
that Claribel / Measure us back to Naples? Keep in Tunis, / And
let Sebastian wake" (2.1.256–58). Kermode dismisses Antonio as
a "moral pervert."[28] Antonio's perversion consists in allowing the
political to form the horizon of his desire, as anything he takes to
be everything must. Ascription of Prospero's motives to ambition
renders incoherent his decision to opt for the comparative impo-
tence of a secular ruler when magic already furnishes him with
more power than his worldly brother can even desire.

None of this is to deny the value of political readings of the
play, especially postcolonial readings. By reducing the play to
an exhibition of "naked power,"[29] however, they neglect to note
that power is not necessarily political in any reasonably narrow

sense of the term. In fact, Prospero admits that in the study of magic, his younger self was "neglecting worldly ends" (1.2.89). He thereby establishes an opposition between magic and politics, if only for his attention. This neglect of politics in favor of magic anticipates his exile; conversely, his surrender of magical power precedes his return. Barbara Howard Traister points out that his changes of clothing symbolize this.[30] Prospero appears "As I was sometime Milan," rather than wearing the cloak that he identifies metonymically with "my art" (5.1.86; 1.2.25). Even on the island, Robin Headlam-Wells argues, Prospero has no intention of constructing any sort of colony, instead seeking the earliest possible return.[31] Schneider claims that "colonialist critics," as he terms them, must "simply erase the climax of the play," which he finds in "Prospero's renunciation of revenge and his abjuration of magic."[32] Orgel, one of Schneider's targets, argues that the earlier answer as to why Prospero renounces his magic is insufficient: "To say that Prospero no longer needs his magic is to beg all the most important questions."[33] Moreover, if magic proves useful on the island, one would expect it to be absolutely necessary in Milan, to which Prospero returns in the company of his murderous sibling and the latter's equally untrustworthy henchman. Prospero's decision to abjure his magic is analogous to the opposition between the metaphysical and the physical: it has less to do with its practical uses as a means of surveillance and manipulation than with its opposition to politics. Lewis argues that in *The Tempest*, "true sacrifice requires engaging in affairs of state and of the family."[34] Prospero's abandonment of magic is violent, like overcoming an addiction: "I'll break my staff, / Bury it certain fathoms in the earth, / And deeper than did ever plummet sound / I'll drown my book" (5.1.54–57). Prospero painfully renounces his magical power because it is incompatible with political life in a community with others.

To be fair, the conflation of artistic power, magical power, and political power is a Renaissance commonplace, and in his "art" Prospero might refer to them all at once. Kermode argues,

"The self-discipline of the magician is the self-discipline of the prince...and Prospero labours to regain a worldly as well as a heavenly power."[35] In the humanist tradition, knowledge produces power.[36] "Mastery" conflates concepts "of intellectual comprehension and economic and political domination."[37] On the other hand, Prospero's past clearly demonstrates a failure to rule. Humanist education characteristically warned against a neglect of politics;[38] Prospero, who neglects it anyway, proves a poor product of an education that conflates political and magical power. His particular experience of magic leads him to become estranged from his society and social obligations. He "grew stranger" to his own state, and his activities were marked by "closeness" and "being so retired" (1.2.76; 1.2.90–91). Notwithstanding the Renaissance humanist tendency to conflate magic and politics, the play opposes them.

Karol Berger argues that the power of a magician would in any event render human relationships impossible: "By annihilating the free will of others," the magus "reduces them to the subhuman level of animals or things." As a result, "he is alone. This situation never happens to a politician, even a most powerful one; he is always a man among men."[39] The spirits who accompany Prospero merely reflect his own thoughts, enacting his "present fancies" in the masque (4.1.122). Ariel claims to be incapable of tenderness (5.1.20). Greeting the Neapolitans at the end of the play, on the other hand, Prospero embraces both Alonso and Gonzalo, returning to the society of men among whom he finds himself "one of their kind, that relish all as sharply" (5.1.23). If Prospero evades the political and social realm in his library, "dukedom large enough" (1.2.110), then his return to Milan represents a recognition of others in their corporeal selves. Jane Kingsley-Smith argues that Prospero receives reciprocal recognition for his bodily humanity in his return to the world.[40] Alonso is surprised to find that Prospero's "pulse / Beats as of flesh and blood" (5.1.113–14). Only as a member of society can Prospero be truly human.

This movement back into the world defies being understood as an expression of power. Prospero's response to Sebastian's "The devil speaks in him!" with a simple "No" is bathetically weak (5.1.129). Moreover, Prospero does not embrace his brother, or the equally fratricidal Sebastian, perhaps because he has a renewed sense of the danger they pose. "The choice of a Machiavellian prince," John D. Cox argues, would not be to preserve Antonio,[41] but Prospero abnegates power, a choice that a Machiavellian would never make, by definition. Prospero places himself in a position where, A. Lynne Magnusson writes, "the Antonios of this world will continue to be Antonios and their actions will require continued vigilance."[42] Such vigilance, however, measures the price of living in the world as a man among men—not as a master above slaves, a magician above spirits, or a god above mortals. In moving into politics, Prospero sacrifices physical safety as well as power. He finds himself in the opposite position to the boatswain, able to command the elements but not men, at least not if he is to live among them as one of their kind.

Hunt argues that rather than manipulating with magic, Prospero is reduced in the final scene to "the ordinary, sanctioned means of human persuasion: moral authority, mutual indebtedness, sympathetic identification, dispensation of favors, intimidation, construction of a public image."[43] In reducing himself to an attenuated, political power, Prospero enters a social, political, and economic world constituted by reciprocal obligations. The play repeatedly depicts the return to an economic world in the abandonment of utopian ideals. Gonzalo presents such an ideal most obviously, not to mention naively, when he expostulates on how he would construct and rule an anarchic society. Gonzalo's vision suffers from a number of weaknesses, not the least of which is the self-contradiction that Antonio and Sebastian point out: "The latter end of his commonwealth forgets the beginning" (2.1.155–56). Moreover, as Leslie Fiedler notes, "the beginning" might be read as a Biblical reference to the fall of man in

Genesis.[44] Gonzalo gives his own ambition "T'excel the Golden Age" pagan expression and therefore renders it suspect to anyone believing in any sort of doctrine of original sin (2.1.166). Antonio, who possesses in his own soul an example of human depravity, points out that abolishing social regulations would merely reduce the population to "whores and knaves" (2.1.164). Perhaps more importantly, Gonzalo's utopia, like Thomas More's, depicts an escape from economic existence into primitive communism, without "contract, succession, / Bourn, bound of land, tilth, vineyard" or even any "occupation" (2.1.149–52). More's Raphael Hythloday explains that "it is not to be hoped for" that poverty be eliminated "whiles every man is master of his own to himself."[45] Without scarcity or property, Gonzalo argues, violence also would cease:

> All things in common nature should produce
> Without sweat or endeavour. Treason, felony,
> Sword, pike, knife, gun, or need of any engine,
> Would I not have; but nature should bring forth
> Of its own kind all foison, all abundance,
> To feed my innocent people.   (2.1.157–62)

Antonio and Sebastian are unable to imagine such a world, claiming only that Gonzalo should "Scape being drunk, for want of wine" (2.1.144). One will note the irony that Stephano floated ashore on the "whole butt" (2.2.128), defined by the *Oxford English Dictionary* as "from 108 to 140 gallons,"[46] or more than enough to induce lethal alcohol poisoning. Nevertheless, Antonio correctly identifies the problem with Gonzalo's utopia as following from its exclusion of economics in general, if not viticulture in particular.

Prospero's own image of a perfect society, projected in the masque that he produces for Ferdinand and Miranda, endorses what Gonzalo rejects in his: "Where Gonzalo's commonwealth would abolish contract, succession, property, riches and work, the masque presents these elements as blessings, celebrating especially the fruits of agricultural labour, which are variegated crops, pruned vineyards, winter forage, controlled rivers and the efforts of sunburned sicklemen."[47] Nevertheless, Prospero's vision is also utopian and even, in Ferdinand's estimation, paradisal (4.1.124). Like Gonzalo, Prospero imagines a world freed from scarcity, with "Barns and garners never empty" and where spring immediately follows harvest (4.1.111, 114–15). The masque depicts a physical world in which the married couple is promised earthly, gustatory abundance, and where even the queen of goddesses is known "by her gait" (4.1.110–17; 4.1.102). One might argue that the banishment of Venus and sexual passion contradicts an acceptance of nature (4.1.94–98). Whatever its internal incoherence, however, the masque represents Prospero's own vision of natural, political, and sexual order. "Nothing," writes Traister, "shows more clearly Prospero's rage for order than the betrothal masque he creates: measured, harmonious, and to be completed by a dance."[48] Other critics concur.[49] However, as Magnusson recognizes, Prospero clearly differentiates his dream from the rest of the play, both dramaturgically and prosodically.[50] The outside world interrupts, moreover, in the form of Caliban's inept but murderous expedition. Remembering "that foul conspiracy, / Of the beast Caliban and his confederates," Prospero aborts the production (4.1.139–40). His sudden awareness of mortality and time—that the conspirators aim "Against my life" and that "The minute of their plot / Is almost come" (4.1.141–42)—drags him out of his dreams and inspires existentialist ruminations on mutability and mortality. In comparison to the exigencies of life, he must admit the masque to be an "insubstantial pageant" (4.1.155). Whereas Gonzalo entertains a Montaignian vision of noble savagery, and Prospero produces a Jacobean masque of idealized order, Stephano, were he given to theory, might imagine a perpetual carnival. Certainly he imagines an extended period of inebriation: "When the butt is out, we will drink water; not a drop before" (3.2.1–2). Caliban promises him sex with Miranda, who "will become thy bed, I warrant" (3.2.102). Finally, Stephano betrays a fatal fascination with nice clothes. In sum, he imagines the island as a locus of consumption: gustatory, sexual, and even sartorial. Gonzalo suffers disillusionment and fear, calling on "Some heavenly power" to "guide us / Out of this fearful country" (5.1.105–06); Prospero ponders the grave; Stephano suffers a hangover, or at least cramps (5.1.286–88). All utopias reveal their insubstantiality. In *The Tempest,* escape from the world proves only temporary.

Prospero's steady goal is return, not escape. Moreover, this return is not for his own sake but for Miranda's. "I have done nothing but in care of thee," he reassures her with nearly his first lines (1.2.16). This may imply, as Harry Berger argues, reforming Naples so that Miranda will have somewhere to which she may return,[51] but we should not lose track of the motive. Miranda provides Prospero with his only human relationship on the island, at least after his break with Caliban, and his only salvation from complete isolation.[52] Later, when Alonso complains of the loss of his son Ferdinand, Prospero claims that he also has lost a child, "and supportable / To make the dear loss have I means much weaker / Than you may call to comfort you" (5.1.145–47). Both losses prove temporary or at least metaphorical, because both fathers lose their children to marriage rather than death. Prospero's loss of Miranda would nevertheless be worse than Alonso's of Ferdinand, because Prospero would be deprived entirely of children and of all the company he has known for twelve years. Earlier, describing to Miranda their voyage to the island, Prospero exclaims, "O, a cherubin / Thou wast that did preserve me" (1.2.152–53). Her smile, he says, "raised in me / An undergoing stomach, to bear up / Against what should ensue" (1.2.156–58). Orgel considers this a birth fantasy, in which Prospero usurps the role of mother.[53] Prospero's statement, however, makes the baby Miranda the active party, endowed with angelic powers of inspiration. At a practical level, she provides a reason for him to stay alive in order that she not die of neglect. Unlike Faustus, Prospero never lacks human company altogether. Rather than the description of the voyage representing a fantasy of self-sufficiency, it presents Miranda as an Other, a call to responsibility in the Levinasian sense. She contrasts, therefore, with the children Caliban imagines himself siring who would only multiply his self: "I had peopled else / This isle with Calibans" (1.2.349–50). In offering her as a temptation to Stephano, Caliban promises that Miranda will "bring thee forth brave brood" (3.2.103). Prospero, in contrast, views his child as a motive for self-sacrifice.

Such self-sacrifice qualifies as peculiarly generous because Prospero's paternal care has never before been rewarded with anything but disappointment. Antonio's betrayal years earlier still stings him into incoherence. He relates how

> my trust,
> Like a good parent, did beget of him
> A falsehood in its contrary as great
> As my trust was, which had, indeed, no limit,
> A confidence sans bound. (1.2.93–97)

Prospero presents his trust as the temptation suborning Antonio's evil; moreover, reflecting on the greatest pain in his experience, Prospero's mind grasps at images of paternity. Antonio, represented synecdochically by his evil, appears as a rebellious child. Caliban also rebels against the man who, as he says, "strok'st me and made much of me" (1.2.333) and who educated him. Prospero's brokenhearted disappointment drives him to violent revenge:

> A devil, a born devil, on whose nature
> Nurture can never stick; on whom my pains
> Humanely taken, all, all lost, quite lost;
> And as with age his body uglier grows,
> So his mind cankers. I will plague them all,
> Even to roaring. (4.1.188–93)

Only Miranda has not betrayed Prospero's trust and even she defies him in favoring Ferdinand.[54] Prospero achieves a rare generosity of spirit in not allowing a lifetime of betrayal to poison his love for Miranda.

Prospero both expresses and obfuscates his generosity under the form of exchange. In the act of forgiving his enemies, Prospero gives them more than they can earn. Similarly, his surrender of

Miranda to Ferdinand is a gift, but he carefully presents it as an exchange, dressed in legal language.[55] He claims to "ratify this rich gift" and to do so "afore heaven," and therefore by oath (4.1.7–8). In fact, he gives Miranda to Ferdinand at least three times. A few lines after telling Ferdinand (in the past tense), "I have given you here a third of my own life" (4.1.2–3), he ratifies the gift. Then, following a brief response by Ferdinand, Prospero moves into the present tense: "Then as my gift, and thine own acquisition / Worthily purchased, take my daughter" (4.1.13–14). Despite claiming that the gift has already been given, he gives it again. His repetition demonstrates his determination to ensure that the transfer actually occurs and has legal status. Moreover, he constructs his gift as an exchange, one that Ferdinand has earned. Ferdinand is assigned the same task as Caliban, piling logs (3.1.9–11), and in neither case does the task have any convincing utility. "All thy vexations," Prospero assures him, "were but my trials of thy love" (4.1.5–6). What Black recognizes as Prospero's extraordinary demand for premarital celibacy[56] might be understood as another test that Ferdinand must endure and that turns his achievement of Miranda into something deserved, an exchange in a world of exchanges.

Alonso indulges only political motives in arranging Claribel's Tunisian marriage, a fact that oppresses him with guilt:

> Would I had never
> Married my daughter there, for, coming thence,
> My son is lost, and, in my rate, she too,
> Who is so far from Italy removed
> I ne'er again shall see her.   (2.1.105–09)

Sebastian concurs in viewing the shipwreck as punishment for this dynastic marriage: "Sir, you may thank yourself for this great loss, / That would not bless our Europe with your daughter" (2.1.121–22). The whole court party seems to forget about Prospero, believing instead that their shipwreck punishes Alonso for Claribel's marriage, until Ariel, as the harpy, corrects them. Claribel enters into marriage "Weighed between loathness and obedience" (2.1.128). On the other hand, Miranda's initiative in proposing to Ferdinand demonstrates her enthusiasm (3.1.83). Nevertheless, both brides live in a world in which the exchange of women ratifies political alliances. When Prospero gives Miranda away, he makes the donation in the form of an exchange and therefore grants it legal and social validity.

Like Prospero's return, or the marriage of Miranda, Prospero's forgiveness of his enemies is often read as a political gambit. Certainly, there are a number of problems with Prospero's explanation for his decision to forgive his enemies, as Orgel explains: "Alonso is penitent, but the chief villain, the usurping younger brother Antonio, remains obdurate. Nothing, not all Prospero's magic, can redeem Antonio from his essential badness."[57] Traister notes similarly: "Caliban, though he says he will sue for grace, is still Caliban."[58] Harry Berger notes, "Ariel has said nothing about [the Neapolitans] being penitent."[59] One may ask, with Hunt, if Prospero's magic inspires penitence even in Alonso, or merely terror and despair.[60] In a sense, however, the answer does not matter, because Prospero's forgiveness responds to nobody's penitence. He accuses and then forgives each while there is "Not one of them / That yet looks on me, or would know me" (5.1.82–83).[61] The members of the court party can offer nothing, not even penitence. Prospero's forgiveness is therefore not an exchange to be understood in the quasi-economical terms of a trade in pardons.

In an extended treatment of the influence of humanism on *The Tempest*, Schneider argues that the gifts that end the play are mutual. In particular, "When Alonso and Prospero give each other their children in the denouement, this ancient ritual of gift-exchange signifies peace between them."[62] He cites Cicero and Seneca on the importance of gifts. Certainly, Prospero claims to be entering into exchange, not only exchanging children but also exchanging the revelation of Ferdinand's survival for his dukedom: "My dukedom since you have given me again, / I will requite you with as good a thing" (5.1.168–69). Hunt argues that the epilogue describes "in Christian language a state of reciprocal relation between human beings."[63] According to a number of sympathetic critics, Prospero's generosity constitutes an exchange, into which the audience as much as the other characters are conscripted as agents.

Prospero's enemies are helpless to earn forgiveness, however, not only because Prospero manipulates them, or because he offers them no chance, or because incurable evil possesses them, but also because, in keeping with the Protestant soteriology explored by *Doctor Faustus*, one always is helpless to earn forgiveness. As the harpy, Ariel offers them escape from "Ling'ring perdition, worse than any death / Can be at once," in exchange for "heart's sorrow / And a clear life ensuing" (3.3.77–78; 3.3.81–82). However, quite apart from the fact that they might not experience heartfelt sorrow, they have no opportunity to live "a clear life." The offer of forgiveness in exchange for penitence makes no sense.

Instead of Prospero disguising the exercise of naked power with the language of grace, he does the opposite, obfuscating gratuitous forgiveness under a tissue of exchange. By expressing his forgiveness in the terms of politics, he grants it being in a political world of exchanges and negotiations. To paraphrase Rimbaud, true forgiveness is elsewhere, but Prospero must make it live in the world. He not only accuses Antonio but also ascribes remorse to him in order to explain his own forgiveness and endow it with reality in the world:

> You, brother mine, that entertained ambition,
> Expelled remorse and nature, whom, with Sebastian—
> Whose inward pinches therefore are most strong—
> Would here have killed your king, I do forgive thee,
> Unnatural though thou art.   (5.1.75–79)

Here, as elsewhere, Prospero's pain deranges his grammar. Nevertheless, he offers an entirely unjustified forgiveness. Antonio remains obstinately "[u]nnatural." Later, Prospero adds that he requires "My dukedom of thee, which perforce I know / Thou must restore" (5.1.133–34). The politically unwarranted forgiveness of Antonio takes political expression as an exchange of sovereignty for forgiveness. Prospero's forgiveness, like Antonio's extraordinary love for Bassanio, Edward's for Gaveston, or Titus's for Lavinia, calls for expression in the world. Unlike these other protagonists, however, Prospero obscures his generosity under a pretense of exchange and thereby saves it from its own betrayal.

In keeping with his newfound powerlessness, claims of need and even abjection fill Prospero's epilogue. Having given up his power, he now finds his strength "most faint" (5.1.321). He must beg rather than command. Prayer, in Prospero's image, "assaults / Mercy itself, and frees all faults" (5.1.335–36), but apparently his own prayers are insufficient, because he must beg the audience to pray for him. The final lines—"As you from crimes would pardoned be, / Let your indulgence set me free" (5.1.337–38)—echoes the Lord's Prayer, as a number of critics have noted.[64] In neither the epilogue nor the prayer, however, is the pardoning of sins reciprocal. "Them that trespasse against us" in the Lord's Prayer,[65] are not called upon or capable of forgiving the sins of the speaker of the prayer. Similarly, Prospero does not place himself in any position to grant forgiveness for the audience's sins. On the contrary, the relationship of Prospero's forgiveness to ours is exemplary, not reciprocal. In fact, his earlier lines seem to make his acts of forgiveness into things that require our forgiveness, as if we must forgive his mercy: "Let me not, / Since I have my dukedom got, / And pardoned the deceiver, dwell / In this bare island by your spell" (5.1.323–26). The events beginning with "Since" might furnish a reason to forgive, but they seem more immediately a reason for Prospero to "dwell / In this bare island." Prospero's effort to obtain forgiveness for his own forgiveness does not mark forgiveness as mutual, something offered in exchange. Instead, it places Prospero's forgiveness at a double remove from mutual exchange. In forgiving Prospero's forgiveness, we release him from any chance of being repaid in kind.

Prospero renounces power generously, for the sake of another. His claim that he will "retire me to my Milan" expresses the paradox of giving up power in favor of rule (5.1.310), conflating a return to political responsibility with retreat and seclusion. In a movement opposite to that of King Lear, Prospero retires from power and from his life's work precisely by regaining political office. One need not draw biographical parallels to the author's life to see in the end of *The Tempest* a movement away from magic and toward the mundane. If generosity finds economic and political expression, this does not demonstrate Prospero's bad faith. Instead, it shows his need to give generosity expression in the political world. He must promise his fellow aristocrats a rational explanation of everything that has befallen them and so offers them "the story of my life, / And the particular accidents gone by / Since I came to this isle" (5.1.246–50; 5.1.304–06). The story he tells may be less interesting than that which the audience has witnessed, but its pedestrian character would merely reflect his own move from magic to mortality. Prospero embraces his return, with all its disempowering but social consequences. His move into the economic world—out of utopias and masques and off the island—constitutes an act of generosity, a gift.

Conclusion

To the frustration of biographical criticism, Shakespeare writes almost entirely in the voices of characters. In response, James S. Shapiro turns away from Shakespeare's psychology and personal views to "what can be known with greater certainty: the 'form and pressure' of the time that shaped Shakespeare's writing."[1] Nevertheless, in his reconstruction of Shakespeare's rivalry with the comic actor Will Kemp, Shapiro ascribes unprecedented importance to the one speech written in Shakespeare's own voice, from the epilogue to the second part of *Henry IV*. Unfortunately, ironies and textual difficulties hedge and plague this epilogue.

The New Variorum text ascribes to Frederick Gard Fleay, writing in 1891, the notion that the epilogue as printed in early texts conflates more than one speech.[2] Fleay's reading has attained wide acceptance. A. R. Humphreys's 1967 Arden edition, for instance, declares, "Not all three paragraphs would be delivered at the same time," separating the first paragraph, spoken by Shakespeare, from the last two, spoken by a dancer.[3] René Weis follows him in this division and uses it as part of his argument on the dating of the play.[4] Giorgio Melchiori not only accepts but compounds the division of the epilogue in his 1989 Cambridge edition, declaring that the epilogue "is divided into three sections written at different times and serving different purposes."[5] The layout of the first quarto seems to endorse Melchiori's reading, because it inserts blank lines between each paragraph. The first paragraph, Shapiro

185

argues, probably constitutes the epilogue delivered at court, because the quarto ends it with a prayer for the queen.[6] The other paragraphs, spoken by a dancer and incorporating tasteless jokes on Falstaff's "fat meat"[7] would have been more appropriate to the public theater, where performances concluded with a jig.[8] The first paragraph, on the other hand, significantly fails to contain any reference to the speaker dancing. Its speaker admits, "If you look for a good speech now, you undo me, for what I have to say is of mine own making."[9] This seems a confession of Shakespeare's own authorship, especially as he proceeds to apologize for an earlier "displeasing play."

The fact that in the first performance the speaker and playwright would be identical, marks this speech as unique in Shakespeare's canon. Shakespeare takes this opportunity to playfully compare his relationship to his audience with commercial exchange. He begins as he intends to continue, "and so to the venture." Shakespeare presents himself as a deadbeat who owes the audience a play: "I meant indeed to pay you with this; which, if like an ill venture it come unluckily home, I break, and you, my gentle creditors, lose. Here I promised you I would be, and here I commit my body to your mercies. Bate me some, and I will pay you some, and, as most debtors do, promise you infinitely."[10] Shakespeare wrote *Henry IV, Part 2* about two years after *The Merchant of Venice*, and he recalls the earlier play in his imagery, placing himself in Antonio's situation, fearing the wreck of his "venture," and subject to the mercy of his "creditors." Shapiro remarks, "The analogy between a theatrical joint-stock company like the Chamberlain's men and joint-stock mercantile enterprises is not far-fetched." Moreover, Shakespeare wrote *Hamlet* within a year or two, thereby discharging even his most extravagant promise. Nevertheless, he clearly waxes ironic in his choice of imagery. The worst that the audience could reasonably deliver would be some sort of raspberry, not physical punishment or death. The Lord Chamberlain's men was a commercial enterprise and indeed handsomely profitable, but its relationship to the playhouse audience was much more obviously commercial than its relationship to the court audience, to whom this epilogue was probably delivered.[11] "And so I kneel down before you," Shakespeare ends the speech, maintaining the pretense of addressing a body of creditors who wield power of life and death like Shylock's knife, "but indeed," he adds, "to pray for the Queen."[12] He abandons the facade of abjection to the audience, an abjection described as debt, in favor of a subservience that apparently requires no explanation and that finds expression not in the reciprocal obligations of debt but in the gratuity of prayer. Shakespeare dedicates the only speech written to be delivered in his own voice to a playful exploration of the relationship of playwright and audience, described in an elaborate conceit as debtor and creditor.

In his playfulness, however, and the turn to the sovereign with which he ends his speech, Shakespeare undermines and finally deflates his conceit. He exploits the distinction latent in every metaphor when he reveals that he has only figuratively placed himself in the audience's power, not literally. The metaphorical debt to the audience does not constitute a power relationship. On the contrary, state power replaces and overrides this metaphorical debt. Shakespeare hereby refuses to treat commercial relationships of exchange as ubiquitous and foundational to power relations. He acknowledges the network of commercial and quasi-commercial relationships that Greenblatt describes as "a subtle, elusive set of exchanges, a network of trades and trade-offs, a jostling of competing representations, a negotiation between joint-stock companies."[13] On the other hand, Shakespeare refuses to take this network of exchanges entirely seriously, and certainly does not confuse it with the world itself.

While both Shakespeare and Marlowe explore exchange relationships and the societies they constitute, characters who over-rely on mechanisms of exchange prove tragic, like King Lear, or vicious, like Edmund. Even in a comedy like *The Merchant of Venice*, exchange displaces doctrines of salvation, leaving the audience with a slight but definite unease in spite of the conventional happy ending. The prologue on *Faustus* shows that a belief in the ubiquity of exchange proves incompatible with Reformation theology and leads Faustus to Hell, still desperately—in the literal and theological sense—trying to cut a deal. An excessive belief in exchange would lead to agreement with Faustus, with King Lear, with Edmund, with Shylock, and indeed with all the merchants of Venice. In other words, to raise such a belief to a worldview condemns us to impoverished human relationships. As Shylock's desire to claim Antonio's flesh shows, such an all-embracing circulation conflates the human and inhuman, leading to the treatment of persons as things, constituted by and available for purchase within networks of exchange. Even murder and slavery, however, appear merely symptomatic of the inhumanity implicit in an all-embracing network of exchange, which must treat people as things insofar as it claims ubiquity and therefore can tolerate no truly exceptional importance for people or anything else.

The historical example of Reformation soteriology shows that the logic of exchange did not obtain an all-powerful hold over early modern thought. Elizabethan and Jacobean drama does not merely depict networks of exchange in a negative light; it makes a positive claim for relationships that exceed and violate the structures of exchange. Blessings and acts of countercultural bravery in *King Lear* instance a generosity indifferent to reciprocation. Levinas's distinction between the Saying and the Said reveals the relationship between the radical call of the Other and the social and economic systems in which it finds expression and, indeed, to which it gives rise.

In *The Merchant of Venice*, Antonio's love for Bassanio presents an affection that first appears as mysterious, undefined, and excessive. The loan into which Antonio enters provides his love not only with expression but also with a sign that then defines it. Antonio proceeds to claim Bassanio's love in return and nearly to impose a mortal debt upon him, before Portia's machinations allow her to trump Antonio's claim with her own and indeed to appropriate Antonio's claim, making him Bassanio's "surety" for the final exchange of rings (5.1.254). The love affair that catalyzes Marlowe's *Edward II* defies efforts to understand it as reciprocal and indeed is so thoroughly countercultural that it frustrates efforts to understand it at all. The love of Edward and Gaveston lends itself to analysis neither as a set of self-interested exchanges nor even as their obtuse expression in social conventions.

Similarly, in *Titus Andronicus*, the title character's love of his daughter struggles to find expression but rises to importance only once her violation and mutilation erase her value on the marriage market. Titus's baffled efforts to find a suitable response to his daughter's suffering occur in the gap between what Levinas calls the Saying and the Said, between the excessive claim of the Other and its fixture in signs. There may appear to be a grotesque irony in considering the mute Lavinia as an instance of the Saying, but it is precisely her inability to generate words that ensures her wordless appeal cannot become fixed immediately in signs and therefore alienated from her.

Finally, in *The Tempest*, Prospero confronts the paradox of needing to give his love for his daughter expression, while not surrendering it to an economy where it would become a debt to him and a burden to her. He achieves this by hiding his extraordinary generosity, allowing Ferdinand to believe he has earned Miranda's love, for instance. Even in his final epilogue, Prospero does not exchange forgiveness with the audience. On the contrary, like Gloucester offering a blessing, Prospero invokes the divine to evade the reciprocity of a direct exchange. All of the plays examined in this book illustrate a claim by the Other, a claim excessive to the logic of debt and obligation, if only in the anxious efforts to avoid this claim or reappropriate it to networks of debt.

One way to imagine such an excessive claim would be as a debt that not only remains unpaid in fact but also cannot ever be paid in principle. Levinas uses precisely such language to describe the claim of the Other. In *God, Death and Time*, he describes how "there is no debt in regard to the other, for what is due is unpayable: one is never free of it." Rather than this excessive debt threatening my identity, it constitutes my identity: "The other individuates me in the responsibility I have for him."[14] In an interview in New York, Bernard-Henri Levy, a founder of the Institut d'études lévinassiennes, summarized Levinas's ethics by saying, "I owe more than I am." He proceeded to argue that Levinas's "radical anti-totalitarian thought" consists in finding at the core of totalitarianism "the idea that being is full, is done, is complete. There is an ontological totalitarianism which precedes all the political ones."[15] The difficulty with a reading of Renaissance drama based on the circulation of social energy, or the reciprocation of all gifts, is not that gifts fail to impose debts—they frequently do, as even a cursory reading of *The Merchant of Venice* would indicate. Neither can one argue that such exchanges fail to serve to structure societies, because clearly gratitude and reciprocity constitute social obligations in Shakespeare's commercial Venice, Marlowe's feudal England, and the Roman Empire represented in *Titus Andronicus*. The problem arises in claiming that every gift necessarily imposes a debt. Like Being in the philosophy of Heidegger, the circulation of gifts would reduce people to little more than its agents or objects. It would become, to use the language of Levinas's first great work, a totality. Extending the circulation of gifts from material objects to Greenblatt's "social energy" only renders it more totalizing. To grant to circulation omnipresence and omnipotence is to construct a new "conceptual idol,"[16] endowed with all the worst features of a god but deprived of mercy, love or, as Menenius says of Coriolanus, "a heaven to throne in."[17] A pure gift violates the ubiquity of exchange and thereby avoids such deification.

As Peperzak has argued, maintaining the possibility of such a gift need not require the discovery of some sort of presocial or postsocial gift, unalloyed with cultural influences: "For a phenomenology of giving, it is not necessary to establish that its purest form is an empirical fact; it is sufficient and necessary that we can imagine and think its pure form as a realizable possibility, even if the human condition shows us only contaminated or mixed realizations."[18] Insofar as the gift constitutes the social, in the recognition of the Other, a radically antisocial gift would not be possible. Indeed, Levinas defines "sociology" in "the opposition of conversation."[19] Rather than escaping culture, generosity founds it. Instead of either denying the pure gift in order to deify circulation as ubiquitous, or seeking an uncontaminated gift outside society, therefore, we can find generosity in quotidian and social expressions. In order to be understood at all, a gift must find expression in language, if only the language of gesture by which the gift is presented. Rather than locating the gift prior and superior to culture, one discovers it in culture, as a trace.

From an absolute donation, the gift becomes imbricated in systems of exchange, both on the early modern stage and in the world generally. This, I argue with reference to both *Edward II* and *The Merchant of Venice,* is the price that the gift's manifestation demands. A gift becomes real—finds expression in the physical and social world—by risking betrayal. Edward's expression of his love for Gaveston transforms it into a political alliance when Edward places his love within the feudal state of which he is the head and expresses his love in gifts of land and in competition with marital fidelity. Similarly, Antonio's love for Bassanio appears as little more than a vague unease, the sadness without cause of which he complains in the play's first line, until he expresses it by volunteering his body as surety for Shylock's loan. This generous act, however, proceeding from a radical love, becomes in expression and despite its motive a selfish and exclusive claim on Bassanio and draws Antonio into competition with Portia. Finally, Titus's love for his maimed daughter survives her muteness, her exclusion from the gift economy in which she no longer has value, and even the failure of the expectation of gratitude in Rome and the collapse of Roman norms. It finds a language and achieves expression. The cannibal feast by which Titus avenges Lavinia becomes an event in the reconstruction of the Roman state. Unfortunately, in finding expression, Titus's love loses its radical character: Titus silences Lavinia forever in death, reducing her from an appellant into a mere sign. In each of the three plays, a radical appeal betrays itself into a system of exchange by finding expression.

Such betrayal constitutes the gift, insofar as it must achieve practical expression in the world. *The Tempest* addresses this paradox. Prospero's return to Milan for the sake of his daughter is a triumph of love over experience, because his previous paternal relationships with his brother Antonio and with his servant and student Caliban have ended in betrayals that still torture his mind. Moreover, he surrenders far-reaching power to return to a world of mortality and political exigency. He gives his generosity expression in the world, however, by disguising it under the form of exchange. His abandonment of his claim on Miranda takes the form of a marriage contract, preceded by simulated ordeals through which Ferdinand can prove his love. Similarly, his forgiveness of the court party assumes their penitence, though there is no evidence that they are penitent, rather than simply confused, frightened, and numb. Even if they are penitent, Prospero gives them no opportunity to declare it before offering them forgiveness. Finally, he promises an account of his own life on the island, offering an alternative explanation for events and disguising his own magical agency. Rather than betraying generosity into a system of exchanges, Prospero presents as a gift to Miranda the whole political and social world that Mauss claims such exchanges constitute.

Faustus, Lear, Antonio, and many of their fellow characters share an overconfident and uninformed belief in what Mauss made the central and enabling claim of his anthropology: gifts must be returned and, therefore, there is no true gift. These characters thereby condemn themselves to impoverished and mutually destructive relationships. Marlowe and Shakespeare illustrate in a group of characters—Antonio, Edward, Titus and Prospero—a generosity that does not exhaust itself in exchanges but expresses and threatens to betray a radical love. Such a radical love not only exceeds the networks of exchange that structure society but also initiates these exchanges, inspiring Antonio to enter into his bond, for instance, or Edward to participate in kingly rule. Even in the plays described in this book's earlier chapters, several characters defy their societies' belief in apparently ubiquitous exchange. In *Faustus*, the old man seeks the protagonist's salvation and the scholars never quite abandon their hopes for the protagonist's soul (5.1.35–46; 5.2.53–54). Cordelia, in *King Lear*, insists counterfactually that she has "no cause" to hate her father, and he, in turn, dies listening for her voice and gazing intently on her face (4.7.75; 5.3.270, 310). Conversely, Cornwall erases the eyes of an Other, unable to face their claim upon him. The trace of the Other inspires and informs the networks of gift exchange and the circulations of social energy that dominate the early modern stage.

Of course, the audience experiences the claim of the Other only secondhand. Titus's impotent confusion in the face of Lavinia's suffering is his and not ours, just as the audience does not feel the guilt and anxiety that inspire Cornwall's erasure of Gloucester's accusing eyes. For that matter, we do not feel Faustus's loneliness and lust as our own. Nevertheless, the early modern stage shows an awareness of the radical claim of the Other, dramatizing it in the responses and actions of the characters. We do not, in fact, treat other people as products of economic forces, functions of power, or bundles of sexual drives and anxieties. A literary criticism adequate to how we live in the world must recognize, with the dying Lear or with Prospero returning to his dukedom, an obligation beyond that imposed by circulations of social energy.

Such a recognition runs counter to our postmodern suspicion of the gift. It allows us, therefore, to explore other and potentially liberating ways of living in our world. Specifically, it furnishes a criticism adequate to how we must live in the world with others, to whom we have ethical obligations beyond those chosen by ourselves or imposed by our cultures. Rather than endorsing

Faustus's constricted worldview, such criticism would explore those moments at which the social betrays its origins in responsibility toward the Other. Rather than endorsing the beliefs and actions of Faustus, Goneril, or Edmund, it would take its cue from Cordelia's forgiveness of Lear and Prospero's of the unrepentant Antonio. Moving beyond the misanthropy that characterizes much of contemporary criticism requires that we recognize in the gift a violation of, rather than an extension to, the ubiquity of exchange. We must learn not only to accept or repay but, more importantly, to forgive the gift.

NOTES

Notes to Prologue

1. Christopher Marlowe, *Doctor Faustus: A 1604 Edition*, ed. Michael Keefer, 2nd ed. (Peterborough, ON: Broadview, 2007), Prologue, 8.

2. David Hawkes, *The Faust Myth: Religion and the Rise of Representation* (New York: Palgrave Macmillan, 2007), 59, 1, 52.

3. Diarmaid MacCulloch summarizes this intellectual movement in *The Reformation* (London: Allen Lane, 2003), 106–12.

4. Alister E. McGrath provides a summary of Luther's intellectual development in *Luther's Theology of the Cross: Martin Luther's Theological Breakthrough* (Oxford: Blackwell, 1985; repr., Grand Rapids, MI: Baker Books, 1994). His discussion of how salvation remains external to the sinner is on pages 134–35.

5. MacCulloch, *Reformation*, 122–26.

6. Michael Keefer, Introduction to *Doctor Faustus: The 1604 Edition*, 2nd ed. (Peterborough: Broadview, 2007), 31; Hawkes, *Faust Myth*, 33–34.

7. Keefer, Introduction, 41.

8. Jonathan Dollimore, *Radical Tragedy: Religion, Ideology and Power in the Drama of Shakespeare and His Contemporaries* (Brighton: Harvester, 1984), 109, 114–15.

9. Keefer, Introduction, 42.

10. Dollimore, *Radical Tragedy*, 119.

11. Ibid., 117.

12. McGrath, *Luther's Theology*, 101, 139.

13. Ibid., 59–60.

14. Martin Luther, "The Bondage of the Will," trans. J. I. Packer and A. R. Johnston, in *Martin Luther: Selections From His Writings*, ed. John Dillenberger (New York: Anchor Press, 1961), 199.

15. *Oxford English Dictionary Online*, s.v. "surrender, v. 1a."

16. James I, *Daemonologie in Forme of a Dialogue, Diuided into Three Bookes* (Edinburgh: Robert Walde-graue, 1597), 18.

17. Jean Bodin, *On the Demon-Mania of Witches*, ed. Jonathan L. Pearl and Randy A. Scott, trans. Randy A. Scott, Renaissance and Reformation Texts in Translation (Toronto: Centre for Reformation and Renaissance Studies, 1995), 90, 112.

18. Reginald Scot, *The Discouerie of Witchcraft Wherein the Lewde Dealing of Witches and Witchmongers Is Notablie Detected* (London: [Henry Denham for] William Brome, 1584), 44–45.

19. Keith Vivian Thomas, *Religion and the Decline of Magic: Studies in Popular Beliefs in Sixteenth- and Seventeenth-Century England* (London: Weidenfeld and Nicholson, 1971; repr., Harmondsworth, England: Penguin Books, 1973), 521.

20. Jeffrey Burton Russell, *Lucifer, the Devil in the Middle Ages* (Ithaca, NY: Cornell University Press, 1984), 81.

21. *The Geneva Bible: A Facsimile of the 1560 Edition*, ed. Lloyd Eason Berry and William Whittingham (Madison: University Wisconsin Press, 1969), John 8:44.

22. Scot, *Discouerie of Witchcraft*, 56.

23. McGrath, *Luther's Theology*, 100–03.

24. *Certayne Sermons Appoynted by the Quenes Maiestie, to Be Declared and Read, by All Persones, Vycars, and Curates, Euery Sondaye and Holy Daye in Theyr Churches*, ([London]: R. I[ugge], 1559), sig. D1v.

25. Erasmus's views are described by MacCulloch, *Reformation*, 112–14.

26. For a brief discussion of Luther's defiance at the Diet of Worms, see Patrick Collinson, *The Reformation* (London: Weidenfeld and Nicolson, 2003), 63.

27. Peter Happé, "The Devil in the Interludes, 1550–1577," *Medieval English Theatre* 11, nos. 1–2 (1989): 44.

28. Luke 4:5–7, in *Geneva Bible*.

29. Bodin, *On the Demon-Mania*, 182.

30. David Riggs, *The World of Christopher Marlowe* (London: Faber, 2004), 89.

31. Wolfgang Musculus, *Common Places of Christian Religion*, trans. John Man (London: Henry Bynneman, 1578), 44.

32. Dollimore, *Radical Tragedy*, 118.

33. Keefer, Introduction, 243.

34. William Shakespeare, *King Lear*, ed. R. A. Foakes, 3rd ed., The Arden Shakespeare (London: Thomas Nelson, 2000), 1.4.130.

Notes to Introduction

1. Adriaan Peperzak, "Giving," in *The Enigma of Gift and Sacrifice*, ed. Edith Wyshcogrod, Jean-Joseph Goux, and Eric Boynton (New York: Fordham University Press, 2002), 167.

2. For Greenblatt's acknowledgment of the influence of Geertz and other anthropologists, see Stephen Greenblatt, *Renaissance Self-Fashioning: From More to Shakespeare* (Chicago: University of Chicago Press, 1980), 4.

3. Stephen Greenblatt, *Shakespearean Negotiations: The Circulation of Social Energy in Renaissance England* (Berkeley: University of California Press, 1988), 7.

4. Mary Douglas, "No Free Gifts," in *The Gift: The Form and Reason for Exchange in Archaic Societies*, ed. W. D. Halls (London: Routledge, 1990), x.

5. Emmanuel Levinas, *Time and the Other and Additional Essays*, trans. and ed. Richard A. Cohen (Pittsburgh: Duquesne University Press, 1987), 72.

6. Richard A. Cohen, "Some Reflections on Levinas and Shakespeare," in *Levinasian Meditations: Ethics, Philosophy, and Religion* (Pittsburgh: Duquesne University Press, 2010), 152, 151.

7. Levinas, *Time and the Other*, 73.

8. Emmanuel Levinas, "The Bad Conscience and the Inexorable," in *Of God Who Comes to Mind*, trans. Bettina Bergo (Stanford: Stanford University Press, 1998), 177. In the opening page of *Otherwise than Being*—originally published in French in 1974—Levinas also writes, "To be or not to be is not the question where transcendence is concerned." Emmanuel Levinas, *Otherwise than Being or Beyond Essence*, trans. Alphonso Lingis (Pittsburgh: Duquesne University Press, 1981), 3.

9. Emmanuel Levinas, "Ethics as First Philosophy," in *The Levinas Reader*, ed. Seán Hand (Oxford: Blackwell, 1989), 86.

10. Jacques Derrida, *Adieu to Emmanuel Levinas*, trans. Pascale-Anne Brault and Michael Naas (Stanford: Stanford University Press, 1999), 8.

11. Cohen, "Some Reflections," 155.

12. Jacques Derrida, *Given Time: 1. Counterfeit Money*, trans. Peggy Kamuf (Chicago: University Chicago Press, 1992), 24.

13. Marcel Mauss, *The Gift: The Form and Reason for Exchange in Archaic Societies*, trans. W. D. Halls (New York: W. W. Norton, 1990), 3; Jonathan Parry, "*The Gift*, the Indian Gift, and the 'Indian Gift,'" *Man*, n.s., 21 (1986): 455–56. Parry takes umbrage with the term "self-interest" in an earlier translation.

14. Ilana F. Silber, "Beyond Purity and Danger: Gift-Giving in the Monotheistic Religions," in *Gifts and Interests*, ed. Antoon Vandevelde (Leuven: Peeters, 2000), 116.

15. Mauss, *Gift*, 6, 39. All italics within quoted materials are original.

16. Ibid., *Gift*, 23, 73; Douglas, vii–viii; Parry, *"The Gift*, the Indian Gift, "* 463–64.

17. Mauss, *Gift*, 75.

18. Ibid., 10, 69, 65.

19. Simon Jarvis, "The Gift in Theory," *Dionysius* 17 (Dec. 1999): 206.

20. Parry, *"The Gift*, the Indian Gift, "* 455.

21. Mauss, *Gift*, 72–73, 69, 70.

22. Ibid., 4, 100n29, 32, 37.

23. Ibid., 47, 65, 72.

24. Douglas, "No Free Gifts," xvi, xiv.

25. Mauss, *Gift*, 74.

26. Ibid., 70, 3.

27. Ibid., 5–6, 78.

28. Douglas, "No Free Gifts," ix–x.

29. Mauss, *Gift*, 71.

30. Christian Arnsperger, "Gift-Giving Practice and Noncontextual Habitus: How (Not) to Be Fooled by Mauss," in Vandevelde, *Gifts and Interests*, 71, 74–75. Arnsperger repeats the second observation in "Methodological Altruism as an Alternative Foundation for Individual Optimization," *Ethical Theory and Moral Practice* 3 (2000): 118.

31. Mauss, *Gift*, 3.

32. Ibid., 46, 47.

33. Parry, *"The Gift*, the Indian Gift," 456.

34. Mauss, *Gift*, 5, 30.

35. Parry, *"The Gift*, the Indian Gift," 456.

36. Marin Terpstra, "Social Gifts and the Gift of Sociality: Some Thoughts on Mauss' *The Gift* and Hobbes' *Leviathan*," in Vandevelde, *Gifts and Interests*, 195.

37. Mauss, *Gift*, 76, 77.

38. Ibid., 65.

39. Douglas, "No Free Gifts," vii.

40. Mauss, *Gift*, 16, 17.

41. Parry, *"The Gift*, the Indian Gift," 461.

42. Camille Tarot, "Gift and Grace: A Family to Be Recomposed?" in Vandevelde, *Gifts and Interests*, 139.

43. Parry, *"The Gift*, the Indian Gift," 469.

44. Ibid., 467.

45. Mauss, *Gift*, 39.

46. Emmanuel Levinas, *Ethics and Infinity: Conversations with Philippe Nemo*, trans. Richard A. Cohen (Pittsburgh: Duquesne University Press, 1985), 86.

47. Emmanuel Levinas, *Totality and Infinity: An Essay on Exteriority*, trans. Alphonso Lingis (Pittsburgh: Duquesne University Press, 1969), 213.

48. Levinas, *Ethics and Infinity*, 86, 87–88.

49. Levinas, *Totality and Infinity*, 95.

50. Ibid., 197.

51. Ibid., 170–171, 216, 172.

52. Emmanuel Levinas, "Meaning and Sense," in *Emmanuel Levinas: Basic Philosophical Writings*, ed. Adriaan T. Peperzak, Simon Critchley, and Robert Bernasconi (Bloomington: Indiana University Press, 1996), 45, 44, 47.

53. Ibid., 49; Robert Bernasconi, "The Logic of the Gift: Toward an Ethic of Generosity," in *The Logic of the Gift*, ed. Alan D. Schrift (New York: Routledge, 1997), 258 examines this passage. Levinas earlier used the term "works" very differently in *Totality and Infinity* (177–80), to distinguish between the Other's expression of signs and her expression of herself. This roughly corresponds to the distinction between the Said and the Saying, explained later in this prologue.

54. Levinas, "Meaning and Sense," 49; Emmanuel Levinas, "The Trace of the Other," in *Deconstruction in Context: Literature and Philosophy*, ed. Mark C. Taylor (Chicago: University of Chicago Press, 1986), 348–49.

55. Peperzak, "Giving," 162, 163, 166, 170. Peperzak is also the translator of the versions of both "Trace of the Other" and "Meaning and Sense" to which I refer.

56. Peperzak, "Giving," 162.

57. Derrida, *Given*, 24, 13, 24.

58. Peperzak, "Giving," 167–68.

59. Derrida, *Given*, 12–14, 16, 7, 37.

60. Bernasconi, "Logic of the Gift," 256.

61. Derrida, *Given*, 48, 10.

62. Ibid., 6.

63. Mauss, *Gift*, 21–22; Derrida, *Given*, 25, 7.

64. Levinas, "Trace," 348; Peperzak, "Giving," 162.

65. Paul Ricoeur, "Asserting Personal Capacities and Pleading for Mutual Recognition," Kluge Prize acceptance speech, John W. Kluge Center, Washington, DC, 2004, http://www.loc.gov/loc/kluge/prize/ricoeur-transcript.html.

66. Paul Ricoeur, *The Course of Recognition* (Cambridge, MA: Harvard University Press, 2005), 225, 235, 227, 240, 242, 243, 263, 259.

67. Ibid., 260–62.

68. Arnsperger, "Gift-giving Practice," 75, 90.

69. Arnsperger, "Methodological Altruism," 119.

70. Emmanuel Levinas, *Entre Nous: On Thinking-of-the-Other* (New York: Columbia University Press, 1998), 100–01; Arnsperger, "Methodological Altruism," 122.

71. Levinas, *Time and the Other*, 79.

72. Emmanuel Levinas, "Reality and Its Shadow," in *The Levinas Reader*, ed. Seán Hand (Oxford: Blackwell, 1989), 138, 132, 142.

73. Jill Robbins, *Altered Reading: Levinas and Literature* (Chicago: University of Chicago Press, 1999), 53.

74. Robert Eaglestone, *Ethical Criticism: Reading after Levinas* (Edinburgh: Edinburgh University Press, 1997), 109.

75. Levinas, "Reality and Its Shadow," 142.

76. Robbins, *Altered Reading*, 161.

77. Eaglestone, *Ethical Criticism*, 177, 165, 177.

78. Graham Good, "The Hegemony of Theory," *University of Toronto Quarterly* 65, no. 3 (Summer 1996): 535.

79. Eaglestone, *Ethical Criticism*, 158.

80. Emmanuel Levinas, *Proper Names*, trans. Michael B. Smith (London: Athlone Press, 1996), 61.

81. Emmanuel Levinas, "Diachrony and Representation," in *Time and the Other and Additional Essays*, ed. Richard A. Cohen (Pittsburgh: Duquesne University Press, 1987), 100, 103–04.

82. Levinas, *Totality and Infinity*, 92.

83. Levinas, *Ethics and Infinity*, 88.

84. On the Saying and the Said, see Levinas, *Otherwise than Being*, 5–7, 9–10, 37–38, 45–48, 77–78, 153–62, 188–91.

85. Robbins, *Altered Reading*, 6–8.

86. Ibid., xiv.

87. William Shakespeare, *Titus Andronicus*, ed. Eugene Waith (Oxford: Oxford University Press, 1984), 2.3.185.

88. Robbins, *Altered Reading*, xxiii.

89. Ibid., 11.

90. Levinas, "Diachrony and Representation," 101.

91. Levinas, "Reality and Its Shadow," 137. The figure of the idol becomes very important in the philosophy of Jean-Luc Marion.

92. Robbins, *Altered Reading*, 68.

93. Stanley Cavell, *Disowning Knowledge in Six Plays of Shakespeare* (Cambridge: Cambridge University Press, 1988), 334 comments on this, though using his own particular vocabulary.

94. Levinas, *Time and the Other*, 72–73. Levinas also discusses the subject of Macbeth and death in *Otherwise than Being*, 3.

95. Cohen, "Some Reflections," 155, 158.

96. Levinas, "Reality and Its Shadow," 143.

97. Levinas, *Proper Names*, 59.

98. Alan Jacobs, *A Theology of Reading: The Hermeneutics of Love* (Boulder: Westview, 2001), 78.

99. Greenblatt, *Negotiations*, 19.

100. Ricoeur, *Course of Recognition*, 237.

101. Greenblatt, *Negotiations*, 12.

102. Douglas, "No Free Gifts," xiv.

103. Stephen Greenblatt, *Hamlet in Purgatory* (Princeton: Princeton University Press, 2001), 4.

104. *King Lear*, 1.1.90, 1.4.130.

105. Greenblatt, *Purgatory*, 4.

106. Ibid., 250.

107. Greenblatt, *Negotiations*, 7.

108. Greenblatt, *Purgatory*, 51.

109. Levinas, "Meaning and Sense," 50.

110. Greenblatt, *Purgatory*, 59.

111. Ibid., 130–32.

112. Ibid., 143–44.

113. Ibid., 149.

114. Ibid., 23–24, 60.

115. Peperzak, "Giving," 163.

116. Ibid., 161.

117. Parry argues that both a highly calculated system for purchasing salvation or "an ideal of purely disinterested action" can arise from religions making a strong distinction between this world and the next ("*The Gift*, the Indian Gift," 468).

118. Greenblatt, *Self-Fashioning*, 113.

119. Ibid.

120. I have argued elsewhere that Greenblatt's commitment to the thesis that it is not possible to speak with the dead embargoes the ethical relationship described by Levinas. See Sean Kevin Lawrence, "'As a Stranger, Bid It Welcome': Alterity and Ethics in *Hamlet* and the New Historicism," *European Journal of English Studies* 4, no. 2 (Aug. 2000): 155–69.

121. William Shakespeare, *The Merchant of Venice*, edited by Jay L. Halio (Oxford: Oxford University Press, 1993), 1.1.138.

Notes to Chapter One

An earlier version of this essay appeared as Sean Kevin Lawrence, "'To Give and to Receive': Performing Exchanges in *The Merchant of Venice*," in *Shakespeare and the Cultures of Performance*, ed. Paul Yachnin and Patricia Badir, 41–51 (Aldershot, England: Ashgate, 2008). Used by permission.

1. John Cunningham and Stephen Slimp, "The Less Into the Greater: Emblem, Analogue and Deification in *The Merchant of Venice*," in *The Merchant of Venice: New Critical Essays*, ed. John W. Mahon and Ellen Macleod Mahon (New York: Routledge, 2002), 240.

2. Douglas, "No Free Gifts," viii–ix.

3. Arnsperger uses this phrase to describe one way of understanding the Maussian model of social organization. See Arnsperger, "Gift-Giving Practice," 71.

4. René Girard, "'To Entrap the Wisest': A Reading of *The Merchant of Venice*," in *Literature and Society*, ed. Edward W. Said (Baltimore: Johns Hopkins University Press, 1980), 112.

5. Gabriel Egan, *Shakespeare and Marx* (Oxford: Oxford University Press, 2004), 105.

6. Marc Shell, "The Wether and the Ewe: Verbal Usury in *The Merchant of Venice*," *Kenyon Review* n.s. 1, no. 4 (1979): 86.

7. Girard, "To Entrap," 103. Girard's "vassality" is presumably derived from the French *vassalité*.

8. Lowell Gallagher argues that "some of the subliminal provocations produced by Gobbo's gift help redirect the basic questions arising from Mauss's anthropological horizon." He concentrates especially on how this particular gift is surrounded by malapropisms and does not, in fact, ever seem to be presented. I discuss the limitations of Mauss's paradigm for *The Merchant* in a subsequent chapter. For the time being, it suffices to note that Gobbo feels compelled to make at least a symbolic gift, imbricating his son's service into systems of clientage and patronage. Gallagher, "Waiting for Gobbo" in *Spiritual Shakespeares*, ed. Ewan Fernie (London: Routledge, 2005), 76.

9. Lars Engle, *Shakespearean Pragmatism: Market of His Time* (Chicago: University of Chicago Press, 1993), 20, 37.

10. Tony Tanner, "Which Is the Merchant Here? And Which the Jew? The Venice of Shakespeare's *Merchant of Venice*," in *Venetian Views, Venetian Blinds: English Fantasies of Venice*, ed. Manfred Pfister and Barbara Schaff (Amsterdam: Rodopi, 1999), 51.

11. Geoff Baker, "Other Capital: Investment, Return, Alterity and *The Merchant of Venice*," *Upstart Crow* 22 (2002): 31.

12. Richard Henze, "'Which Is the Merchant Here? And Which the Jew?'" *Criticism: A Quarterly for Literature and the Arts* 16 (1974): 287.

13. Avraham Oz, "'Which Is the Merchant Here? And Which the Jew?': Riddles of Identity in *The Merchant of Venice*" in *Shakespeare and Cultural Traditions*, ed. Tetsuo Kishi, Roger Pringle, and Stanley Wells (Newark: University of Delaware Press; Associated University Presses, 1994); Robert Zaslavsky, "'Which Is the Merchant Here? And Which the Jew?': Keeping the Book and Keeping the Books in *The Merchant of Venice*," *Judaism* 44 (1995); James Shapiro, "'Which Is *The Merchant* Here, and Which *The Jew*?': Shakespeare and the Economics of Influence," *Shakespeare Studies* 20 (1988); Tanner, "Which Is the Merchant Here?"

14. John Russell Brown, Introduction to *The Merchant of Venice*, by William Shakespeare (London: Methuen, 1955), li.

15. John W. Velz, "Portia and Ovidian Grotesque" in *The Merchant of Venice: New Critical Essays*, ed. John W. Mahon and Ellen Macleod Mahon (New York: Routledge, 2002), 179.

16. Hugh Short, "Shylock Is Content: A Study in Salvation," in *The Merchant of Venice: New Critical Essays*, ed. John W. Mahon and Ellen Macleod Mahon (New York: Routledge, 2002), 208.

17. Richard Weisberg, "Antonio's Legalistic Cruelty," *College Literature* 25 (1998): 14.

18. *King Lear*, 1.1.90, 1.4.130; Greenblatt, *Hamlet in Purgatory*, 4.

19. Lawrence W. Hyman, "The Rival Lovers in *The Merchant of Venice*," *Shakespeare Quarterly* 21, no. 2 (1970): 110.

20. Ibid.

21. Coghill quoted in Brown, Introduction, l. David N. Beauregard points out that because "two virtues cannot be opposed," neither of these oppositions are tenable. "Sidney, Aristotle, and *The Merchant of Venice*: Shakespeare's Triadic Images of Liberality and Justice," *Shakespeare Studies* 20 (1988): 40–41.

22. Hyman, "Rival Lovers," 109.

23. Cynthia Lewis, *Particular Saints: Shakespeare's Four Antonios, Their Contexts, and Their Plays* (Newark: University of Delaware Press, 1997), 47.

24. Lorenzo labels himself as a thief; 2.6.21–24.

25. Shell, "Wether and the Ewe," 69–70; Francis Bacon, "On Usury," in *The Works of Francis Bacon*, ed. James Douglas Denon, Robert Leslie Ellis, and Douglas Denon Heath, new ed., 6, Literary and Professional Works, vol. 1 (London: Longmans and Company, et al., 1890), 475.

26. Lewis, *Particular Saints*, 59–60.

27. Edward Andrew, *Shylock's Rights: A Grammar of Lockian Claims* (Toronto: University of Toronto Press, 1988), 35.

28. Moody E. Prior, "Which Is the Jew That Shakespeare Drew? Shylock Among the Critics," *American Scholar* 50, no. 4 (1981): 496.

29. Shell, "Wether and the Ewe," 69–70.

30. Brown, Introduction, xlix.

31. Velz, "Portia," 183; Anne Barton, "The Merchant of Venice," in *The Riverside Shakespeare*, ed. G. Blakemore Evans et al. (Boston: Houghton Mifflin Company, 1974), 252.

32. Harry Berger, "Marriage and Mercifixion in *The Merchant of Venice*: The Casket Scene Revisited," *Shakespeare Quarterly* 32, no. 2 (1981): 160.

33. Lewis, *Particular Saints*, 74.

34. Engle, *Shakespearean Pragmatism*, 24, 27

35. Ben Ross Schneider Jr., "Granville's *Jew of Venice* (1701): A Close Reading of Shakespeare's *Merchant*," *Restoration: Studies in English Literary Culture* 17, no. 2 (1993): 122.

36. Levinas, *Totality and Infinity*, 39.
37. Lester G. Crocker, "*The Merchant of Venice* and Christian Conscience," *Diogenes* 30, no. 118 (1982): 93.
38. Alan Holaday, "Antonio and the Allegory of Salvation," *Shakespeare Studies* 4 (1968): 111.
39. Barbara Lewalski, "Biblical Allusion and Allegory in *The Merchant of Venice*," *Shakespeare Quarterly* 13 (1962): 331.
40. *Oxford English Dictionary (OED) Online*, s.v. "kind, adj. 5."
41. *OED Online*, s. v. "kind, adj. 1–3."
42. Douglas, "No Free Gifts," viii–ix.
43. Mauss, *Gift*, 69.
44. Andrew, *Shylock's Rights*, 71.
45. Girard, "To Entrap," 105; Ralph Berry, *Shakespeare's Comedies: Explorations in Form* (Princeton: Princeton University Press, 1972), 112.
46. Girard, "To Entrap," 100.
47. Crocker, "*Merchant*," 83; Tanner, "Which Is the Merchant," 53; Prior, "Which Is the Jew," 485; Thomas Fujimura, "Mode and Structure in *The Merchant of Venice*," *PMLA* 81 (1966): 503; Michael Shapiro, "Shylock the Jew Onstage: Past and Present," *Shofar* 4, no. 2 (1986): 4.
48. Patrick Grant, "The Bible and *The Merchant of Venice*: Hermeneutics, Ideology, and Displaced Persons," *English Studies in Canada* 16 (1990): 258.
49. Andrew, *Shylock's Rights*, 32.
50. Catherine S. Cox, "Neither Gentile Nor Jew: Performative Subjectivity in *The Merchant of Venice*," *Exemplaria* 12, no. 2 (2000): 359; Lewis, *Particular Saints*, 59; Klaus L. Berghahn, "Comedy without Laughter: Jewish Characters in Comedies from Shylock to Nathan," in *Laughter Unlimited: Essays on Humor, Satire, and the Comic*, ed. Reinhold Grimm and Jost Hermand (Madison: University of Wisconsin Press, 1991), 16; Henze, 300.
51. Girard, "To Entrap," 116, 109, 110.
52. Parry argues that all commercial societies must deny the ubiquity of gift exchange in order to maintain themselves. "*The Gift*," 460.
53. *OED Online*, s.v. "bond, n. 1."
54. *OED Online*, s.v. "bond, n. 3."
55. *OED Online*, s.v. "bond, n. 1 9a."
56. Berry, *Shakespeare's Comedies*, 127.
57. Grant notes that Saint Jerome makes this association, "Bible," 257.
58. Andrew, *Shylock's Rights*, 45.
59. "If every ducat in six-thousand ducats / Were in six parts, and every part a ducat, / I would not draw them" (4.1.84–86).
60. Short, "Shylock Is Content," 205.

61. Brown, Introduction, xxxi.

62. Shell, "Wether and the Ewe," 80.

63. Hope Traver provides a useful history of the series of narratives in which Lucifer attempts to sue for man's soul: "The Four Daughters of God: A Mirror of Changing Doctrine," *PMLA: Publications of the Modern Language Association of America* 40 (1925), 71.

64. Camille Pierre Laurent, "Dog, Fiend and Christian, or Shylock's Conversion," *Cahiers Elisabethains: Late Medieval and Renaissance Studies* 26 (1984): 22.

65. Girard, "To Entrap," 101–02.

66. Grant, "Bible," 261.

67. Lewis, *Particular Saints,* 56.

68. Catherine Belsey, "Love in Venice," *Shakespeare Survey* 44 (1992): 46n.

69. Alexander Pope, ed. *The Works of Mr. William Shakespear,* vol. 2, *Merchant of Venice* (London: Mr. Pope and Dr. Sewell, 1728) 189.

70. Berry, *Shakespeare's Comedies,* 138.

71. John Russell Brown, *Shakespeare and His Comedies* (London: Methuen, 1957), 74.

72. Girard, "To Entrap," 100.

73. Karoline Szatek, "*The Merchant of Venice* and the Politics of Commerce," in *The Merchant of Venice: New Critical Essays,* ed. John W. Mahon and Ellen Macleod Mahon (New York: Routledge, 2002), 326–27.

74. Mauss, *Gift,* 69.

Notes to Chapter Two

1. Lewalski, "Biblical Allusion," 341; Frank Kermode, "The Mature Comedies," in *Early Shakespeare,* ed. John Russell Brown (New York: Schocken Books, 1961), 221. Lawrence Danson and Roland Frye are also ascribed this view in Crocker, "*Merchant,*" 82, 95;

2. Cunningham and Slimp, "Less into the Greater," 251; Short, "Shylock Is Content," 210–11.

3. Brown, Introduction, xxxiv; Horst Meller, "A Pound of Flesh and the Economics of Christian Grace: Shakespeare's *Merchant of Venice,*" in *Essays on Shakespeare in Honour of A. A. Ansari,* ed. T. R. Sharma (Meerut, India: Shalabh Book House, 1986), 152.

4. René E. Fortin, "Launcelot and the Uses of Allegory in *The Merchant of Venice,*" *Studies in English Literature* 14 (1974): 260; Crocker, "*Merchant,*" 97.

5. Meller, "Pound of Flesh," 165.

6. Steven R. Mentz, "The Fiend Gives Friendly Counsel: Lancelot Gobbo and Polyglot Economics in *The Merchant of Venice,*" in *Money*

and the Age of Shakespeare: Essays in New Economic Criticism, ed. Linda Woodbridge (New York: Palgrave Macmillan, 2003), 182.

7. Fortin, "Launcelot," 261.

8. Cox, "Neither Gentile," 372.

9. Berger, "Marriage and Mercifixion," 161.

10. Lars Engle, "'Thrift Is Blessing': Exchange and Explanation in *The Merchant of Venice*," *Shakespeare Quarterly* 37, no. 1 (1986): 21.

11. Stephen Marx, *Shakespeare and the Bible* (Oxford: Oxford University Press, 2000), 120.

12. Harold Ford considers the play "a powerful indictment of Christless Christianity"; Crocker, "*Merchant*," 81.

13. Emmanuel Levinas, "Ideology and Idealism," in *The Levinas Reader*, ed. Seán Hand (Oxford: Blackwell, 1989), 247.

14. Levinas, *Entre Nous*, 115.

15. Baker, "Other Capital," 28.

16. René Girard and James G. Williams, *The Girard Reader* (New York: Crossroad, 1996), 273.

17. Kermode, "Mature Comedies," 221.

18. Richard Marius, *Martin Luther: The Christian Between God and Death* (Cambridge, MA: Belknap Press of Harvard University Press, 1999), 247.

19. Tyndale, *Tyndale's New Testament*, 207–08n.

20. John King, "John Foxe and Tudor Humanism," in *Reassessing Tudor Humanism*, ed. Jonathan Woolfson (New York: Palgrave Macmillan, 2002), 178.

21. John Craig, "Erasmus' *Paraphrases* in English Parishes, 1547–1666," in *Holy Scripture Speaks: The Production and Reception of Erasmus' Paraphrases on the New Testament*, ed. Mark Vessey and Hilmar M. Pabel (Toronto: University of Toronto Press, 2002), 335.

22. MacCulloch, *Reformation*, 109–13.

23. McGrath, *Luther's Theology*, 114.

24. Tyndale, *Tyndale's New Testament*, 207.

25. Matthew 6:12 (Geneva). In quite a different context, Ricoeur notes that this is the only use of the term "debt" in the Greek New Testament. His own emphasis is on remission. *The Symbolism of Evil*, trans. Emerson Buchanan (Boston: Beacon Press, 1969), 276.

26. Lewalski, "Biblical Allusion," 338.

27. Tyndale, *Tyndale's New Testament*, 218.

28. Quoted in Lewalski, "Biblical Allusion," 338.

29. Tyndale, *Tyndale's New Testament*, 218.

30. Ibid., 215.

31. Desiderius Erasmus, *The Seconde Tome or Volume of the Paraphrase of Erasmus Vpon the Newe Testamente*, trans. Miles Coverdale and John Olde (London: Edwarde Whitchurche, 1549), sig. A5r, sig. B1v.

32. Col. 3:11 (Geneva).

33. Erasmus, sig. bb.6v; Gal. 3:28.

34. Zaslavky, "'Which Is the Merchant?,'" 185–86.

35. Erasmus, *Second Tome*, c.iii. *The Seconde Tome* is listed twice in *Early English Books Online*, with the same date and publisher but different page numbering. Only the copies held by Harvard University and the Huntington Library include this "Argument."

36. Marius, *Martin Luther*, 372–73, 377.

37. Thomas H. Luxon, "A Second Daniel: The Jew and the 'True Jew' in *The Merchant of Venice*," *Early Modern Literary Studies: A Journal of Sixteenth and Seventeenth Century English Literature* 4, no. 3 (1999): para. 7, para. 33.

38. Cunningham and Slimp, "Less into the Greater," 228.

39. Fujimura, "Mode and Structure," 506.

40. Luxon, "Second Daniel," para. 3.

41. Cox, "Neither Gentile," 379.

42. Marx, *Shakespeare and the Bible*, 118.

43. Stephen A. Cohen, "'The Quality of Mercy': Law, Equity and Ideology in *The Merchant of Venice*," *Mosaic* 27, no. 4 (1994): 36.

44. William Chester Jordan, "Approaches to the Court Scene in the Bond Story: Equity and Mercy or Reason and Nature," *Shakespeare Quarterly* 33, no. 1 (1982): 49, 52–53.

45. Ibid., 58.

46. Crocker, "*Merchant of Venice*," 101.

47. Short, "Shylock Is Content," 210, 199, 210–11.

48. Quoted in Szatek, "*Merchant*," 335–36.

49. Lewalski, "Biblical Allusion," 341.

50. Cohen, "'Quality of Mercy,'" 44.

51. William Shakespeare, *Henry VI, Part Three*, ed. Randall Martin (Oxford: Oxford University Press, 2001), 1.1.175–89.

52. William Shakespeare, *Henry V*, ed. Gary Taylor (Oxford: Oxford University Press, 1982), 5.2.313.

53. Sigurd Burckhardt, "*The Merchant of Venice*: The Gentle Bond," *Shakespeare Quarterly* 29, no. 3 (September 1962): 260.

54. Shell, "Wether and the Ewe," 82–83.

55. Lewalski, "Biblical Allusion," 341.

56. J. Madison Davis and Sylvie L. F. Richards, "The Merchant and the Jew: A Fourteenth-Century French Analogue to *The Merchant of Venice*," *Shakespeare Quarterly* 36, no. 1 (1985): 63.

57. Cox, "Neither Gentile," 377; Holaday, 112–13; Burckhardt, 250.

58. Lynda E. Boose, "The Comic Contract and Portia's Golden Ring," *Shakespeare Studies* 20 (1987): 252.

59. Anne Parten, "Re-establishing Sexual Order: The Ring Episode in *The Merchant of Venice*," *Women's Studies* 9, no. 2 (1982): 147.

60. Exodus 16:15n (Geneva).

Notes to Chapter Three

1. Mauss, *Gift*, 3.
2. William Flesch, *Generosity and the Limits of Authority: Shakespeare, Herbert, Milton* (Ithaca: Cornell University Press, 1992), 148.
3. Cavell, *Disowning Knowledge*, 61.
4. Ibid.
5. S. L. Goldberg, *An Essay on "King Lear"* (Cambridge: Cambridge University Press, 1974), 105, 106.
6. Dollimore, *Radical Tragedy*, 197.
7. Douglas, "No Free Gifts," viii–ix.
8. Dollimore, *Radical Tragedy*, 194.
9. Leonard Tennenhouse, *Power on Display: The Politics of Shakespeare's Genres* (New York: Methuen, 1986), 2.
10. Stephanie Chamberlain, "'She Is Herself a Dowry': *King Lear* and the Problem of Female Entitlement in Early Modern England," in *Domestic Arrangements in Early Modern England*, ed. Kari Boyd McBride (Pittsburgh: Duquesne University Press, 2002), 183.
11. William O. Scott, "Contracts of Love and Affection: Lear, Old Age, and Kingship," *Shakespeare Survey: An Annual Survey of Shakespeare Studies and Production* 55 (2002): 39–40.
12. G. R. Hibbard, "*King Lear*: A Retrospect, 1939–79," *Shakespeare Survey: An Annual Survey of Shakespeare Studies and Production* 33 (1980): 3.
13. Lionel Basney, "Enacting the Bonds of Love in *King Lear*," in *Literature and the Renewal of the Public Sphere*, ed. Susan VanZanten Gallagher and M. D. Walhout (Basingstoke, Eng.: St. Martin's Press, 2000), 14.
14. Emmanuel Levinas, "Philosophy and the Idea of the Infinite," in *To the Other: An Introduction to the Philosophy of Emmanuel Levinas*, ed. Adriaan Peperzak (West Lafayette: Purdue University Press, 1993), 96.
15. Sean Lawrence, "'Gods that We Adore': The Divine in *King Lear*," *Renascence: Essays on Values in Literature* 56, no. 3 (Spring 2004): 143–59.
16. Mauss, *Gift*, 17.
17. Frederick Turner argues against the claim that economic thought alienates man from God, but pays more attention to Lear's denial of creation than to his denial of Grace. *Shakespeare's Twenty-First Century Economics: The Morality of Love and Money* (New York: Oxford University Press, 1999), 35
18. Paula Blank, "Shakespeare's Equalities: Checking the Math of *King Lear*," *Exemplaria: A Journal of Theory in Medieval and Renaissance Studies* 15, no. 2 (Fall 2003): 482.
19. Levinas, *Totality and Infinity*, 298.

20. Chamberlain, "'She Is Herself a Dowry,'" 183.

21. Blank, "Shakespeare's Equalities," 483.

22. Harry Berger Jr., *Making Trifles of Terrors: Redistributing Complicities in Shakespeare*, ed. Peter Erickson (Stanford: Stanford University Press, 1997), 57.

23. Charles Spinosa, "'The Name and All Th'Addition': *King Lear*'s Opening Scene and the Common Law Use," *Shakespeare Studies* 23 (1995): 159–60.

24. *Oxford English Dictionary (OED) Online*, s.v. "account," sb. II; the first recorded use is from 1300.

25. Nicholas Visser, "Shakespeare and Hanekom, *King Lear* and Land," *Textual Practice* 11, no. 1 (Spring 1997): 28.

26. Spinosa, "'Name,'" 160.

27. Berger, *Trifles of Terrors*, 57.

28. Grigori Kozintsev, *"King Lear": The Space of Tragedy: The Diary of a Film Director*, trans. Mary Mackintosh (Berkeley: University of California Press, 1977), 35.

29. Scott, "Contracts," 42.

30. *The True Chronicle History of King Leir, and His Three Daughters, Gonorill, Ragan, and Cordella* (London: Simon Stafford for John Wright, 1605), TLN 2089–90. Brian Vickers, "Thomas Kyd, Secret Sharer," *Times Literary Supplement*, April 18, 2008, 13, argues that this play was written by Thomas Kyd.

31. Scott, "Contracts," 39.

32. Berger, *Trifles of Terrors*, 30.

33. Basney, "Enacting the Bonds," 19.

34. Dan Brayton, "Angling in the Lake of Darkness: Possession, Dispossession, and the Politics of Discovery in *King Lear*," *ELH* 70, no. 2 (Summer 2003): 407.

35. Peter Holbrook, "The Left and *King Lear*," *Textual Practice* 14, no. 2 (Summer 2000): 346.

36. Cavell, *Disowning Knowledge*, 60, 62.

37. Berger, *Trifles of Terrors*, 41.

38. The quarto text reads "More richer."

39. Cavell, *Disowning Knowledge*, 65.

40. Spinosa, "'Name,'" 165.

41. Levinas, *Time and the Other*, 91.

42. It should be noted that this comment appears in the context of Tolstoy's famous essay characterizing admiration for Shakespeare as a popular hysteria, akin to "the belief in witches, in the utility of torture for the discovery of truth, the search for the elixir of life, for the philosopher's stone, and the passion for tulips valued at several thousand guilders a bulb, which overran Holland." Leo Tolstóy, "Shakespeare and the Drama," in *Recollections and Essays*, trans. Aylmer Maude (London: Oxford University Press, 1937), 336, 366.

43. Berger, *Trifles of Terrors*, 55.

44. Michel de Montaigne, *The Essayes or, Morall, Politike, and Militarie Discovrses of Lord Michael De Montaigne*, 3rd ed., trans. by John Florio (London: M. Flesher, 1632), 90.

45. Berger, *Trifles of Terrors*, 55.

46. These words do not appear in the folio.

47. Berger, *Trifles of Terrors*, 59.

48. Ibid., 34.

49. Cherrell Guilfoyle, "The Redemption of King Lear," *Comparative Drama* 23, no. 1 (Spring 1989): 60.

50. William Shakespeare, *Hamlet*, ed. G. R. Hibbard (Oxford: Oxford University Press, 1994), 4.5.148.

51. Marlowe, *Faustus*, 5.2.71.

52. Guilfoyle, "Redemption," 60.

53. Ben Ross Schneider Jr., "*King Lear* in Its Own Time: The Difference that Death Makes," *Early Modern Literary Studies* 1, no. 1 (1995): para. 27.

54. Blank, "Shakespeare's Equalities," 501.

55. Holbrook, "Left," 357.

56. Richard Strier, "Faithful Servants: Shakespeare's Praise of Disobedience," in *The Historical Renaissance: New Essays on Tudor and Stuart Literature and Culture*, ed. Heather Dubrow and Richard Strier (Chicago: University of Chicago Press, 1988), 119.

57. In fairness, it should be pointed out that the question mark is found in the folio and conflated texts but not in the first two quartos.

58. Basney, "Enacting the Bonds," 23.

59. Dollimore, *Radical Tragedy*, 193.

60. Strier, "Faithful Servants," 104, 118.

61. Basney, "Enacting the Bonds," 22.

62. Turner, *Shakespeare's Twenty-First Century Economics*, 46.

63. Dollimore, *Radical Tragedy*, 191.

64. In the folio text, these words are placed in brackets and therefore seem to refer to Lear and Cordelia. In the quarto text, on the other hand, they are not placed in brackets and would indicate their interlocutors, perhaps fellow prisoners.

65. I have written elsewhere on "The Difficulty of Dying in *King Lear*," *English Studies in Canada* 31, no. 4 (December 2005): 35–52.

66. Emmanuel Levinas, "God and Philosophy," in *The Levinas Reader*, ed. Seán Hand (Oxford: Blackwell, 1989), 180.

Notes to Chapter Four

1. Graham Midgley, "*The Merchant of Venice*: A Reconsideration," *Essays in Criticism: A Quarterly Journal of Literary Criticism* 10, no. 2 (1960): 126.

2. Alan Sinfield, "How to Read *The Merchant of Venice* Without Being Heterosexist," in *Shakespeare, Feminism and Gender,* ed. Kate Chedgzoy (Basingstoke: Palgrave, 2001), 129, 126, 121, 117.

3. Lewis, *Particular Saints,* 57.

4. Sinfield, "How to Read," 126.

5. Alan Bray, "Homosexuality and the Signs of Male Friendship in Elizabethan England," *History Workshop* 29 (1990); Montaigne, *Essayes,* 90.

6. Bray, "Homosexuality," 3, 4.

7. Montaigne, *Essayes,* 93. John D. Cox discusses *The Merchant of Venice* in an argument to the effect that Shakespeare shows suspicion toward Stoic ideals of friendship ultimately derived from Aristotle, but by way of Cicero. "Shakespeare and the Ethics of Friendship," *Religion and Literature* 40, no. 3 (Aut. 2008): 1–29.

8. "Oh my friends, there is no friend!"; Michel de Montaigne, *Essais,* ed. Maurice Rat (Paris: Garnier frères, 1971), 206.

9. Jacques Derrida, "The Politics of Friendship," *Journal of Philosophy* 85, no. 11 (November 1988): 635–36.

10. Derrida, "Politics of Friendship," 633–34, 644n.

11. Derrida, *Adieu,* 8.

12. Derrida, "Politics of Friendship," 641–42.

13. Montaigne, *Essayes,* 91. "En l'amitié, il n'y a affaire ny commerce que d'elle mesme"; Montaigne, *Essais,* 201.

14. Montaigne, *Essayes,* 91.

15. Ibid., 93.

16. Ibid., 92.

17. Alberto Manguel, *The City of Words,* Massey Lectures Series (Toronto: House of Anansi Press, 2007), 52–53. Manguel does not cite a translation of Montaigne, but he easily could have made his own. I have substituted Florio's.

18. Montaigne, *Essayes,* 94.

19. Ricoeur, "Asserting Personal Capacities."

20. Ricoeur, *Course of Recognition,* 263.

21. It should nevertheless be noted that relationships between schoolmasters and their charges were not unknown in Elizabethan England. They seem even to have been tolerated, because both Nicholas Udall (also the translator of the first volume of Erasmus's *Paraphrases*) and one Mr. Cooke of Great Tey in Essex continued their careers despite accusations and even trials. Marie Rutkoski, "Breeching the Boy in Marlowe's *Edward II,*" *SEL: Studies in English Literature, 1500–1900* 46, no. 2 (Spring 2006): 295.

22. Montaigne, *Essayes,* 90.

23. Levinas, "Trace," 351.

24. Montaigne, *Essayes,* 91.

25. Levinas, "Trace," 353, 349.

26. Montaigne, *Essayes*, 94, 90.

27. Schneider, "Granville's *Jew of Venice*," 118.

28. Murray J. Levith, "Shakespeare's *Merchant* and Marlowe's Other Play," in *The Merchant of Venice: New Critical Essays*, ed. John W. Mahon and Ellen Macleod Mahon (New York: Routledge, 2002), 97.

29. William Shakespeare, *Measure for Measure*, ed. N. W. Bawcutt (Oxford: Oxford University Press, 1991), 5.1.525–26.

30. Levinas, *Otherwise than Being*, 121.

31. Brown, "Introduction," liv.

32. Lewis, *Particular Saints*, 47.

33. Ibid., 83.

34. Girard, "To Entrap," 102, 106–07.

35. Girard and Williams, *Girard Reader*, 272.

36. Levinas, *Otherwise than Being*, 120.

37. Girard, "To Entrap," 114.

38. Paul Whitfield White, "'Reforming Mysteries' End': A New Look At Protestant Intervention in English Provincial Drama," *Journal of Medieval and Early Modern Studies* 29 (1999): 130.

39. Jordan, "Approaches," 53.

40. Traver, "Four Daughters," 76.

41. Lewis, *Particular Saints*, 30–31, 21, 47.

42. Lewalski, "Biblical Allusion," 334.

43. Cf. Matt. 27.11, Mark 15.2, Luke 23.3.

44. R. Chris Hassel, "Frustrated Communion in *The Merchant of Venice*," *Cithara: Essays in the Judaeo-Christian Tradition* 13, no. 2 (1974): 23, 25.

45. Engle, "Thrift Is Blessing," 24.

46. Montaigne, *Essayes*, 94, 91.

47. Berry, *Shakespeare's Comedies*, 127.

48. Montaigne, *Essayes*, 94.

49. Mark Netzloff, "The Lead Casket: Capital, Mercantilism, and *The Merchant of Venice*," in *Money and the Age of Shakespeare: Essays in New Economic Criticism*, ed. Linda Woodbridge (New York: Palgrave Macmillan, 2003), 162–63; *Oxford English Dictionary Online*, s. v. "rack, vl. 2a."

50. Fujimura, "Mode and Structure," 503.

51. Lewis, *Particular Saints*, 19.

52. Shell, "Wether and the Ewe," 84.

53. Szatek, "*Merchant of Venice*," 384.

54. Engle, "Thrift Is Blessing," 37.

55. Barton, Introduction, 253.

56. Short, "Shylock Is Content," 204.

57. Engle, "Thrift Is Blessing," 34. The exclamation mark is present in both the quarto and folio texts but not in the Oxford edition I am using.

58. Ricoeur, *Course of Recognition,* 160.
59. Ibid., 161, citing Levinas, *Otherwise than Being,* 190n35 and Levinas, *Totality and Infinity,* 64.
60. Levinas, *Otherwise than Being,* 157, 161.
61. Levinas, *Entre Nous,* 195, 107.
62. Ibid., 165.

Notes to Chapter Five

1. Louis Ule, *A Concordance to the Works of Christopher Marlowe,* The Elizabethan Concordance Series (New York: Olms, 1979), s.v. "friend, friends, friendly."
2. Christopher Marlowe, *Edward the Second,* ed. Martin Wiggins and Robert Lindsey, New Mermaids (New York: W. W. Norton, 1997), 1.2.
3. Lawrence Normand, "'What Passions Call You These?': *Edward II* and James VI," in *Christopher Marlowe and English Renaissance Culture,* ed. Darryll Grantley and Peter Roberts (Hants, Eng.: Scolar, 1996), 179.
4. Rutkoski, "Breeching," 286–87.
5. Bray, "Homosexuality and Signs," 101.
6. Levinas, *Ethics and Infinity,* 79, 89–90.
7. Levinas, *Otherwise than Being,* 157, 158–59.
8. Emmanuel Levinas, *Existence and Existents,* trans. Alphonso Lingis (The Hague: Martinus Nijhoff, 1978), 98.
9. Levinas, *Time and the Other,* 85, 86.
10. Stella Sandford, "Levinas, Feminism and the Feminine," in *The Cambridge Companion to Levinas,* ed. Simon Critchley and Robert Bernasconi (Cambridge: Cambridge University Press, 2002), 142–43.
11. Levinas, *Totality and Infinity,* 266.
12. Bray, "Homosexuality and the Signs," 7, 1.
13. Claude J. Summers, "Sex, Politics, and Self-Realization in *Edward II,*" in *"A Poet and a Filthy Play-Maker": New Essays on Christopher Marlowe,* ed. Kenneth Friedenreich, Roma Gill, and Constance B. Kuriyama (New York: AMS, 1988), 225.
14. Purvis E. Boyette, "Wanton Humour and Wanton Poets: Homosexuality in Marlowe's *Edward II,*" *Tulane Studies in English* 22 (1977): 37–38.
15. J. A. Nicklin, "Marlowe's 'Gaveston,'" *Free Review* 5 (December 1895): 324.
16. James Voss, "*Edward II*: Marlowe's Historical Tragedy," *English Studies: A Journal of English Language and Literature* 63, no. 6 (December 1982): 520. A new relevance was recently given this

passage in Christopher Wessman, "Marlowe's *Edward II* as 'Actaeonesque History,'" *Connotations: A Journal for Critical Debate* 9, no. 1 (2000): 19–22.

17. The *Oxford English Dictionary* witnesses the currency of both the meaning of "peer" as a nobleman (the fourth noun definition) and as "a companion, a fellow, a mate" (the third noun definition).

18. Riggs, *World*, 71.

19. Sharon Tyler, "Bedfellows Make Strange Politics: Christopher Marlowe's *Edward II*," in *Drama, Sex and Politics*, ed. James Redmond (Cambridge: Cambridge University Press, 1985), 63–64.

20. Voss, "*Edward II*," 527.

21. Ibid.

22. Curtis Perry, "The Politics of Access and Representations of the Sodomite King in Early Modern England," *Renaissance Quarterly* 53, no. 4 (Winter 2000): 1060.

23. Joan Parks, "History, Tragedy, and Truth in Christopher Marlowe's *Edward II*," *SEL: Studies in English Literature, 1500–1900* 39, no. 2 (Spring 1999): 283; *Edward II* 23.46.

24. Clifford Leech, "Marlowe's *Edward II*: Power and Suffering," *Critical Quarterly* 1 (1959): 195.

25. Boyette, "Wanton Humour," 35.

26. David Stymeist, "Status, Sodomy, and the Theater in Marlowe's *Edward II*," *SEL: Studies in English Literature, 1500–1900* 44, no. 2 (Spring 2004): 239.

27. Stephen Guy-Bray, "Homophobia and the Depoliticizing of *Edward II*," *English Studies in Canada* 17, no. 2 (June 1991): 131.

28. Ian McAdam, "*Edward II* and the Illusion of Integrity," *Studies in Philology* 92, no. 2 (Spring 1995): 204.

29. Scott Giantvalley, "Barnfield, Brayton, and Marlowe: Homoeroticism and Homosexuality in Elizabethan Literature," *Pacific Coast Philology* 16, no. 2 (1981): 21.

30. Stymeist, "Status, Sodomy," 238.

31. Guy-Bray, "Homophobia," 132.

32. Ibid., 131.

33. Wessman, "Marlowe's *Edward II*," 8.

34. Marcie Bianco, "To Sodomize a Nation: *Edward II*, Ireland, and the Threat of Penetration," *Early Modern Literary Studies: A Journal of Sixteenth- and Seventeenth-Century English Literature* Special Issue 16 (2007): para. 1.

35. Siobhan Keenan, "Reading Christopher Marlowe's *Edward II*: The Example of John Newdigate in 1601," *Notes and Queries* 53 (251), no. 4 (2006): 457.

36. Belsey, "Love in Venice," 88.

37. *Faustus*, 1.3.77–80.

38. Jon Surgal, "The Rebel and the Red-Hot Spit: Marlowe's *Edward II* as Anal-Sadistic Prototype," *American Imago: Studies in Psychoanalysis and Culture* 61, no. 2 (Summer 2004): 178.

39. Stymeist, "Status, Sodomy," 242–43; Leech, "Marlowe's *Edward II,*" 192–93; Surgal, "The Rebel," 177–78.

40. Parks, "History, Tragedy," 288.

41. Voss, "*Edward II,*" 517.

42. Jennifer Brady, "Fear and Loathing in Marlowe's *Edward II,*" in *Sexuality and Politics in Renaissance Drama,* ed. Carole Levin and Karen Robertson (Lewiston, NY: Mellen, 1991), 186.

43. McAdam, "*Edward II* and the Illusion," 213.

44. Boyette, "Wanton Humour," 41; Summers, "Sex, Politics," 236–37.

45. Levinas, *Time and the Other,* 86.

46. Normand, "What Passions," 189.

47. Eugene Waith, "*Edward II*: The Shadow of Action," *Tulane Drama Review* 8, no. 4 (Summer 1964): 59–74.

Notes to Chapter Six

An earlier version of this essay appeared in *Through a Glass Darkly: Suffering, the Sacred, and the Sublime in Literature and Theory,* ed. Holly Faith Nelson, Lynn R. Szabo and Jens Zimmermann, 57–69 (Waterloo, ON: Wilfrid Laurier University Press, 2010). I am grateful to Wilfrid Laurier University Press for permission to reproduce it here.

1. Eugene Waith, Introduction to *Titus Andronicus* (Oxford: Oxford University Press, 1984), 1. Waith confuses Thomas Ravenscroft, the composer, with Edward Ravenscroft, the playwright. I am grateful to Robert Eggleston for drawing this to my attention.

2. Brian Vickers, *Shakespeare, Co-Author: A Historical Study of Five Collaborative Plays* (New York: Oxford University Press, 2002), 152.

3. S. Clark Hulse, "Wresting the Alphabet: Oratory and Action in *Titus Andronicus,*" *Criticism* 21, no. 2 (Spring 1979): 106.

4. Gillian Murray Kendall, "'Lend Me Thy Hand': Metaphor and Mayhem in *Titus Andronicus,*" *Shakespeare Quarterly* 40, no. 3 (Fall 1989): 309, 314.

5. Levinas, *Totality and Infinity,* 216.

6. Bernasconi, "Logic of the Gift," 261.

7. Levinas, *Otherwise than Being,* 5.

8. Levinas, "God and Philosophy," 183.

9. Bernice Harris, "Sexuality as a Signifier for Power Relations: Using Lavinia, of Shakespeare's *Titus Andronicus,*" *Criticism: A Quarterly for Literature and the Arts* 38, no. 3 (Summer 1996): 385.

10. Emily Detmer-Goebel, "The Need for Lavinia's Voice: *Titus Andronicus* and the Telling of Rape," *Shakespeare Studies* 29 (2001): 77–78; Carolyn D. Williams, "'Silence, Like a Lucrece Knife': Shakespeare and the Meanings of Rape," *Yearbook in English Studies* 23 (1993): 99–100.

11. Harris, "Sexuality," 389.

12. Vickers, *Shakespeare, Co-Author*, 243.

13. Linda Woodbridge, Introduction to *Money and the Age of Shakespeare: Essays in New Economic Criticism*, ed. Linda Woodbridge (New York: Palgrave Macmillan, 2003), 8.

14. Sara Eaton, "A Woman of Letters: Lavinia in *Titus Andronicus*," in *Shakespearean Tragedy and Gender*, ed. Shirley Nelson Garner and Madelon Sprengnether (Bloomington: Indiana University Press, 1996), 64.

15. Alexander Leggatt, *Shakespeare's Tragedies: Violation and Identity* (New York: Cambridge University Press, 2005), 18.

16. Karen Cunningham, "'Scars Can Witness': Trials by Ordeal and Lavinia's Body in *Titus Andronicus*," in *Women and Violence in Literature: An Essay Collection*, ed. Katherine Anne Ackley (New York: Garland, 1990), 144.

17. Eaton, "Woman of Letters," 59.

18. Levinas, "Ethics as First Philosophy," 43.

19. Brian Gibbons, *Shakespeare and Multiplicity* (New York: Cambridge University Press, 1993), 55.

20. Ibid., 56.

21. Stephen Greenblatt, *Will in the World: How Shakespeare Became Shakespeare* (New York: W. W. Norton, 2004), 152.

22. Pascale Aebischer, *Shakespeare's Violated Bodies: Stage and Screen Performance* (Cambridge: Cambridge University Press, 2003), 31.

23. Leggatt, *Shakespeare's Tragedies*, 19.

24. Cunningham, "'Scars Can Witness,'" 145, 149.

25. Leggatt, *Shakespeare's Tragedies*, 21.

26. Stanley Cavell, *Must We Mean What We Say? A Book of Essays* (New York: Charles Scribner's Sons, 1969), 253.

27. Grace Starry West, "Going by the Book: Classical Allusions in Shakespeare's *Titus Andronicus*," *Studies in Philology* 79, no. 1 (1982): 67.

28. Kendall, "'Lend Me Thy Hand,'" 299.

29. Mary Laughlin Fawcett, "Arms/Words/Tears: Language and the Body in *Titus Andronicus*," *ELH* 50, no. 2 (Summer 1983): 271.

30. West, "Going by the Book," 65.

31. Fawcett, "Arms/Words/Tears," 269; West, "Going by the Book," 68.

32. Kendall, "'Lend Me Thy Hand,'" 300.

33. Levinas, *Otherwise than Being*, 6.

34. Leggatt, *Shakespeare's Tragedies*, 18.

35. *OED Online*, s. v., "villian, adj. 4b."

36. Waith, Introduction, 58.

37. William W. E. Slights, "The Sacrificial Crisis in *Titus Andronicus*," *University of Toronto Quarterly* 49, no. 1 (Fall 1979): 20.

38. Stephen X. Mead, "The Crisis of Ritual in *Titus Andronicus*," *Exemplaria: A Journal of Theory in Medieval and Renaissance Studies* 6, no. 2 (1994): 463.

39. Kendall, "'Lend Me Thy Hand,'" 304.

40. Detmer-Goebel, "The Need for Lavinia's Voice," 87.

41. Ovid, *Shakespeare's Ovid*, ed. W. H. D. Rouse, trans. Arthur Golding (New York: W. W. Norton and Company, 1966), 15.910.

42. Deborah Willis, "The Gnawing Vulture: Revenge, Trauma Theory, and *Titus Andronicus*," *Shakespeare Quarterly* 53, no. 1 (Spring 2002): 49.

43. *The Tragical History of Titus Andronicus, & c.*, in *Titus Andronicus*, ed. Eugene Waith (Oxford: Oxford University Press, 1984), 203.

44. Kendall, "'Lend Me Thy Hand,'" 314.

45. Ibid., 305n.

46. Umberto Eco, *A Theory of Semiotics*, Advances in Semiotics (Bloomington: Indiana University Press, 1976), 7.

47. Levinas, *Otherwise than Being*, 6.

Notes to Chapter Seven

1. Levinas, *Totality and Infinity*, 33.

2. William Shakespeare, *The Tempest*, ed. Stephen Orgel (Oxford: Oxford University Press, 1987), 1.2.56–57.

3. Frank Kermode, Introduction to *The Tempest*, by William Shakespeare (1954; London: Routledge, 1994), xlix; 4.1.118–23, for instance.

4. Meredith Anne Skura, "Discourse and the Individual: The Case of Colonialism in *The Tempest*," *Shakespeare Quarterly* 40, no. 1 (Spring 1989): 60.

5. James Black, "The Latter End of Prospero's Commonwealth," *Shakespeare Survey* 44 (1991): 33.

6. A few possibilities are listed in Leslie Fiedler, *The Stranger in Shakespeare* (New York: Stein and Day, 1972), 251.

7. David Evett, "Luther, Cranmer, Service, and Shakespeare," in *Centered on the Word: Literature, Scripture, and the Tudor-Stuart Middle Way*, ed. Daniel W. Doerksen and Christopher Hodgkins (Newark: University of Delaware Press, 2004), 103.

8. William M. Hamlin, "Men of Inde: Renaissance Ethnography and *The Tempest*," *Shakespeare Studies* 22 (1994): 36.

9. Lewis, *Particular Saints*, 157.

10. Harry Berger, "Miraculous Harp: A Reading of Shakespeare's *Tempest*," *Shakespeare Studies* 5 (1969): 270.

11. John S. Hunt, "Prospero's Empty Grasp," *Shakespeare Studies* 22 (1994): 289.

12. Kermode, Introduction, xxiv; Walter Clyde Curry, *Shakespeare's Philosophical Patterns* (Baton Rouge: Louisiana State University Press, 1959), 166–69; Jane Kingsley-Smith, *Shakespeare's Drama of Exile* (Houndmills: Palgrave Macmillan, 2004), 228; Laura Kolb, "Playing with Demons: Interrogating the Supernatural in Jacobean Drama," *Forum for Modern Language Studies* 43, no. 4 (2007): 346, 343.

13. Karol Berger, "Prospero's Art," *Shakespeare Studies* 10 (1977): 211.

14. Stephen Orgel, "Prospero's Wife," *Representations* 8 (Fall 1984): 10.

15. Hunt, "Prospero's Empty Grasp," 294.

16. Curry, *Shakespeare's Philosophical Patterns*, 182.

17. *Faustus*, 2.1.60.

18. David Lucking, "Our Devils Now Are Ended: A Comparative Analysis of *The Tempest* and *Doctor Faustus*," *Dalhousie Review* 80, no. 2 (Summer 2000): 160–61.

19. Peter Lindenbaum, "Prospero's Anger," *Massachusetts Review* 25, no. 1 (March 1984): 162.

20. Hunt, "Prospero's Empty Grasp," 299.

21. Berger, "Miraculous Harp," 268.

22. William Shakespeare, *A Midsummer Night's Dream*, ed. Peter Holland, the Oxford Shakespeare (Oxford: Oxford University Press, 1994), 1.2.24–25.

23. *Edward II*, 20.60–85 and stage direction.

24. John D. Cox, "Recovering Something Christian about *The Tempest*," *Christianity and Literature* 50, no. 1 (Fall 2000): 37.

25. Skura, "Discourse and the Individual," 44.

26. Hunt, "Prospero's Empty Grasp," 277.

27. Orgel, "Prospero's Wife," 12.

28. Kermode, Introduction, liv.

29. Ben Ross Schneider, Jr., "'Are We Being Historical Yet?' Colonialist Interpretations of Shakepeare's *Tempest*," *Shakespeare Studies* 23 (1995): 122.

30. Barbara Howard Traister, "Prospero: Master of Self-Knowledge," in *William Shakespeare's The Tempest*, ed. Harold Bloom (New York: Chelsea House, 1988), 125.

31. Robin Headlam-Wells, "An Orpheus for a Hercules: Virtue Redefined in *The Tempest*," in *Neo-Historicism: Studies in Renaissance Literature, History and Politics*, ed. Robin Headlam-Wells, Glenn Burgess and Rowland Wymer (Cambridge: D. S. Brewer, 2000), 251.

32. Schneider, "Historical," 124.

33. Orgel, "Prospero's Wife," 10.

34. Lewis, *Particular Saints,* 155.

35. Kermode, Introduction, xlix.

36. Goran Stanivukovic, *"The Tempest* and the Discontents of Humanism," *Philological Quarterly* 85, no. 1–2 (2006): 100–01.

37. Hunt, "Prospero's Empty Grasp," 238.

38. Stanivukovic, *"The Tempest* and the Discontents," 104.

39. Berger, "Prospero's Art," 220.

40. Kingsley-Smith, *Shakespeare's Drama,* 225.

41. Cox, "Recovering Something," 37.

42. A. Lynne Magnusson, "Interruption in *The Tempest,"* *Shakespeare Quarterly* 37, no. 1 (Spring 1986): 62.

43. Hunt, "Prospero's Empty Grasp," 304.

44. Fiedler, *Stranger,* 231.

45. Thomas More, *Utopia,* ed. David Harris Sacks, trans. Ralph Robynson (Boston: Bedford/St. Martin's, 1999), 125.

46. *OED Online,* s.v. "butt," n2.

47. Black, "Latter End," 35.

48. Traister, "Prospero: Master," 123.

49. Magnusson, "Interruption," 65; Robert Egan, "This Rough Magic: Perspectives of Art and Morality in *The Tempest,"* *Shakespeare Quarterly* 23, no. 2 (1972): 178; Hunt, "Prospero's Empty Grasp," 301; Black, "Latter End," 33.

50. Magnusson, "Interruption," 64.

51. Berger, "Miraculous Harp," 268.

52. Hunt, "Prospero's Empty Grasp," 297.

53. Orgel, "Prospero's Wife," 4.

54. Melissa E. Sanchez, "Seduction and Service in *The Tempest,"* *Studies in Philology* 105, no. 1 (Winter 2008): 66.

55. Black, "Latter End," 33.

56. Ibid., 32.

57. Orgel, "Prospero's Wife," 9.

58. Traister, "Prospero: Master," 126.

59. Berger, "Miraculous Harp," 273.

60. Hunt, "Prospero's Empty Grasp," 294.

61. Black, "Latter End," 38.

62. Schneider, "Historical," 136.

63. Hunt, "Prospero's Empty Grasp," 308.

64. Hunt, "Prospero's Empty Grasp," 308; Berger, "Prospero's Art," 237; Fiedler, *Stranger,* 252; *Tempest,* 5.1.337–38n.

65. "An Order for Morning Prayer Dayly Throughout the Yeare," in *The First and Second Prayer Books of Edward VI* (London: J. M. Dent and Sons, 1960), 349.

Notes to Conclusion

1. James S. Shapiro, *A Year in the Life of William Shakespeare, 1599* (New York: Harper Collins, 2005), 33.

2. William Shakespeare, *The Second Part of Henry the Fourth*, ed. Matthias A. Shaaber (Philadelphia: J. B. Lippincott and Company, 1940), epilogue, 14n.

3. William Shakespeare, *The Second Part of King Henry IV*, ed. A. R. Humphreys (London: Methuen, 1966), note to epilogue.

4. William Shakespeare, *Henry IV, Part 2*, ed. René Weis (New York: Clarendon Press, 1998), 14.

5. William Shakespeare, *The Second Part of King Henry IV*, ed. Giorgio Melchiori (Cambridge: Cambridge University Press, 1989), note to epilogue.

6. Shapiro, *Year*, 33.

7. *Henry IV, Part 2* (ed. Weis), epilogue.26.

8. Frank Kermode, *The Age of Shakespeare* (London: Weidenfeld and Nicolson, 2004), 99.

9. *Henry IV, Part 2* (ed. Weis), epilogue, 3–5.

10. Ibid., epilogue, 7, 9–15.

11. Shapiro, *Year*, 35, 14.

12. *Henry IV, Part 2* (ed. Weis), epilogue, 15–16.

13. Greenblatt, *Negotiations*, 7.

14. Emmanuel Levinas, *God, Death and Time*, trans. Bettina Bergo (Stanford: Stanford University Press, 2000), 12.

15. Bernard-Henri Levy and Adam Gopnick, "Bernard-Henri Levy on America, France, and the Jews, At the 92nd Street Y" (New York: 92nd Street Y, 2006). Audio podcast.

16. Jean-Luc Marion, *God Without Being: "Hors Texte,"* trans. Thomas A. Carlson (Chicago: University of Chicago Press, 1991), 29–33 uses this term, though with specific reference to Being.

17. William Shakespeare, *The Tragedy of Coriolanus*, ed. R. B. Parker (Oxford: Oxford University Press, 1994), 5.2.24.

18. Peperzak, "Giving," 163.

19. Levinas, *Totality and Infinity*, 197.

BIBLIOGRAPHY

Aebischer, Pascale. *Shakespeare's Violated Bodies: Stage and Screen Performance.* Cambridge: Cambridge University Press, 2003.

Andrew, Edward. *Shylock's Rights: A Grammar of Lockian Claims.* Toronto: University of Toronto Press, 1988.

Arnsperger, Christian. "Gift-Giving Practice and Noncontextual Habitus: How (Not) to Be Fooled by Mauss." In Vandevelde, *Gifts and Interests,* 71–92.

———. "Methodological Altruism as an Alternative Foundation for Individual Optimization." *Ethical Theory and Moral Practice* 3 (2000): 115–36.

Bacon, Francis. "On Usury." In *The Works of Francis Bacon,* edited by James Spedding, Robert Leslie Ellis and Douglas Denon Heath. New edition, vol. 6. *Literary and Professional Works, vol. 1.* 473–76. London: Longmans and Company, et al., 1890.

Baker, Geoff. "Other Capital: Investment, Return, Alterity and *The Merchant of Venice.*" *Upstart Crow* 22 (2002): 21–36.

Barton, Anne. Introduction to *The Merchant of Venice.* In *The Riverside Shakespeare,* edited by G. Blakemore Evans, Harry Levin, Herschel Baker, Anne Barton, Frank Kermode, Hallett Smith and Marie Edel, 250–53. Boston: Houghton Mifflin Company, 1974.

Basney, Lionel. "Enacting the Bonds of Love in *King Lear.*" In *Literature and the Renewal of the Public Sphere,* edited by Susan VanZanten Gallagher and M. D. Walhout, 14–31. Basingstoke, England: St. Martin's Press, 2000.

Beauregard, David N. "Sidney, Aristotle, and *The Merchant of Venice*: Shakespeare's Triadic Images of Liberality and Justice." *Shakespeare Studies* 20 (1988): 33–51.

Belsey, Catherine. "Love in Venice." *Shakespeare Survey* 44 (1992): 41–53.

Berger, Harry. *Making Trifles of Terrors: Redistributing Complicities in Shakespeare.* Edited by Peter Erickson. Stanford: Stanford University Press, 1997.

———. "Marriage and Mercifixion in *The Merchant of Venice:* The Casket Scene Revisited." *Shakespeare Quarterly* 32, no. 2 (1981): 155–62.

———. "Miraculous Harp: A Reading of Shakespeare's *Tempest.*" *Shakespeare Studies* 5 (1969): 253–83.

Berger, Karol. "Prospero's Art." *Shakespeare Studies* 10 (1977): 211–39.

Berghahn, Klaus L. "Comedy without Laughter: Jewish Characters in Comedies From Shylock to Nathan." In *Laughter Unlimited: Essays on Humor, Satire, and the Comic,* edited by Reinhold Grimm and Jost Hermand, 3–27. Madison: University of Wisconsin Press, 1991.

Bernasconi, Robert. "The Logic of the Gift: Toward an Ethic of Generosity." In *The Logic of the Gift,* edited by Alan D. Schrift, 256–73. New York: Routledge, 1997.

Berry, Ralph. *Shakespeare's Comedies: Explorations in Form.* Princeton: Princeton University Press, 1972.

Bianco, Marcie. "To Sodomize a Nation: *Edward II,* Ireland, and the Threat of Penetration." *Early Modern Literary Studies: A Journal of Sixteenth- and Seventeenth-Century English Literature* Special Issue 16 (2007).

Black, James. "The Latter End of Prospero's Commonwealth." *Shakespeare Survey* 44 (1991): 29–41.

Blank, Paula. "Shakespeare's Equalities: Checking the Math of *King Lear.*" *Exemplaria: A Journal of Theory in Medieval and Renaissance Studies* 15, no. 2 (Fall 2003): 473–508.

Bodin, Jean. *On the Demon-Mania of Witches.* Renaissance and Reformation Texts in Translation, 7. Edited by Jonathan L. Pearl and Randy A. Scott. Translated by Randy A. Scott. Toronto: Centre for Reformation and Renaissance Studies, 1995.

Boose, Lynda E. "The Comic Contract and Portia's Golden Ring." *Shakespeare Studies* 20 (1987): 241–54.

Boyette, Purvis E. "Wanton Humour and Wanton Poets: Homosexuality in Marlowe's *Edward II.*" *Tulane Studies in English* 22 (1977): 33–50.

Brady, Jennifer. "Fear and Loathing in Marlowe's *Edward II*." In *Sexuality and Politics in Renaissance Drama*, edited by Carole Levin and Karen Robertson. 175–91. Lewiston, NY: Mellen, 1991.

Bray, Alan. "Homosexuality and the Signs of Male Friendship in Elizabethan England." *History Workshop* 29 (1990): 1–19.

Brayton, Dan. "Angling in the Lake of Darkness: Possession, Dispossession, and the Politics of Discovery in *King Lear*." *ELH* 70, no. 2 (Summer 2003): 399–426.

Brown, John Russell. Introduction to *The Merchant of Venice*, ix–lviii. The Arden Shakespeare. London: Methuen, 1955.

———. *Shakespeare and His Comedies*. London: Methuen, 1957.

Burckhardt, Sigurd. "*The Merchant of Venice*: The Gentle Bond." *Shakespeare Quarterly* 29, no. 3 (September 1962): 239–62.

Cavell, Stanley. *Disowning Knowledge in Six Plays of Shakespeare*. Cambridge: Cambridge University Press, 1988.

———. *Must We Mean What We Say? A Book of Essays*. New York: Charles Scribner's Sons, 1969.

Certayne Sermons Appoynted by the Quenes Maiestie, to Be Declared and Read, by All Persones, Vycars, and Curates, Euery Sondaye and Holy Daye in Theyr Churches. [London]: R. I[ugge], 1559. Early English Books Online.

Chamberlain, Stephanie. "'She Is Herself a Dowry': *King Lear* and the Problem of Female Entitlement in Early Modern England." In *Domestic Arrangements in Early Modern England*, edited by Kari Boyd McBride, 169–87. Pittsburgh: Duquesne University Press, 2002.

Cohen, Richard A. "Some Reflections on Levinas and Shakespeare." In *Levinasian Meditations: Ethics, Philosophy, and Religion*, 150–68. Pittsburgh: Duquesne University Press, 2010.

Cohen, Stephen A. "'The Quality of Mercy': Law, Equity and Ideology in *The Merchant of Venice*." *Mosaic* 27, no. 4 (1994): 35–55.

Collinson, Patrick. *The Reformation*. London: Weidenfeld and Nicolson, 2003.

Cox, Catherine S. "Neither Gentile nor Jew: Performative Subjectivity in *The Merchant of Venice*." *Exemplaria* 12, no. 2 (2000): 359–83.

Cox, John D. "Recovering Something Christian About *The Tempest*." *Christianity and Literature* 50, no. 1 (Fall 2000): 31–51.

———. "Shakespeare and the Ethics of Friendship." *Religion and Literature* 40, no. 3 (Aut. 2008): 1–29.

Craig, John. "Erasmus' *Paraphrases* in English Parishes, 1547–1666." In *Holy Scripture Speaks: The Production and Reception of Erasmus' Paraphrases on the New Testament*, edited by Mark Vessey and Hilmar M. Pabel, 313–59. Toronto: University of Toronto Press, 2002.

Crocker, Lester G. "*The Merchant of Venice* and Christian Conscience." *Diogenes* 30, no. 118 (1982): 77–102.

Cunningham, John, and Stephen Slimp. "The Less into the Greater: Emblem, Analogue and Deification in *The Merchant of Venice*." In *The Merchant of Venice: New Critical Essays*, edited by John W. Mahon and Ellen Macleod Mahon, 225–82. New York: Routledge, 2002.

Cunningham, Karen. "'Scars Can Witness': Trials by Ordeal and Lavinia's Body in *Titus Andronicus*." In *Women and Violence in Literature: An Essay Collection*, edited by Katherine Anne Ackley, 139–62. New York: Garland, 1990.

Curry, Walter Clyde. *Shakespeare's Philosophical Patterns*. Baton Rouge: Louisiana State University Press, 1959.

Davis, J. Madison, and Sylvie L. F. Richards. "The Merchant and the Jew: A Fourteenth-Century French Analogue to *The Merchant of Venice*." *Shakespeare Quarterly* 36, no. 1 (1985): 56–63.

Derrida, Jacques. *Adieu to Emmanuel Levinas*. Translated by Pascale-Anne Brault and Michael Naas. Stanford: Stanford University Press, 1999.

———. *Given Time: 1. Counterfeit Money*. Translated by Peggy Kamuf. Chicago: University of Chicago Press, 1992.

———. "The Politics of Friendship." *Journal of Philosophy* 85, no. 11 (November 1988): 632–44.

Detmer-Goebel, Emily. "The Need for Lavinia's Voice: *Titus Andronicus* and the Telling of Rape." *Shakespeare Studies* 29 (2001): 75–93.

Dollimore, Jonathan. *Radical Tragedy: Religion, Ideology and Power in the Drama of Shakespeare and His Contemporaries*. Brighton: Harvester, 1984.

Douglas, Mary. "No Free Gifts." In *The Gift: The Form and Reason for Exchange in Archaic Societies*. Edited by W. D. Halls, vii–xviii. London: Routledge, 1990.

Eaglestone, Robert. *Ethical Criticism: Reading after Levinas*. Edinburgh: Edinburgh University Press, 1997.

Eaton, Sara. "A Woman of Letters: Lavinia in *Titus Andronicus*." In *Shakespearean Tragedy and Gender*, edited by Shirley Nelson Garner and Madelon Sprengnether, 54–74. Bloomington: Indiana University Press, 1996.

Eco, Umberto. *A Theory of Semiotics*. Advances in Semiotics. Bloomington: Indiana University Press, 1976.

Egan, Gabriel. *Shakespeare and Marx*. Oxford: Oxford University Press, 2004.

Egan, Robert. "This Rough Magic: Perspectives of Art and Morality in *The Tempest*." *Shakespeare Quarterly* 23, no. 2 (1972): 171–82.

Engle, Lars. "'Thrift Is Blessing': Exchange and Explanation in *The Merchant of Venice*." *Shakespeare Quarterly* 37, no. 1 (1986): 20–37.

———. *Shakespearean Pragmatism: Market of His Time*. Chicago: University of Chicago Press, 1993.

Erasmus, Desiderius. *The Seconde Tome of the Paraphrase of Erasmus Vpon the Newe Testamente*. Translated by Miles Coverdale and John Olde. [London]: Edwarde Whitchurche, 1549.

Evett, David. "Luther, Cranmer, Service, and Shakespeare." In *Centered on the Word: Literature, Scripture, and the Tudor-Stuart Middle Way*, edited by Daniel W. Doerksen and Christopher Hodgkins, 87–109. Newark: University of Delaware Press, 2004.

Fawcett, Mary Laughlin. "Arms/Words/Tears: Language and the Body in *Titus Andronicus*." *ELH* 50, no. 2 (Summer 1983): 261–77.

Fiedler, Leslie. *The Stranger in Shakespeare*. New York: Stein and Day, 1972.

Flesch, William. *Generosity and the Limits of Authority: Shakespeare, Herbert, Milton*. Ithaca: Cornell University Press, 1992.

Fortin, René E. "Launcelot and the Uses of Allegory in *The Merchant of Venice*." *Studies in English Literature* 14 (1974): 259–70.

Fujimura, Thomas. "Mode and Structure in *The Merchant of Venice*." *PMLA* 81 (1966): 499–511.

Gallagher, Lowell. "Waiting for Gobbo." In *Spiritual Shakespeares*, edited by Ewan Fernie, 73–93. London: Routledge, 2005.

The Geneva Bible: A Facsimile of the 1560 Edition. Edited by Lloyd Eason Berry and William Whittingham. Madison: University of Wisconsin Press, 1969.

Giantvalley, Scott. "Barnfield, Brayton, and Marlowe: Homoeroticism and Homosexuality in Elizabethan Literature." *Pacific Coast Philology* 16, no. 2 (1981): 9–24.

Gibbons, Brian. *Shakespeare and Multiplicity.* New York: Cambridge University Press, 1993.

Girard, René. "'To Entrap the Wisest': A Reading of *The Merchant of Venice.*" In *Literature and Society,* edited by Edward W. Said, 100–19. Baltimore: Johns Hopkins University Press, 1980.

Girard, René, and James G. Williams. *The Girard Reader.* New York: Crossroad, 1996.

Goldberg, S. L. *An Essay on "King Lear."* Cambridge: Cambridge University Press, 1974.

Good, Graham. "The Hegemony of Theory." *University of Toronto Quarterly* 65, no. 3 (Summer 1996): 534–55.

Grant, Patrick. "The Bible and *The Merchant of Venice:* Hermeneutics, Ideology, and Displaced Persons." *English Studies in Canada* 16 (1990): 248–62.

Greenblatt, Stephen. *Hamlet in Purgatory.* Princeton: Princeton University Press, 2001.

———. *Renaissance Self-Fashioning: From More to Shakespeare.* Chicago: University of Chicago Press, 1980.

———. *Shakespearean Negotiations: The Circulation of Social Energy in Renaissance England.* Berkeley: University of California Press, 1988.

———. *Will in the World: How Shakespeare Became Shakespeare.* New York: W. W. Norton, 2004.

Guilfoyle, Cherrell. "The Redemption of King Lear." *Comparative Drama* 23, no. 1 (Spring 1989): 50–69.

Guy-Bray, Stephen. "Homophobia and the Depoliticizing of *Edward II.*" *English Studies in Canada* 17, no. 2 (June 1991): 125–33.

Hamlin, William M. "Men of Inde: Renaissance Ethnography and *The Tempest.*" *Shakespeare Studies* 22 (1994): 15–44.

Happé, Peter. "The Devil in the Interludes, 1550–1577." *Medieval English Theatre* 11, nos. 1–2 (1989): 42–56.

Harris, Bernice. "Sexuality as a Signifier for Power Relations: Using Lavinia, of Shakespeare's *Titus Andronicus.*" *Criticism: A Quarterly for Literature and the Arts* 38, no. 3 (Summer 1996): 383–406.

Hassel, R. Chris. "Frustrated Communion in *The Merchant of Venice.*" *Cithara: Essays in the Judaeo-Christian Tradition* 13, no. 2 (1974): 19–33.

Hawkes, David. *The Faust Myth: Religion and the Rise of Representation.* New York: Palgrave Macmillan, 2007.

Headlam-Wells, Robin. "An Orpheus for a Hercules: Virtue Redefined in *The Tempest.*" In *Neo- Historicism: Studies in Renaissance Literature, History and Politics*. Edited by Robin Headlam-Wells, Glenn Burgess, and Rowland Wymer, 240–62. Cambridge: D. S. Brewer, 2000.

Henze, Richard. "'Which Is the Merchant Here? And Which the Jew?'" *Criticism: A Quarterly for Literature and the Arts* 16 (1974): 287–300.

Hibbard, G. R. "*King Lear*: A Retrospect, 1939–79." *Shakespeare Survey* 33 (1980): 1–12.

Holaday, Alan. "Antonio and the Allegory of Salvation." *Shakespeare Studies* 4 (1968): 109–18.

Holbrook, Peter. "The Left and *King Lear.*" *Textual Practice* 14, no. 2 (Summer 2000): 343–62.

Hulse, S. Clark. "Wresting the Alphabet: Oratory and Action in *Titus Andronicus.*" *Criticism: A Quarterly for Literature and the Arts* 21 (1979): 106–18.

Hunt, John S. "Prospero's Empty Grasp." *Shakespeare Studies* 22 (1994): 277–313.

Hyman, Lawrence W. "The Rival Lovers in *The Merchant of Venice.*" *Shakespeare Quarterly* 21, no. 2 (1970): 109–16.

Jacobs, Alan. *A Theology of Reading: The Hermeneutics of Love.* Boulder: Westview, 2001.

James I. *Daemonologie in Forme of a Dialogue, Diuided into Three Bookes.* Edinburgh: Robert Walde-graue, 1597. Early English Books Online.

Jarvis, Simon. "The Gift in Theory." *Dionysius* 17 (December 1999): 201–22.

Jordan, William Chester. "Approaches to the Court Scene in the Bond Story: Equity and Mercy or Reason and Nature." *Shakespeare Quarterly* 33, no. 1 (1982): 49–59.

Keefer, Michael. Introduction. In Marlowe, *Doctor Faustus*, 15–58.

Keenan, Siobhan. "Reading Christopher Marlowe's *Edward II*: The Example of John Newdigate in 1601." *Notes and Queries* 53 (251), no. 4 (2006): 452–58.

Kendall, Gillian Murray. "'Lend Me Thy Hand': Metaphor and Mayhem in *Titus Andronicus.*" *Shakespeare Quarterly* 40, no. 3 (Fall 1989): 299–316.

Kermode, Frank. Introduction to *The Tempest*, by William Shakespeare, xi–xciii. 1954; London: Routledge, 1994.

———. *The Age of Shakespeare*. London: Weidenfeld and Nicolson, 2004.

———. "The Mature Comedies." In *Early Shakespeare*, edited by John Russell Brown, 211–27. New York: Schocken Books, 1961.

King, John. "John Foxe and Tudor Humanism." In *Reassessing Tudor Humanism*, edited by Jonathan Woolfson, 174–85. New York: Palgrave Macmillan, 2002.

Kingsley-Smith, Jane. *Shakespeare's Drama of Exile*. Houndmills, Hampshire: Palgrave Macmillan, 2004.

Kolb, Laura. "Playing with Demons: Interrogating the Supernatural in Jacobean Drama." *Forum for Modern Language Studies* 43, no. 4 (2007): 337–50.

Kozintsev, Grigori. *"King Lear": The Space of Tragedy: The Diary of a Film Director*. Translated by Mary Mackintosh. Berkeley: University of California Press, 1977.

Laurent, Camille Pierre. "Dog, Fiend and Christian, or Shylock's Conversion." *Cahiers Elisabethains: Late Medieval and Renaissance Studies* 26 (1984): 15–27.

Lawrence, Sean Kevin. "'As a Stranger, Bid It Welcome': Alterity and Ethics in *Hamlet* and the New Historicism." *European Journal of English Studies* 4, no. 2 (August 2000): 155–69.

———. "The Difficulty of Dying in *King Lear*." *English Studies in Canada* 31, no. 4 (December 2005): 35–52.

———. "'Gods that We Adore': The Divine in *King Lear*." *Renascence: Essays on Values in Literature* 56, no. 3 (Spring 2004): 143–59.

———. "Listening to Lavinia: Emmanuel Levinas's Saying and Said in *Titus Andronicus*." In *Through a Glass Darkly: Suffering, the Sacred, and the Sublime in Literature and Theory*, edited by Holly Faith Nelson, Lynn R. Szabo, and Jens Zimmermann, 57–69. Waterloo, ON: Wilfrid Laurier University Press, 2010.

———. "'To Give and to Receive': Performing Exchanges in *The Merchant of Venice*." In *Shakespeare and the Cultures of Performance*, edited by Paul Yachnin and Patricia Badir, 41–51. Aldershot, Eng.: Ashgate, 2008.

Leech, Clifford. "Marlowe's *Edward II*: Power and Suffering." *Critical Quarterly* 1 (1959): 181–96.

Leggatt, Alexander. *Shakespeare's Tragedies: Violation and Identity*. New York: Cambridge University Press, 2005.

Levinas, Emmanuel. "The Bad Conscience and the Inexorable." In *Of God Who Comes to Mind*, translated by Bettina Bergo, 172–77. Stanford: Stanford University Press, 1998.

———. "Diachrony and Representation." In *Time and the Other and Additional Essays*, translated and edited by Richard A. Cohen, 97–120. Pittsburgh: Duquesne University Press, 1987.

———. *Entre Nous: On Thinking-of-the-Other*. Translated by Michael B. Smith and Barbara Harshav. New York: Columbia University Press, 1998.

———. *Ethics and Infinity: Conversations with Philippe Nemo*. Translated by Richard A. Cohen. Pittsburgh: Duquesne University Press, 1985.

———. "Ethics as First Philosophy." In *The Levinas Reader*, edited by Seán Hand, 75–87. Oxford: Blackwell, 1989.

———. *Existence and Existents*. Translated by Alphonso Lingis. The Hague: Martinus Nijhoff, 1978.

———. "God and Philosophy." In *The Levinas Reader*, edited by Seán Hand, 166–89. Oxford: Blackwell, 1989.

———. *God, Death and Time*. Translated by Bettina Bergo. Stanford: Stanford University Press, 2000.

———. "Ideology and Idealism." In *The Levinas Reader*, edited by Seán Hand. 236–48. Oxford: Blackwell, 1989.

———. "Meaning and Sense." In *Emmanuel Levinas: Basic Philosophical Writings*, edited by Adriaan T. Peperzak, Simon Critchley and Robert Bernasconi, 33–64. Bloomington: Indiana University Press, 1996.

———. *Otherwise than Being or Beyond Essence*. Translated by Alphonso Lingis. Pittsburgh: Duquesne University Press, 1998.

———. "Philosophy and the Idea of the Infinite." In *To the Other: An Introduction to the Philosophy of Emmanuel Levinas*, edited by Adriaan Peperzak, 88–119. West Lafayette: Purdue University Press, 1993.

———. *Proper Names*. Translated by Michael B. Smith. London: Athlone Press, 1996.

———. "Reality and Its Shadow." In *The Levinas Reader*, edited by Seán Hand, 129–43. Oxford: Blackwell, 1989.

———. *Time and the Other and Additional Essays*. Translated and edited by Richard A. Cohen. Pittsburgh: Duquesne University Press, 1987.

————. *Totality and Infinity: An Essay on Exteriority.* Translated by Alphonso Lingis. Pittsburgh: Duquesne University Press, 1969.

————. "The Trace of the Other." In *Deconstruction in Context: Literature and Philosophy,* edited by Mark C. Taylor, 345–59. Chicago: University of Chicago Press, 1986.

Levith, Murray J. "Shakespeare's *Merchant* and Marlowe's Other Play." In *The Merchant of Venice: New Critical Essays,* edited by John W. Mahon and Ellen Macleod Mahon, 95– 107. New York: Routledge, 2002.

Levy, Bernard-Henri, and Adam Gopnick. "Bernard-Henri Levy on America, France, and the Jews, At the 92nd Street Y." New York: 92nd Street Y, 2006. Podcast.

Lewalski, Barbara. "Biblical Allusion and Allegory in *The Merchant of Venice.*" *Shakespeare Quarterly* 13 (1962): 327–43.

Lewis, Cynthia. *Particular Saints: Shakespeare's Four Antonios, Their Contexts, and Their Plays.* Newark: University of Delaware Press, 1997.

Lindenbaum, Peter. "Prospero's Anger." *Massachusetts Review* 25, no. 1 (March 1984): 161–71.

Lucking, David. "Our Devils Now Are Ended: A Comparative Analysis of *The Tempest* and *Doctor Faustus.*" *Dalhousie Review* 80, no. 2 (Summer 2000): 151–67.

Luther, Martin. "The Bondage of the Will." Translated by J. I. Packer and A. R. Johnston. Originally published in *The Bondage of the Will.* London: James Clark, 1957. Reprinted in *Martin Luther: Selections From His Writings,* edited by John Dillenberger, 166–203. New York: Anchor Press, 1961.

Luxon, Thomas H. "A Second Daniel: The Jew and the 'True Jew' in *The Merchant of Venice.*" *Early Modern Literary Studies: A Journal of Sixteenth and Seventeenth Century English Literature* 4, no. 3 (1999).

MacCulloch, Diarmaid. *The Reformation.* London: Allen Lane, 2003.

Magnusson, A. Lynne. "Interruption in *The Tempest.*" *Shakespeare Quarterly* 37, no. 1 (Spring 1986): 52–65.

Manguel, Alberto. *The City of Words.* Toronto: House of Anansi Press, 2007.

Marion, Jean-Luc. *God Without Being: "Hors Texte."* Translated by Thomas A. Carlson. Chicago: University of Chicago Press, 1991.

Marius, Richard. *Martin Luther: The Christian Between God and Death.* Cambridge, MA: Belknap Press of Harvard University Press, 1999.

Marlowe, Christopher. *Doctor Faustus: A 1604 Edition*. 2nd ed. Edited by Michael Keefer. Peterborough, ON: Broadview Press, 2007.

———. *Edward the Second*. New Mermaids. New York: W. W. Norton, 1997.

Marx, Stephen. *Shakespeare and the Bible*. Oxford: Oxford University Press, 2000.

Mauss, Marcel. *The Gift: The Form and Reason for Exchange in Archaic Societies*. Translated by W. D. Halls. New York: W. W. Norton, 1990.

McAdam, Ian. "*Edward II* and the Illusion of Integrity." *Studies in Philology* 92, no. 2 (Spring 1995): 203–29.

McGrath, Alister E. *Luther's Theology of the Cross: Martin Luther's Theological Breakthrough*. Oxford: Blackwell, 1985. Grand Rapids: Baker Books, 1994.

Mead, Stephen X. "The Crisis of Ritual in *Titus Andronicus*." *Exemplaria: A Journal of Theory in Medieval and Renaissance Studies* 6, no. 2 (1994): 459–79.

Meller, Horst. "A Pound of Flesh and the Economics of Christian Grace: Shakespeare's *Merchant of Venice*." In *Essays on Shakespeare in Honour of A. A. Ansari*, edited by T. R. Sharma, 150–74. Meerut, India: Shalabh Book House, 1986.

Mentz, Steven R. "The Fiend Gives Friendly Counsel: Lancelot Gobbo and Polyglot Economics in *The Merchant of Venice*." In *Money and the Age of Shakespeare: Essays in New Economic Criticism*, edited by Linda Woodbridge, 177–87. New York: Palgrave Macmillan, 2003.

Midgley, Graham. "*The Merchant of Venice*: A Reconsideration." *Essays in Criticism: A Quarterly Journal of Literary Criticism* 10, no. 2 (1960): 119–33.

Montaigne, Michel de. *Essais*. Edited by Maurice Rat. Paris: Garnier frères, 1971.

———. *The Essayes or, Morall, Politike, and Militarie Discovrses of Lord Michael De Montaigne*. 3rd ed. Translated by John Florio. London: M. Flesher, 1632.

More, Thomas. *Utopia*. Translated by Ralph Robynson. Edited by David Harris Sacks. Boston: Bedford/St. Martin's, 1999.

Musculus, Wolfgang. *Common Places of Christian Religion*. Translated by John Man. London: Henry Bynneman, 1578. Early English Books Online.

Netzloff, Mark. "The Lead Casket: Capital, Mercantilism, and *The Merchant of Venice*." In *Money and the Age of Shakespeare: Essays in*

New Economic Criticism, edited by Linda Woodbridge, 159–76. New York: Palgrave Macmillan, 2003.

Nicklin, J. A. "Marlowe's 'Gaveston.'" *Free Review* 5 (December 1895): 323–27.

Normand, Lawrence. "'What Passions Call You These?' Edward II and James VI." In *Christopher Marlowe and English Renaissance Culture*, edited by Darryll Grantley and Peter Roberts, 172–97. Hants, Eng.: Scolar, 1996.

"An Order for Morning Prayer Dayly Throughout the Yeare." In *The First and Second Prayer Books of Edward VI*, 347–55. London: J. M. Dent and Sons, 1960.

Orgel, Stephen. "Prospero's Wife." *Representations* 8 (Fall 1984): 1–13.

Ovid. *Shakespeare's Ovid*. Edited by W. H. D. Rouse. Translated by Arthur Golding. New York: W. W. Norton and Company, 1966.

Oz, Avraham. "'Which Is the Merchant Here? And Which the Jew?': Riddles of Identity in *The Merchant of Venice*." In *Shakespeare and Cultural Traditions*, edited by Tetsuo Kishi, Roger Pringle, and Stanley Wells, 155–73. Newark: University of Delaware Press; Associated University Presses, 1994.

Parks, Joan. "History, Tragedy, and Truth in Christopher Marlowe's *Edward II*." *SEL: Studies in English Literature, 1500–1900* 39, no. 2 (Spring 1999): 275–90.

Parry, Jonathan. "*The Gift*, the Indian Gift, and the 'Indian Gift,'" *Man*, n.s., 21 (1986): 453–73.

Parten, Anne. "Re-establishing Sexual Order: The Ring Episode in *The Merchant of Venice*." *Women's Studies* 9, no. 2 (1982): 145–55.

Peperzak, Adriaan. "Giving." In *The Enigma of Gift and Sacrifice*, edited by Edith Wyschogrod, Jean-Joseph Goux and Eric Boynton, 161–75. New York: Fordham University Press, 2002.

Perry, Curtis. "The Politics of Access and Representations of the Sodomite King in Early Modern England." *Renaissance Quarterly* 53, no. 4 (Winter 2000): 1054–83.

Pope, Alexander, ed. *The Works of Mr. William Shakespear*. Vol. 2, *Merchant of Venice*. London: Mr. Pope and Dr. Sewell, 1728.

Prior, Moody E. "Which Is the Jew That Shakespeare Drew? Shylock Among the Critics." *American Scholar* 50, no. 4 (1981): 479–98.

Ricoeur, Paul. "Asserting Personal Capacities and Pleading for Mutual Recognition." Kluge Prize acceptance speech, John W. Kluge Center, Washington, DC, 2004. http://www.loc.gov/loc/kluge/prize/ricoeur-transcript.html. Transcript of webcast.

———. *The Course of Recognition*. Translated by David Pellauer. Cambridge, MA: Harvard University Press, 2005.

———. *The Symbolism of Evil*. Translated by Emerson Buchanan. Boston: Beacon Press, 1969.

Riggs, David. *The World of Christopher Marlowe*. London: Faber, 2004.

Robbins, Jill. *Altered Reading: Levinas and Literature*. Chicago: University of Chicago Press, 1999.

Russell, Jeffrey Burton. *Lucifer, the Devil in the Middle Ages*. Ithaca: Cornell University Press, 1984.

Rutkoski, Marie. "Breeching the Boy in Marlowe's *Edward II*." *SEL: Studies in English Literature, 1500–1900* 46, no. 2 (Spring 2006): 281–304.

Sanchez, Melissa E. "Seduction and Service in *The Tempest*." *Studies in Philology* 105, no. 1 (Winter 2008): 50–82.

Sandford, Stella. "Levinas, Feminism and the Feminine." In *The Cambridge Companion to Levinas*, edited by Simon Critchley and Robert Bernasconi, 139–60. Cambridge: Cambridge University Press, 2002.

Schneider, Ben Ross, Jr. "'Are We Being Historical Yet?' Colonialist Interpretations of Shakepeare's *Tempest*." *Shakespeare Studies* 23 (1995): 120–45.

———. "Granville's *Jew of Venice* (1701): A Close Reading of Shakespeare's *Merchant*." *Restoration: Studies in English Literary Culture* 17, no. 2 (1993): 111–34.

———. "*King Lear* in Its Own Time: The Difference That Death Makes." *Early Modern Literary Studies* 1, no. 1 (1995).

Scot, Reginald. *The Discouerie of Witchcraft VVherein the Lewde Dealing of Witches and Witchmongers Is Notablie Detected*. London: [Henry Denham for] William Brome, 1584. Early English Books Online.

Scott, William O. "Contracts of Love and Affection: Lear, Old Age, and Kingship." *Shakespeare Survey: An Annual Survey of Shakespeare Studies and Production* 55 (2002): 36–42.

Shakespeare, William. *Hamlet*. Edited by G. R. Hibbard. 1987. Reprint. Oxford: Oxford University Press, 1994.

———. *Henry IV, Part 2*. Edited by René Weis. New York: Clarendon Press, 1998.

———. *Henry V*. Edited by Gary Taylor. Oxford: Oxford University Press, 1982.

———. *Henry VI, Part Three*. Edited by Randall Martin. Oxford: Oxford University Press, 2001.

———. *King Lear*. Edited by R. A. Foakes. The Arden Shakespeare. 3rd ed. London: Thomas Nelson, 2000.

———. *Measure for Measure*. Edited by N. W. Bawcutt. Oxford: Oxford University Press, 1991.

———. *The Merchant of Venice*. Edited by Jay L. Halio. Oxford: Oxford University Press, 1993.

———. *A Midsummer Night's Dream*. Edited by Peter Holland. The Oxford Shakespeare. Oxford: Oxford University Press, 1994.

———. *The Second Part of Henry the Fourth*. Edited by Matthias A. Shaaber Philadelphia: J. B. Lippincott and Company, 1940.

———. *The Second Part of King Henry IV*. Edited by A. R. Humphreys. The Arden Shakespeare. Revised ed. London: Methuen, 1966.

———. *The Second Part of King Henry IV*. Edited by Giorgio Melchiori. Cambridge: Cambridge University Press, 1989.

———. *The Tempest*. Edited by Stephen Orgel. Oxford: Oxford University Press, 1987.

———. *Titus Andronicus*. Edited by Eugene Waith. Oxford: Oxford University Press, 1984.

———. *The Tragedy of Coriolanus*. Edited by R. B. Parker. New York: Oxford University Press, 1994.

Shapiro, James. "'Which Is *The Merchant* Here, and Which *The Jew*?': Shakespeare and the Economics of Influence." *Shakespeare Studies* 20 (1988): 269–82.

Shapiro, James S. *A Year in the Life of William Shakespeare, 1599*. New York: HarperCollins Publishers, 2005.

Shapiro, Michael. "Shylock the Jew Onstage: Past and Present." *Shofar* 4, no. 2 (1986): 1–11.

Shell, Marc. "The Wether and the Ewe: Verbal Usury in *The Merchant of Venice*." *Kenyon Review* n.s. 1, no. 4 (1979): 65–92.

Short, Hugh. "Shylock Is Content: A Study in Salvation." In *The Merchant of Venice: New Critical Essays*, edited by John W. Mahon and Ellen Macleod Mahon, 199–212. New York: Routledge, 2002.

Silber, Ilana F. "Beyond Purity and Danger: Gift-Giving in the Monotheistic Religions." In Vandevelde, *Gifts and Interests*, 115–32.

Sinfield, Alan. "How to Read The Merchant of Venice Without Being Heterosexist." In *Shakespeare, Feminism and Gender*, edited by Kate Chedgzoy, 115–34. Basingstoke, Eng.: Palgrave, 2001.

Skura, Meredith Anne. "Discourse and the Individual: The Case of Colonialism in *The Tempest.*" *Shakespeare Quarterly* 40, no. 1 (Spring 1989): 42–69.

Slights, William W. E. "The Sacrificial Crisis in *Titus Andronicus.*" *University of Toronto Quarterly* 49, no. 1 (Fall 1979): 18–32.

Spinosa, Charles. "'The Name and All Th'Addition': *King Lear*'s Opening Scene and the Common Law Use." *Shakespeare Studies* 23 (1995): 146–86.

Stanivukovic, Goran. "*The Tempest* and the Discontents of Humanism." *Philological Quarterly* 85, no. 1–2 (2006): 91–119.

Strier, Richard. "Faithful Servants: Shakespeare's Praise of Disobedience." In *The Historical Renaissance: New Essays on Tudor and Stuart Literature and Culture,* edited by Heather Dubrow and Richard Strier, 104–33. Chicago: University of Chicago Press, 1988.

Stymeist, David. "Status, Sodomy, and the Theater in Marlowe's *Edward II.*" *SEL: Studies in English Literature, 1500–1900* 44, no. 2 (Spring 2004): 233–53.

Summers, Claude J. "Sex, Politics, and Self-Realization in *Edward II.*" In *"A Poet and a Filthy Play-Maker": New Essays on Christopher Marlowe,* edited by Kenneth Friedenreich, Roma Gill and Constance B. Kuriyama, 221–40. New York: AMS, 1988.

Surgal, Jon. "The Rebel and the Red-Hot Spit: Marlowe's *Edward II* as Anal-Sadistic Prototype." *American Imago: Studies in Psychoanalysis and Culture* 61, no. 2 (Summer 2004): 165–200.

Szatek, Karoline. "*The Merchant of Venice* and the Politics of Commerce." In *The Merchant of Venice: New Critical Essays,* edited by John W. Mahon and Ellen Macleod Mahon, 325–52. New York: Routledge, 2002.

Tanner, Tony. "Which Is the Merchant Here? And Which the Jew? The Venice of Shakespeare's *Merchant of Venice.*" In *Venetian Views, Venetian Blinds: English Fantasies of Venice,* edited by Manfred Pfister and Barbara Schaff, 45–62. Amsterdam: Rodopi, 1999.

Tarot, Camille. "Gift and Grace: A Family to Be Recomposed?" In Vandevelde, *Gifts and Interests,* 133–55.

Tennenhouse, Leonard. *Power on Display: The Politics of Shakespeare's Genres.* New York: Methuen, 1986.

Terpstra, Marin. "Social Gifts and the Gift of Sociality: Some Thoughts on Mauss' *The Gift* and Hobbes' *Leviathan.*" In Vandevelde, *Gifts and Interests,* 191–208.

Thomas, Keith Vivian. *Religion and the Decline of Magic: Studies in Popular Beliefs in Sixteenth- and Seventeenth-Century England.* Harmondsworth, Eng.: Penguin Books, 1973.

Tolstóy, Leo. "Shakespeare and the Drama." In *Recollections and Essays,* translated by Aylmer Maude, 307–83. London: Oxford University Press, 1937.

Traister, Barbara Howard. "Prospero: Master of Self-Knowledge." In *William Shakespeare's The Tempest,* edited by Harold Bloom, 113–30. New York: Chelsea House, 1988.

Traver, Hope. "The Four Daughters of God: A Mirror of Changing Doctrine." *PMLA: Publications of the Modern Language Association of America* 40 (1925): 44–92.

The True Chronicle History of King Leir, and His Three Daughters, Gonorill, Ragan, and Cordella. London: Simon Stafford for John Wright, 1605.

Turner, Frederick. *Shakespeare's Twenty-First Century Economics: The Morality of Love and Money.* New York: Oxford University Press, 1999.

Tyler, Sharon. "Bedfellows Make Strange Politics: Christopher Marlowe's *Edward II*." In *Drama, Sex and Politics,* edited by James Redmond, 55–68. Cambridge: Cambridge University Press, 1985.

Tyndale, William. *Tyndale's New Testament.* Edited by David Daniell. New Haven: Yale University Press, 1989.

Ule, Louis. *A Concordance to the Works of Christopher Marlowe.* The Elizabethan Concordance Series. Hildesheim; New York: Olms, 1979.

Vandevelde, Antoon, ed. *Gifts and Interests.* Leuven: Peeters, 2000.

Velz, John W. "Portia and Ovidian Grotesque." In *The Merchant of Venice: New Critical Essays,* edited by John W. Mahon and Ellen Macleod Mahon, 179–86. New York: Routledge, 2002.

Vickers, Brian. *Shakespeare, Co-Author: A Historical Study of Five Collaborative Plays.* New York: Oxford University Press, 2002.

———. "Thomas Kyd, Secret Sharer." *Times Literary Supplement,* April 18, 2008.

Visser, Nicholas. "Shakespeare and Hanekom, King Lear and Land." *Textual Practice* 11, no. 1 (Spring 1997): 25–37.

Voss, James. "*Edward II*: Marlowe's Historical Tragedy." *English Studies: A Journal of English Language and Literature* 63, no. 6 (December 1982): 517–30.

Waith, Eugene. *"Edward II:* The Shadow of Action." *Tulane Drama Review* 8, no. 4 (Summer 1964): 59–74.

———. Introduction to *Titus Andronicus,* 1–69. Oxford: Oxford University Press, 1984.

Weisberg, Richard. "Antonio's Legalistic Cruelty." *College Literature* 25 (1998): 12–21.

Wessman, Christopher. "Marlowe's *Edward II* as 'Actaeonesque History.'" *Connotations: A Journal for Critical Debate* 9, no. 1 (2000): 1–33.

West, Grace Starry. "Going by the Book: Classical Allusions in Shakespeare's *Titus Andronicus." Studies in Philology* 79, no. 1 (1982): 62–77.

White, Paul Whitfield. "'Reforming Mysteries' End': A New Look at Protestant Intervention in English Provincial Drama." *Journal of Medieval and Early Modern Studies* 29 (1999): 121–47.

Williams, Carolyn D. "'Silence, Like a Lucrece Knife': Shakespeare and the Meanings of Rape." *Yearbook in English Studies* 23 (1993): 93–110.

Willis, Deborah. "The Gnawing Vulture: Revenge, Trauma Theory, and *Titus Andronicus." Shakespeare Quarterly* 53, no. 1 (Spring 2002): 21–52.

Woodbridge, Linda. Introduction to *Money and the Age of Shakespeare: Essays in New Economic Criticism,* edited by Linda Woodbridge, 1–18. New York: Palgrave Macmillan, 2003.

Zaslavsky, Robert. "'Which Is the Merchant Here? And Which the Jew?': Keeping the Book and Keeping the Books in *The Merchant of Venice." Judaism* 44 (1995): 181–92.

INDEX

239